W9-CMH-031

THE SPIRIT OF THE LITURGY

THE SPIRIT
OF THE LITURGY

by

JOSEPH CARDINAL RATZINGER

───────────────

with

THE SPIRIT OF THE LITURGY

by

FATHER ROMANO GUARDINI

Commemorative Edition

IGNATIUS PRESS　　SAN FRANCISCO

Joseph Ratzinger, *The Spirit of the Liturgy*
Original German edition:
Einführung in den Geist der Liturgie
© 2000 by Herder, Freiburg im Breisgau
Original English edition:
© 2000 by Ignatius Press, San Francisco
All rights reserved

Romano Guardini, *The Spirit of the Liturgy*
Original German edition: *Vom Geist der Liturgie*
1918 by Herder, Freiburg im Breisgau
Original English ed.: London: Sheed & Ward, 1930

Unless otherwise indicated, Scripture quotations are from Revised Standard Version of the Bible—Second Catholic Edition (Ignatius Edition) copyright © 2006 National Council of the Churches of Christ in the United States of America. Used by permission. All rights reserved worldwide.

Cover art: *The Tree of Life*
Pacino di Bonaguida (active circa 1303–about 1347)
Accademia, Florence, Italy
© Alinari/Art Resource, New York

Cover design by Roxanne Mei Lum

Published in 2018 by Ignatius Press, San Francisco
Paperback edition published 2020
All rights reserved
ISBN 978-1-62164-429-3 (PB)
ISBN 978-1-64229-054-7 (eBook)
Library of Congress control number 2018938708
Printed in the United States of America ∞

Contents

THE SPIRIT OF THE LITURGY

by Joseph Cardinal Ratzinger

THE SPIRIT OF THE LITURGY

by Father Romano Guardini

Foreword

by

ROBERT CARDINAL SARAH

Forty years ago, as the ecclesiastical turmoil of the 1970s continued, a thirty-seven-year-old American Jesuit founded a new publishing house with the objective, as he would later assert, "to support the teachings of the Church". This year, as we celebrate the fortieth anniversary of Ignatius Press, it is only appropriate to give thanks to Almighty God for the vision and courage of this loyal son of Saint Ignatius, Father Joseph Fessio, S.J., and for his fidelity, tenacity, and perseverance these past four decades. Through his inspiration and his leadership in establishing and maintaining a faithful team of cooperators in this publishing house, not only has he succeeded in supporting the teachings of the Church in an age when they have all too often been called into question, or even denied by those whose God-given ministry is to transmit them faithfully, his initiative has also served to inform and to form generations of young clergy, religious, and laity in the truths and riches of our Catholic faith, tradition, and culture.

In selecting *The Spirit of the Liturgy*, written by his former teacher Joseph Cardinal Ratzinger (now our beloved Pope Emeritus Benedict XVI), as the title with which to mark the fortieth anniversary of Ignatius Press, Father

Fessio himself does not fail to teach us. For of all the excellent theological, philosophical, spiritual, catechetical, historical, literary, and other works he has published, this title makes manifest the heart and soul of all his endeavors. While Ignatius Press is an exemplary and utterly professional publisher, it is the sacred liturgy that is the veritable "source and summit" of its life and mission.[1] How many publishing houses have at the center of their premises a chapel in which their staff daily participate in the Holy Sacrifice of the Mass or pray the Divine Office together? The "spirit and power" of the sacred liturgy[2] permeates all of their professional work in a truly exemplary and edifying manner.

This, surely, must bring great joy and consolation to the Pope Emeritus Benedict XVI, whose preface to his own *The Spirit of the Liturgy* expresses the hope that: "If this book were to encourage, in a new way, something like a 'liturgical movement', a movement toward the liturgy and toward the right way of celebrating the liturgy, inwardly and outwardly, then the intention that inspired its writing would be richly fulfilled."[3]

How much we owe Cardinal Ratzinger for what has come to be known as "the new Liturgical Movement". How much the English-speaking world, and beyond, owes Ignatius Press for making Cardinal Ratzinger's writings on the sacred liturgy available, writings that have truly become beacons lighting the path for that "movement toward the liturgy and toward the right way of cel-

---

[1] Cf. *Second Vatican Council*, Constitution on the Sacred Liturgy, *Sacrosanctum Concilium*, 4 December 1963, n. 10.

[2] Cf. *Sacrosanctum Concilium*, n. 14.

[3] Joseph Cardinal Ratzinger, *The Spirit of the Liturgy*, Ignatius Press, San Francisco 2000, pp. 22–23.

ebrating the liturgy, inwardly and outwardly", which I believe is growing and steadily advancing even today.

It is opportune to underline briefly this twofold dimension of the sacred liturgy—its internal and external realities—for it is always necessary to guard against the two temptations about which Pope Saint John Paul II warned us, namely, that "sacramental life is impoverished and very soon turns into hollow ritualism if it is not based on serious knowledge of the meaning of the sacraments, and catechesis becomes intellectualized if it fails to come alive in the sacramental practice."[4]

Let us develop this teaching, substituting the word "liturgy" for "sacramental"; after all, we in fact celebrate all the sacraments liturgically. We can say, then, that our *liturgical* life is impoverished and very soon turns into hollow ritualism if it is not based on serious knowledge of the meaning of the *liturgy* and that catechesis becomes intellectualized if it fails to come alive in liturgical practice.

That is to say, we must penetrate the inner meaning of the sacred liturgy and not simply perform its external rituals without what is essential: the engagement of our hearts, minds, and souls. Certainly, this presupposes an understanding of the meaning of the rites and prayers appropriate to our age, ability, and state in life—that is why thorough liturgical catechesis and formation at every level is a crucial need of the Church in our times. As our Holy Father Pope Francis has reminded us, "it is necessary to unite a renewed willingness to go forward along the path indicated by the Council Fathers, as there remains much to be done for a correct and complete assimilation of the Constitution on the Sacred Liturgy on

[4] Pope St. John Paul, Apostolic Exhortation, *Catechesi Tradendae* 16 October 1979, n. 23.

the part of the baptized and ecclesial communities. I refer, in particular, to the commitment to a solid and organic liturgical initiation and formation, both of lay faithful as well as of clergy and consecrated persons."[5] Here, *The Spirit of the Liturgy* is a singularly rich resource and guide in our day, as are the other personal liturgical writings of the Pope Emeritus Benedict XVI[6] and, indeed, his liturgical magisterium as Supreme Pontiff, which retains its validity.[7] So too are the classical writings of the twentieth century liturgical movement that nourished the Pope Emeritus' own liturgical formation, and for this reason I am delighted that Father Fessio is also publishing here the text of Romano Guardini's *The Spirit of the Liturgy* —a "decisive" text that, in Cardinal Ratzinger's words, "helped us to rediscover the liturgy in all its beauty, hidden wealth, and time-transcending grandeur, to see it as the animating center of the Church, the very center of Christian life".[8]

But it is also to say—and this is indispensable—that our external liturgical practices must be acts of love and adoration that truly arise from the reality of our intrinsically ecclesial and profoundly personal worship of Almighty God. We know this from the simple acts of making the sign of the cross or of genuflecting: they can be merely

[5] Pope Francis, Message to participants in the Symposium "*Sacrosanctum Concilium*: Gratitude and Commitment for a Great Ecclesial Movement" 18 February 2014.

[6] Cf. Joseph Ratzinger, *Theology of the Liturgy*, Collected Works vol. 11, Ignatius Press, San Francisco 2014.

[7] In addition to his many papal discourses reflecting the primacy of the Sacred Liturgy in the life and mission of the Church, I would highlight Pope Benedict XVI's Post Synodal Apostolic Exhortation *Sacramentum Caritatis* (22 February 2007) and his Apostolic Letter given motu proprio, *Summorum Pontificum* (7 July 2007), together with his Letter of the same date to Bishops accompanying *Summorum Pontificum*.

[8] Joseph Cardinal Ratzinger, *The Spirit of the Liturgy*, p. 21.

routine acts largely devoid of meaning, or they can become small but intimate expressions of the heart and soul of one who truly loves and worships and, indeed, places God at the center of his life and gives him primacy in all of his activities. "This does not mean that we must always be thinking of God, but that we must really be penetrated by the reality of God so that our whole life . . . may be a liturgy, may be adoration."[9] Let us live the sacred liturgy with reverential awe and rejoice in and draw from the wealth and richness of its traditional signs, gestures, and rites, large and small, as true lovers of Almighty God— quite the opposite of those somehow "obliged" to perform servile acts of obeisance. Where necessary, let us rediscover why our Holy Mother the Church introduced the powerful symbols with which the sacred liturgy is replete and let Christ acting in and through them inform, enrich, guide, and sustain our lives of faith and our particular mission in the world, which is none other than the sanctification of the whole of humanity.

Let us, then, truly live from the sacred liturgy, which surpasses all other acts, for no other action of the Church can equal its efficacy by the same title and to the same degree.[10] In so doing we discover the spirit and power of the sacred liturgy, and, if I may be so bold, this is the right way of celebrating the liturgy, inwardly and outwardly, that Pope Emeritus Benedict XVI has so earnestly sought.

In 1997, two years before publishing the German edition of *The Spirit of the Liturgy*, Cardinal Ratzinger wrote:

> The Church stands and falls with the liturgy. When the adoration of the divine Trinity declines, when the faith no longer appears in its fullness in the liturgy of the Church,

---

[9] Pope Benedict XVI, *Lectio divina*, Seminary of the Diocese of Rome, 15 February 2012.

[10] Cf. *Sacrosanctum Concilium*, n. 7.

when man's words, his thoughts, his intentions are suffocating him, then faith will have lost the place where it is expressed and where it dwells. For that reason, the true celebration of the sacred liturgy is the center of any renewal of the Church whatever.[11]

Our Pope Emeritus Benedict XVI has captured in these breathtaking words the essence of our present dilemma, and so, before closing, I wish to take this opportunity once again to express my deep gratitude to His Holiness for his precious contributions, which have, I believe, only just begun to shower forth their blessings upon Holy Mother Church, both for her life of prayer and for faith, for indeed *lex orandi, lex credendi!*

Father Fessio knows this truth. Ignatius Press daily lives and works from it. For that reality, and for the witness and good example that they continue to give us, in this their fortieth anniversary year we give thanks to Almighty God, asking him to continue to bless and inspire their faithful apostolate, that it might continue to play an important role in the renewal of the faith and life of the Church at the beginning of the third Christian millennium. Indeed, I feel very privileged and honored to be associated with these joyful celebrations in commemoration of the fortieth anniversary of Ignatius Press.

Robert Cardinal Sarah
Prefect, Congregation for Divine Worship
and the Discipline of the Sacraments
January 13, 2018

[11] Preface to Franz Breid, ed., *Die heilige Liturgie*, papers from the "Internationale Theologische Sommerakademie 1997" of the Priests' Circle of Linz, Ennsthaler Verlag, Steyr 1997.

Preface

by

POPE EMERITUS BENEDICT XVI

I heartily congratulate Ignatius Press on its forty years of existence. For me this is an occasion for giving very personal thanks, since it was Ignatius Press that first opened for me the door to America and gave me a voice in American Catholicism.

But my gratitude goes far beyond the merely personal, for Ignatius Press has rendered, and at present continues to render, an important service in the spiritual struggle, particularly that of the Catholic Church in America and the rest of the world. The question of what it means to be Catholic, of what fundamental spiritual decisions today's Catholic must make, has been asked since the Second Vatican Council with a new radicalness. The older Catholic publishing houses were seized worldwide by the new climate, and in part they surrendered to it, then only to disappear or to rise anew. New publishers, among them Ignatius Press, appeared and have left a decisive mark on the spiritual struggle. The names of Hans Urs von Balthasar, Adrienne von Speyr, Louis Bouyer, Josef Pieper, and Joseph Ratzinger are a clear expression of a decision on behalf of a faith that always includes the humility of obedience to the Church. But, precisely for this reason, it is also a faith that investigates bravely the full breadth of truth and can therefore fearlessly oppose the spirit of the times.

It gladdens me, of course, that the editor wishes to celebrate the fortieth anniversary of his publishing house with a new edition of my book *The Spirit of the Liturgy*. The postconciliar drama was largely marked by the battle around the correct renewal of the liturgy. At first a person could have thought that the whole thing was but a paltry internal conflict among Christians concerning, for instance, the question of whether Latin should remain the language of the liturgy or whether it was necessary to admit all the languages of the world. It soon became obvious, however, that a Church that could no longer mediate the encounter with the living God, but instead only enabled little groups to celebrate themselves, would be a meaningless Church. And it became evident as well that this issue concerned far more than just the community of believers. Rather, it was seen that the collapse of the Church, considered a possibility by sociologists, would represent a catastrophe of unforeseeable proportions for the whole of mankind.

For this reason, I am also glad to know that the Press intends to publish a small programmatic writing of Romano Guardini's entitled *The Spirit of the Liturgy*. This is as well the book that for me personally opened the door to the understanding of the liturgy, which is why I retained Guardini's title for my own book.

Above all I would like to address a word of thanks to the founder of Ignatius Press, Father Joseph D. Fessio, S.J. I shall never forget the first visit he paid me. Father de Lubac had commended him to me as a "true Jesuit". And that was my immediate experience of him. During my encounter with him, what kept coming to mind was the Ignatian meditation "On the Two Standards". Father Fessio has always seemed to me to be a man of the "decisive decision", something that for Heinrich Schlier belongs to the very essence of Catholicity. This decision Schlier interprets as the decisive Yes of man to God's definitive decision for man in the incarnate Word. Father Fessio follows the lead of the Ignatian definition of the decision for the Standard of Jesus Christ. As such, he has always appeared to me a man who strives to live the three steps of poverty of which the *Exercises* speak: poverty over against riches, poverty over against contempt, poverty over against arrogance.[1] In my eyes, Father Fessio has something combative about him, combative in the sense defined by Josef Pieper. In his first small book, written in the middle of the Nazi period, Pieper wanted to show, over against the Nazi concept of valor, that true valor does not consist in inflicting blows on others but, rather, in the courage and humility to receive the blows oneself. Father Fessio has received many blows, and it is precisely in this way that he has made credible the tidings for which he stands.

From my heart I wish Ignatius Press another forty years of blessings!

Benedict XVI

Vatican City,
Mater Ecclesiae Monastery
February 2, 2018

---

[1] K. Rahner, *Betrachtungen zum ignatianischen Exerzitienbuch* (Munich, 1965), 177.

JOSEPH CARDINAL RATZINGER

The Spirit
of the Liturgy

TRANSLATED BY JOHN SAWARD

Preface

One of the first books I read after starting my theological studies at the beginning of 1946 was Romano Guardini's first little book, *The Spirit of the Liturgy*. It was published at Easter 1918 as the opening volume in the Ecclesia Orans series edited by Abbot Herwegen, and from then until 1957 it was constantly reprinted. This slim volume may rightly be said to have inaugurated the Liturgical Movement in Germany. Its contribution was decisive. It helped us to rediscover the liturgy in all its beauty, hidden wealth, and time-transcending grandeur, to see it as the animating center of the Church, the very center of Christian life. It led to a striving for a celebration of the liturgy that would be "more substantial" (*wesentlicher*, one of Guardini's favorite words). We were now willing to see the liturgy —in its inner demands and form—as the prayer of the Church, a prayer moved and guided by the Holy Spirit himself, a prayer in which Christ unceasingly becomes contemporary with us, enters into our lives.

I should like to suggest a comparison. Like all comparisons, it is in many ways inadequate, and yet it may aid understanding. We might say that in 1918, the year that Guardini published his book, the liturgy was rather like a fresco. It had been preserved from damage, but it had been almost completely overlaid with whitewash by later generations. In the Missal from which the priest celebrated,

21

the form of the liturgy that had grown from its earliest beginnings was still present, but, as far as the faithful were concerned, it was largely concealed beneath instructions for and forms of private prayer. The fresco was laid bare by the Liturgical Movement and, in a definitive way, by the Second Vatican Council. For a moment, its colors and figures fascinated us. But since then, the fresco has been endangered by climatic conditions as well as by various restorations and reconstructions. In fact, it is threatened with destruction, if the necessary steps are not taken to stop these damaging influences. Of course, there must be no question of its being covered with whitewash again, but what is imperative is a new reverence in the way we treat it, a new understanding of its message and its reality, so that rediscovery does not become the first stage of irreparable loss.

My purpose in writing this little book, which I now lay before the public, is to assist this renewal of understanding. Its basic intentions coincide with what Guardini wanted to achieve in his own time with *The Spirit of the Liturgy*. That is why I deliberately chose a title that would be immediately reminiscent of that classic of liturgical theology. The only difference is that I have had to translate what Guardini did at the end of the First World War, in a totally different historical situation, into the context of our present-day questions, hopes, and dangers. I am not attempting, any more than Guardini was, to involve myself with scholarly discussion and research. I am simply offering an aid to the understanding of the faith and to the right way to give the faith its central form of expression in the liturgy. If this book were to encourage, in a new way, something like a "liturgical movement", a movement toward the liturgy and toward the right way of celebrating the liturgy, inwardly and outwardly, then the intention that inspired its writing would be richly fulfilled.

Rome
The Feast of Saint Augustine of Hippo
August 28, 1999
Joseph Cardinal Ratzinger

PART ONE

THE ESSENCE OF THE LITURGY

CHAPTER ONE

Liturgy and Life:
The Place of the Liturgy in Reality

W HAT *is* the liturgy? What happens during the liturgy? What kind of reality do we encounter here? In the 1920s, the suggestion was made that we should understand the liturgy in terms of "play". The point of the analogy was that a game has its own rules, sets up its own world, which is in force from the start of play but then, of course, is suspended at the close of play. A further point of similarity was that play, though it has a meaning, does not have a purpose and that for this very reason there is something healing, even liberating, about it. Play takes us out of the world of daily goals and their pressures and into a sphere free of purpose and achievement, releasing us for a time from all the burdens of our daily world of work. Play is a kind of other world, an oasis of freedom, where for a moment we can let life flow freely. We need such moments of retreat from the pressure of daily life if its burden is to be bearable. Now there is some truth in this way of thinking, but it is insufficient. It all depends on what we are playing. Everything we have said can be applied to any game, and the trouble is that serious commitment to the rules needed for playing the game soon develops its own burdens and leads to new kinds of purposefulness. Whether we look at modern sport or at chess championships or, indeed, at any game, we find that play, when it does not degenerate into mere fooling about, quickly turns from being another world, a counter-world or non-world, to being a bit of the normal world with its own laws.

We should mention another aspect of this theory of play, something that brings us closer to the essence of the liturgy. Children's play seems in many ways a kind of anticipation of life, a rehearsal for later life, without its burdens and gravity. On this analogy, the liturgy would be a reminder that we are all children, or should be children, in relation to that true life toward which we yearn to go. Liturgy would be a kind of anticipation, a rehearsal, a prelude for the life to come, for eternal life, which Saint Augustine describes, by contrast with life in this world, as a fabric woven, no longer of exigency and need, but of the freedom of generosity and gift. Seen thus, liturgy would be the rediscovery within us of true childhood, of openness to a greatness still to come, which is still unfulfilled in adult life. Here, then, would be the concrete form of hope, which lives in advance the life to come, the only true life, which initiates us into authentic life —the life of freedom, of intimate union with God, of pure openness to our fellowman. Thus it would imprint on the seemingly real life of daily existence the mark of future freedom, break open the walls that confine us, and let the light of heaven shine down upon earth.

This application of play-theory distinguishes the liturgy by its essence from the ordinary kinds of play, which doubtless always contain a longing for the real "game", for a wholly different world in which order and freedom are at one. By contrast with the superficial, utilitarian, or humanly vacuous aspects of ordinary play, the play-theory of liturgy brings out what is special and different about that "play" of Wisdom of which the Bible speaks, the play that can be compared to the liturgy. But this analogy still lacks something, something essential. The idea of a life to come appears only as a vague postulate. The reference to God, without whom the "life to come" would only be a wasteland, remains quite indeterminate. I should like to suggest, therefore, a new approach, this time starting from specific biblical texts.

In the accounts of the events leading up to Israel's flight from Egypt, as well as in those that describe the flight itself, the Exodus appears to have two distinct goals. The first, which is familiar to us all, is the reaching of the Promised Land, in which Israel will at last live on its own soil and territory, with secure borders, as a people with the freedom and independence proper to it. But we also hear repeatedly of another goal. God's original command to Pharaoh runs as follows: "Let my people go, that they may serve me in the wilderness" (Ex 7:16). These words—"Let my people go, that they may serve me"—are repeated four times, with slight variations, in all the meetings of Pharaoh with Moses and Aaron (cf. Ex 8:1; 9:1; 9:13; 10:3). In the course of the negotiations with Pharaoh, the goal becomes more concrete. Pharaoh shows he is willing to compromise. For him the issue is the Israelites' freedom of worship, which he first of all concedes in the following form: "Go, sacrifice to your God within the land" (Ex 8:25). But Moses insists—in obedience to God's command—that they must go out in order to worship. The proper place of worship is the wilderness: "We must go three days' journey into the wilderness and sacrifice to the LORD our God as he will command us" (Ex 8:27). After the plagues that follow, Pharaoh extends his compromise. He now concedes that worship according to the will of the Deity should take place in the wilderness, but he wants only the men to leave: the women and children, together with the cattle, must stay in Egypt. He is assuming the current religious practice, according to which only men are active participants in worship. But Moses cannot negotiate about the liturgy with a foreign potentate, nor can he subject worship to any form of political compromise. The manner in which God is to be worshipped is not a question of political feasibility. It contains its measure within itself, that is, it can only be ordered by the measure of revelation, in dependency upon God. That is why the third and most far-reaching compromise suggested by the earthly ruler is also rejected. Pharaoh now offers women and children the permission to leave with the men: "Only let your flocks and your herds remain" (Ex 10:24). Moses objects: All the livestock must go, too, for "we do not know with what we must serve the LORD until we arrive there" (10:26). In all this, the issue is not the Promised Land: the only goal of the Exodus is shown to be worship, which can only take place according to God's measure and therefore eludes the rules of the game of political compromise.

Israel departs, not in order to be a people like all the others; it departs in order to serve God. The goal of the departure is the still unknown mountain of God, the service of God. Now the objection could be made that focusing on worship in the negotiations with Pharaoh was purely tactical. The real goal of the Exodus, ultimately its only goal, was not worship but land—this, after all, was the real content of the promise to Abraham. I do not think that this does justice to the seriousness that pervades the texts. To oppose land and worship makes no sense. The land is given to the people to be a place for the worship of the true God. Mere possession of the land, mere national autonomy, would reduce Israel to the level of all the other nations. The pursuit of such a goal would be a misunderstanding of what is distinctive about Israel's election. The whole history recounted in the books of the Judges and Kings, which is taken up afresh and given a new interpretation in the Chronicles, is intended to show precisely this, that the land, considered just in itself, is an indeterminate good. It only becomes a true good, a real gift, a promise fulfilled, when it is the place where God reigns. Then it will not be just some independent state or other, but the realm of obedience, where God's will is done and the right kind of human existence developed. Looking at the biblical texts enables us to define more exactly the relationship of the two goals of the Exodus. In its wanderings, Israel discovers the kind of sacrifice God wants, not after three days (as suggested in the conversation with Pharaoh), but after three months, on the day they come "into the wilderness of Sinai" (Ex 19:1). On the third day, God comes down onto the top of the mountain (cf. 19:16, 20). Now he speaks to the people. He makes known his will to them in the Ten Commandments (cf. 20:1–17) and, through the mediation of Moses, makes a covenant with them (cf. Ex 24), a covenant concretized in a minutely regulated form of worship. In this way, the purpose of the wandering in the wilderness, as explained to Pharaoh, is fulfilled. Israel learns how to worship God in the way he himself desires. Cult, liturgy in the proper sense, is part of this worship, but so too is life according to the will of God;

such a life is an indispensable part of true worship. "The glory of God is the living man, but the life of man is the vision of God", says Saint Irenaeus (cf. *Adv. Haer.* 4, 20, 7), getting to the heart of what happens when man meets God on the mountain in the wilderness. Ultimately, it is the very life of man, man himself as living righteously, that is the true worship of God, but life only becomes real life when it receives its form from looking toward God. Cult exists in order to communicate this vision and to give life in such a way that glory is given to God.

Three things are important for the question we are considering. First of all, on Sinai the people receive not only instructions about worship, but also an all-embracing rule of law and life. Only thus can it become a people. A people without a common rule of law cannot live. It destroys itself in anarchy, which is a parody of freedom, its exaltation to the point of abolition. When every man lives without law, every man lives without freedom. This brings me to my second point. In the ordering of the covenant on Sinai, the three aspects of worship, law, and ethics are inseparably interwoven. This is the greatness of the Sinai covenant but also its limitation, as is shown in the transition from Israel to the Church of the Gentiles, where the interweaving was to unravel, to make room for a diversity of legal forms and political structures. In the modern age, this necessary unraveling has led finally to the total secularization of the law and the exclusion of any God-ward perspective from the fashioning of the law. But we must not forget that there is an essential connection between the three orders of worship, law, and ethics. Law without a foundation in morality becomes injustice. When morality and law do not originate in a God-ward perspective, they degrade man, because they rob him of his highest measure and his highest capacity, deprive him of any vision of the infinite and eternal. This seeming liberation subjects him to the dictatorship of the ruling majority, to shifting human standards, which inevitably end up doing him violence. Thus we come to a third point, which takes us back to where we started, to the question of the nature of worship and liturgy. When human affairs are so ordered that there is no recognition of God, there is a belittling of man. That is why, in the final analysis, worship and law cannot be completely separated from each other. God has a right to a response from man, to man himself, and where that right of God totally disappears, the order of law among men is dissolved, because there is no cornerstone to keep the whole structure together.

What does this mean for the question we have been considering? We were looking at the two goals of the Exodus, and we saw that the issue was ultimately about the nature of the liturgy. Now it becomes clear that what took place on Sinai, in the period of rest after the wandering through the wilderness, is what gives meaning to the taking of the land. Sinai is not a halfway house, a kind of stop for refreshment on the road to what really matters. No, Sinai gives Israel, so to speak, its interior land without which the exterior one would be a cheerless prospect. Israel is constituted as a people through the covenant and the divine law it contains. It has received a common rule for righteous living. This and this alone is what makes the land a real gift. Sinai remains present in the Promised Land. When the reality of Sinai is lost, the Land, too, is inwardly lost, until finally the people are thrust into exile. Whenever Israel falls away from the right worship of God, when it turns away from God to the false gods (the powers and values of this world), its freedom, too, collapses. It is possible for it to live in its own land and yet still be as it was in Egypt. Mere possession of your own land and state does not give you freedom; in fact, it can be the grossest kind of slavery. And when the loss of law becomes total, it ends in the loss even of the land. The "service of God", the freedom to give right worship to God, appears, in the encounter with Pharaoh, to be the sole purpose of the Exodus, indeed, its very essence. This fact is evident throughout the Pentateuch. This real "canon in the canon", the very heart of Israel's Bible, is set entirely outside of the Holy Land. It ends on the edge of the wilderness, "beyond the Jordan", where Moses once more sums up and repeats the message of Sinai. Thus we can see what the foundation of existence in the Promised Land must be, the necessary condition for life in community and freedom. It is this: steadfast adherence to the law of God, which orders human affairs rightly, that is, by organizing them as realities that come from God and are meant to return to God.

But, once again, what does all this mean for our problem? First, it becomes clear that "cult", seen in its true breadth and depth, goes beyond the action of the liturgy. Ultimately, it embraces the ordering of the whole of human life in Irenaeus' sense. Man becomes glory for God, puts God, so to speak, into the light (and that is what worship is), when he lives by looking toward God. On the other hand, it is also true that law and ethics do not hold together when they are not anchored in the liturgical center and inspired by it. What kind of reality, then, do we find in the liturgy? As a first answer, we can now say this: The man who puts to one side any consideration of the reality of God is a realist only in appearance. He is abstracting himself from the One in whom we "live and move and have our being" (Acts 17:28). It is only, therefore, when man's relationship with God is right that all of his other relationships—his relationships with his fellowmen, his dealings with the rest of creation—can be in good order. As we have seen, law is essential for freedom and community; worship—that is, the right way to relate to God—is, for its part, essential for law. We can now broaden the insight by taking a further step. Worship, that is, the right kind of cult, of relationship with God, is essential for the right kind of human existence in the world. It is so precisely because it reaches beyond everyday life. Worship gives us a share in heaven's mode of existence, in the world of God, and allows light to fall from that divine world into ours. In this sense, worship—as we said when we were discussing play—has the character of anticipation. It lays hold in advance of a more perfect life and, in so doing, gives our present life its proper measure. A life without such anticipation, a life no longer opened up to heaven, would be empty, a leaden life. That is why there are in reality no societies altogether lacking in cult. Even the decidedly atheistic, materialistic systems create their own forms of cult, though, of course, they can only be an illusion and strive in vain, by bombastic trumpeting, to conceal their nothingness.

And so we come to a final reflection. Man himself cannot simply "make" worship. If God does not reveal himself, man is clutching empty space. Moses says to Pharaoh: "[W]e do not know with what we must serve the LORD" (Ex 10:26). These words display a fundamental law of all liturgy. When God does not reveal himself, man can, of course, from the sense of God within him, build altars "to the unknown god" (cf. Acts 17:23). He can reach out toward God in his thinking and try to feel his way toward him. But real liturgy implies that God responds and reveals how we can worship him. In any form, liturgy includes some kind of "institution". It cannot spring from imagination, our own creativity —then it would remain just a cry in the dark or mere self-affirmation. Liturgy implies a real relationship with Another, who reveals himself to us and gives our existence a new direction.

In the Old Testament, there is a series of very impressive testimonies to the truth that the liturgy is not a matter of "what you please". Nowhere is this more dramatically evident than in the narrative of the golden calf (strictly speaking, "bull calf"). The cult conducted by the high priest Aaron is not meant to serve any of the false gods of the heathen. The apostasy is more subtle. There is no obvious turning away from God to the false gods. Outwardly, the people remain completely attached to the same God. They want to glorify the God who led Israel out of Egypt and believe that they may very properly represent his mysterious power in the image of a bull calf. Everything seems to be in order. Presumably even the ritual is in complete conformity to the rubrics. And yet it is a falling away from the worship of God to idolatry. This apostasy, which outwardly is scarcely perceptible, has two causes. First, there is a violation of the prohibition of images. The people cannot cope with the invisible, remote, and mysterious God. They want to bring him down into their own world, into what they can see and understand. Worship is no longer going up to God, but drawing God down into one's own world.

He must be there when he is needed, and he must be the kind of God that is needed. Man is using God, and in reality, even if it is not outwardly discernible, he is placing himself above God. This gives us a clue to the second point. The worship of the golden calf is a self-generated cult. When Moses stays away for too long, and God himself becomes inaccessible, the people just fetch him back. Worship becomes a feast that the community gives itself, a festival of self-affirmation. Instead of being worship of God, it becomes a circle closed in on itself: eating, drinking, and making merry. The dance around the golden calf is an image of this self-seeking worship. It is a kind of banal self-gratification. The narrative of the golden calf is a warning about any kind of self-initiated and self-seeking worship. Ultimately, it is no longer concerned with God but is concerned only with giving oneself a nice little alternative world, manufactured from one's own resources. Then liturgy really does become pointless, just fooling around. Or, still worse, it becomes an apostasy from the living God, an apostasy in sacral disguise. All that is left in the end is frustration, a feeling of emptiness. There is no experience of that liberation which always takes place when man encounters the living God.

CHAPTER TWO

Liturgy—Cosmos—History

I T IS A WIDELY accepted opinion in modern theology that in the so-called nature religions, as well as in the nontheistic higher religions, cult is focused on the cosmos, while in the Old Testament and Christianity the orientation is toward history. Islam—like post-biblical Judaism —is familiar only with a liturgy of the Word, which is shaped and ordered by the revelation that took place in history, though, in line with the universal tendency of that revelation, it is definitely meant to have a significance for the world as a whole. The idea of worship being either cosmic or historical is not entirely unfounded, but it is false when it leads to an exclusive opposition. It underestimates the sense of history to be found even in the nature religions, and it narrows the meaning of Christian worship of God, forgetting that faith in redemption cannot be separated from faith in the Creator. In this book, we shall discover just how important this question is, even for the apparent externals of liturgical celebration.

I shall try to explain what I am saying in several stages. In the religions of the world, cult and cosmos are always closely bound up with one another. The worship of the gods is never just a kind of act of socialization on the part of the community, the affirmation, through symbols, of its social cohesion. The commonly held idea is that worship involves a circular movement of giving and receiving. The gods sustain the world, while men, by their cultic gifts, feed and sustain the gods. The circle of being has two parts: the power of the gods supporting the world, but also the gift of men, which provides for the gods out of the world's resources. This leads to the idea that man was in fact created in order to sustain the gods and to be an essential link in the circular chain of the universe. However naïve this may seem, it reveals a profound intuition into the meaning of human existence. Man exists for God, and thus he serves the whole. Of course, distortion and abuse also lurk behind the door: man somehow has power over the gods; in some small way, in his relationship to them, he has the key to reality in his hand. The gods need him, but, of course, he also needs them. Should he abuse his power, he would do harm to the gods, but he would also destroy himself.

In the Old Testament's account of creation (Gen 1:1— 2:4), these views are certainly discernible but at the same time transformed. Creation moves toward the Sabbath, to the day on which man and the whole created order participates in God's rest, in his freedom. Nothing is said directly about worship, still less about the Creator needing the gifts of men. The Sabbath is a vision of freedom. On this day, slave and master are equals. The "hallowing" of the Sabbath means precisely this: a rest from all relationships of subordination and a temporary relief from all burden of work. Now some people conclude from this that the Old Testament makes no connection between creation and worship, that it leads to a pure vision of a liberated society as the goal of human history, that from the very beginning its orientation is anthropological and social, indeed, revolutionary. But this is a complete mis-understanding of the Sabbath. The account of creation and the Sinai regulations about the Sabbath come from the same source. To understand the account of creation properly, one has to read the Sabbath ordinances of the Torah. Then everything becomes clear. The Sabbath is the sign of the covenant between God and man; it sums up the inward essence of the covenant. If this is so, then we can now define the intention of the account of creation as follows: creation exists to be a place for the covenant that God wants to make with man. The goal of creation is the covenant, the love story of God and man. The free-dom and equality of men, which the Sabbath is meant to bring about, is not a merely anthropological or sociolog-ical vision; it can only be understood *theo*-logically. Only when man is in covenant with God does he become free. Only then are the equality and dignity of all men made manifest. If, then, everything is directed to the covenant, it is important to see that the covenant is a relationship: God's gift of himself to man, but also man's response to God. Man's response to the God who is good to him is love, and loving God means worshipping him. If creation is meant to be a space for the covenant, the place where God and man meet one another, then it must be thought of as a space for worship. But what does worship really mean? How is it different from the circle of giving and receiving that characterized the pre-Christian world of worship?

Before turning to this vital question, I should like to refer to the text that concludes the giving of the ceremo-nial law in the book of Exodus. It is constructed in close parallel to the account of creation. Seven times it says, "Moses did as the Lord had commanded him", words that

suggest that the seven-day work on the tabernacle repli-
cates the seven-day work on creation. The account of the
construction of the tabernacle ends with a kind of vision
of the Sabbath. "So Moses finished the work. Then the
cloud covered the tent of meeting, and the glory of the
LORD filled the tabernacle" (Ex 40:33f.). The completion
of the tent anticipates the completion of creation. God
makes his dwelling in the world. Heaven and earth are
united. In this connection, we should add that, in the Old
Testament, the verb *bara* has two, and only two, meanings. First, it denotes the process of the world's creation,
the separation of the elements, through which the cosmos emerges out of chaos. Secondly, it denotes the fundamental process of salvation history, that is, the election
and separation of pure from impure and, therefore, the
inauguration of the history of God's dealings with men.
Thus begins the spiritual creation, the creation of the
covenant, without which the created cosmos would be
an empty shell. Creation and history, creation, history,
and worship are in a relationship of reciprocity. Creation
looks toward the covenant, but the covenant completes
creation and does not simply exist along with it. Now if
worship, rightly understood, is the soul of the covenant,
then it not only saves mankind but is also meant to draw
the whole of reality into communion with God.

Once again we face the question: What *is* worship?
What happens when we worship? In all religions, sacrifice is at the heart of worship. But this is a concept that
has been buried under the debris of endless misunderstandings. The common view is that sacrifice has something to do with destruction. It means handing over to
God a reality that is in some way precious to man. Now
this handing over presupposes that it is withdrawn from

use by man, and that can only happen through its destruction, its definitive removal from the hands of man. But this immediately raises the question: What pleasure is God supposed to take in destruction? Is anything really surrendered to God through destruction? One answer is that the destruction always conceals within itself the act of acknowledging God's sovereignty over all things. But can such a mechanical act really serve God's glory? Obviously not. True surrender to God looks very different. It consists—according to the Fathers, in fidelity to biblical thought—in the union of man and creation with God. Belonging to God has nothing to do with destruction or non-being: it is rather a way of being. It means emerging from the state of separation, of apparent autonomy, of existing only for oneself and in oneself. It means losing oneself as the only possible way of finding oneself (cf. Mk 8:35; Mt 10:39). That is why Saint Augustine could say that the true "sacrifice" is the *civitas Dei*, that is, love-transformed mankind, the divinization of creation and the surrender of all things to God: God all in all (cf. 1 Cor 15:28). That is the purpose of the world. That is the essence of sacrifice and worship.

And so we can now say that the goal of worship and the goal of creation as a whole are one and the same—divinization, a world of freedom and love. But this means that the historical makes its appearance in the cosmic. The cosmos is not a kind of closed building, a stationary container in which history may by chance take place. It is itself movement, from its one beginning to its one end. In a sense, creation *is* history.

This can be understood in several ways. For example, against the background of the modern evolutionary world view, Teilhard de Chardin depicted the cosmos as a process of ascent, a series of unions. From very simple beginnings, the path leads to ever greater and more complex unities, in which multiplicity is not abolished but merged into a growing synthesis, leading to the "Noosphere", in which spirit and its understanding embrace the whole and are blended into a kind of living organism. Invoking the epistles to the Ephesians and Colossians, Teilhard looks on Christ as the energy that strives toward the Noosphere and finally incorporates everything in its "fullness". From here, Teilhard went on to give a new meaning to Christian worship: the transubstantiated Host is the anticipation of the transformation and divinization of matter in the christological "fullness". In his view, the Eucharist provides the movement of the cosmos with its direction; it anticipates its goal and at the same time urges it on.

The older tradition starts from a different conceptual model. Its image is not of an upward flying arrow, but of a kind of circular movement, the two essential directions of which can be called *exitus* and *reditus*, departure and return. This "paradigm" is common in the general history of religions as well as in Christian antiquity and the Middle Ages. For Christian thinkers, the circle is seen as the great movement of the cosmos. The nature religions and many non-Christian philosophies think of it as a movement of unceasing repetition. On closer inspection, these two points of view are not as mutually exclusive as at first sight they seem. For in the Christian view of the world, the many small circles of the lives of individuals are inscribed within the one great circle of history as it moves from *exitus* to *reditus*. The small circles carry within themselves the great rhythm of the whole, give it concrete forms that are ever new, and so provide it with the force of its movement. And in the one great circle there are also the many circles of the lives of the different cultures and communities of human history, in which the drama of beginning, development, and end is played out. In these circles, the mystery of beginning is repeated again and again, but they are also the scene of the end of time, of a final collapse, which may in its own way prepare the ground for a new beginning. The totality of the small circles reflects the great circle. The two—the great circle and the small circles—are interconnected and interdependent. And so worship is bound up with all three dimensions of the circular movement: the personal, the social, and the universal.

Before attempting to explain this in more detail, we must take note of the second, and in many respects more important, possibility lying hidden in the pattern of *exitus* and *reditus*. First, there is an idea that received perhaps its most impressive formulation in the work of the great philosopher of late antiquity Plotinus, though, in different forms, it is found in large parts of the non-Christian cults and religions. The exodus by which non-divine being makes its appearance is seen, not as a going out, but as a falling down, a precipitation from the heights of the divine, and by the laws of falling it hurtles into ever greater depths, farther and farther into remoteness from God. This means that non-divine being is itself, as such, fallen being. Finitude is already a kind of sin, something negative, which has to be saved by being brought back into the infinite. And so the journey back—the *reditus*—begins when the fall is arrested in the outer depths, so that now the arrow points upward. In the end, the "sin" of the finite, of not-being-God, disappears, and in that sense God becomes "all in all". The way of *reditus* means redemption, and redemption means liberation from finitude, which is the real burden of our existence. Cult, then, has to do with the movement turning around. It is the sudden awareness that one has fallen, like the Prodigal Son's moment of remorse, when he looks back to where he has come from. According to many of these philosophies, knowledge and being coincide, and so this new view of the beginning is already an ascent back toward it. Cult in the sense of the looking up to what is before and above all being is, of its very nature, knowledge, and as knowledge it is movement, return, redemption.

The philosophies of cult go off in different directions. One theory is that only philosophers, only minds qualified for higher thought, are capable of the knowledge that constitutes the "way". Only they are capable of the ascent, of the full divinization that is redemption and liberation from finitude. For the others, for the simpler souls not yet capable of the full upward vision, there are the different liturgies that offer them a certain redemption without being able to take them to the height of the Godhead. The doctrine of the transmigration of souls often compensates for these inequalities. It offers the hope that at some time in the wanderings of existence the point will be reached when at last we can find an escape from finitude and its torments. *Knowledge* (*gnosis*) is the real power of redemption here and therefore the highest form of our elevation —union with God. That is why conceptual and religious systems of this kind—individually, they are all very different—are called "Gnosticism". In early Christianity, the clash with Gnosticism was the decisive struggle for its own identity. The fascination of such views is very great; they seem so easily identifiable with the Christian message. For example, original sin, so hard otherwise to understand, is identified with the fall into finitude, which explains why it clings to everything stuck in the vortex of finitude. Again, the idea of redemption as deliverance from the burden of finitude is readily comprehensible, and so on. In our own times, too, in a variety of forms, the fascination of Gnosticism is at work. The religions of the Far East have the same basic pattern. That is why the various kinds of teaching on redemption that they offer seem highly plausible. Exercises for relaxing the body and emptying the mind are seen as the path to redemption. They aim at liberation from finitude, indeed, they momentarily anticipate that liberation and so have salvific power.

As we have said, Christian thought has taken up the schema of *exitus* and *reditus*, but, in so doing, it distinguishes the two movements from one another. *Exitus* is not a fall from the infinite, the rupture of being, and thus the cause of all the sorrow in the world. No, *exitus* is first and foremost something thoroughly positive. It is the Creator's free act of creation. It is his positive will that the created order should exist as something good in relation to himself, from which a response of freedom and love can be given back to him. Non-divine being is not, therefore, something negative in itself but, on the contrary, the wholly positive fruit of the divine will. It depends, not on a disaster, but on a divine decree that is good and does good. The act of God's being, which causes created being, is an act of freedom. In this respect, the principle of freedom is present in being itself, from its ground upward. The *exitus*, or rather God's free act of creation, is indeed ordered toward the *reditus*, but that does not now mean the rescinding of created being, but rather it means what we have described above. The creature, existing in its own right, comes home to itself, and this act is an answer in freedom to God's love. It accepts creation from God as his offer of love, and thus ensues a dialogue of love, that wholly new kind of unity which love alone can create. The being of the other is not absorbed or abolished, but rather, in giving itself, it becomes fully itself. Here is a unity that is higher than the unity of indivisible elementary particles. This *reditus* is a "return", but it does not abolish creation; rather, it bestows its full and final perfection. This is how Christians understand God being "all in all". But everything is bound up with freedom, and the creature has the freedom to turn the positive *exitus* of its creation around, as it were, to rupture it in the Fall: this is the refusal to be dependent, saying No to the *reditus*. Love is seen as dependence and is rejected. In its place come autonomy and autarchy: existing from oneself and in oneself, being a god of one's own making. The arch from *exitus* to *reditus* is broken. The return is no longer desired, and ascent by one's powers proves to be impossible. If "sacrifice" in its essence is simply returning to love and therefore divinization, worship now has a new aspect: the healing of wounded freedom, atonement, purification, deliverance from estrangement. The essence of worship, of sacrifice—the process of assimilation, of growth in love, and thus the way into freedom —remains unchanged. But now it assumes the aspect of healing, the loving transformation of broken freedom, of painful expiation. Worship is directed to the Other in himself, to his all-sufficiency, but now it refers itself to the Other who alone can extricate me from the knot that I myself cannot untie. Redemption now needs the Redeemer. The Fathers saw this expressed in the parable of the Lost Sheep. For them, the sheep caught in the thorn bush and unable to find its way home is a metaphor for man in general. He cannot get out of the thicket and find his way back to God. The shepherd who rescues him and takes him home is the Logos himself, the eternal Word, the eternal Meaning of the universe dwelling in the Son. He it is who makes his way to us and takes the sheep onto his shoulders, that is, he assumes human nature, and as the God-Man he carries man the creature home to God. And so the *reditus* becomes possible. Man is given a homecoming. But now sacrifice takes the form of the Cross of Christ, of the love that in dying makes a gift of itself. Such sacrifice has nothing to do with destruction. It is an act of new creation, the restoration of creation to its true identity. All worship is now a participation in this "Pasch" of Christ, in his "passing over" from divine to human, from death to life, to the unity of God and man. Thus Christian worship is the practical application and fulfillment of the words that Jesus proclaimed on the first day of Holy Week, Palm Sunday, in the Temple in Jerusalem: "I, when I am lifted up from the earth, will draw all men to myself" (Jn 12:32).

The circles of the cosmos and of history are now distinguished. The gift of freedom is the center of created as well as of divine being, and so the historical element has its own irrevocable meaning, but it is not for that reason separated from the cosmic element. Ultimately, despite their differences, the two circles continue to be the one circle of being. The historical liturgy of Christendom is and always will be cosmic, without separation and without confusion, and only as such does it stand erect in its full grandeur. Christianity is uniquely new, but it does not spurn the religious quest of human history. It takes up in itself all the prevailing preoccupations of the world's religions, and in that way it maintains a connection with them.

CHAPTER THREE

From Old Testament to New:
The Fundamental Form of the Christian Liturgy
—Its Determination by Biblical Faith

P EACE IN THE UNIVERSE through peace with God, the
union of above and below—that, according to the argument we have presented so far, is how we can describe
the essential intention of worship in all the world's religions. But this basic definition of the attributes of worship
is marked concretely by an awareness of man's fall and
estrangement. Of necessity it takes place as a struggle for
atonement, forgiveness, reconciliation. The awareness of
guilt weighs down on mankind. Worship is the attempt, to
be found at every stage of history, to overcome guilt and
bring back the world and one's own life into right order.
And yet an immense feeling of futility pervades everything. This is the tragic face of human history. How can
man again connect the world with God? How is he supposed to make valid atonement? The only real gift man
should give to God is himself. As his religious awareness
becomes more highly developed, so his awareness that
any gift but himself is too little, in fact absurd, becomes
more intense. Historically, this sense of inadequacy has
been the source of grotesque and horrific forms of cult.
The most extreme example is human sacrifice. Superficially, it seems to give the deity what is best, and yet more

deeply it has to be seen as the most horrific evasion of the gift of self, the most horrific and therefore the most to be rejected. Thus, as religion becomes more highly developed, this terrible attempt at atonement is more and more discarded, but it also becomes clearer that in all worship it is not the real gift but a mere replacement that is given.[1] The sacrificial system of all the world's religions, including Israel's, rests on the idea of representation—but how can sacrificial animals or the fruits of harvest represent man, make expiation for him? This is not representation but replacement, and worship with replacements turns out to be a replacement for worship. Somehow the real thing is missing.

What, then, is special about the liturgy of Israel? First of all, without doubt, the One to whom it is directed. Other religions frequently direct their worship to subordinate powers. Precisely because they know that the only true God cannot be served by the sacrifice of animals, they leave him without worship. Sacrifices are aimed at the "principalities and powers" with which man has to deal on a daily basis. These are what he has to fear, to propitiate, to placate. Israel did not merely deny the existence of these "gods" but saw them more and more as demons, which increasingly alienate man from himself and from God. Adoration is due to God alone: that is the

---

[1] Cardinal Ratzinger here uses the German word *Ersatz*, which is generally translated as "substitute" (as in *Ersatzkaffee*, coffee made out of a substitute for coffee beans such as acorns). I have not used "substitute" because of the more positive theological connotations of that English word when used as a translation of *Stellvertreter*. The cardinal is contrasting the two ways in which one thing can take the place of another. In the first case, there is mere absence: something that should be there is missing (cf. "a poor substitute for real coffee"). In the second case, there is mysterious presence: somehow one thing is present in the other. This explains the contrast I have put into the English between "replacement" (*Ersatz*) sacrifices and "representation" (*Vertretung*) sacrifices.—TRANS.

first commandment. Now this one God is worshipped through an extensive sacrificial system, the meticulous regulations for which are set out in the Torah. However, when we look at the cultic history of Israel more closely, we run up against a second characteristic, which leads finally, by its inner logic, to Jesus Christ, to the New Testament. It is precisely when we read the New Testament in terms of cultic theology that we see how much it is bound up, in its deepest implications, with the Old. The New Testament corresponds to the inner drama of the Old. It is the inner mediation of two elements that at first are in conflict with one another and find their unity in the form of Jesus Christ, in his Cross and Resurrection. What at first seems to be a break turns out, on closer inspection, to be a real fulfillment, in which all the paths formerly followed converge.

Anyone who would read the book of Leviticus by itself—without looking at chapter 26, with its threat of exile and its promise of new blessings—would come to the conclusion that it sets up an eternally valid form of worship. Here is an apparently everlasting world order, with no further history to come, because in the course of the year it constantly brings about new expiation, purification, restoration. It seems to be a static or, if you like, cyclical world order. It always remains the same, because it contains weights and counterweights in perfect balance. But chapter 26, to a certain extent, shatters this appearance. More importantly, Leviticus has to be read in the context of the whole Torah and the whole Bible. It seems to me to be of some importance that, at the beginning of cultic history, Genesis and Exodus place two events in which the problem of representation is quite clearly addressed. First of all, there is Abraham's sacrifice. Out of obedience, Abraham is willing to do something that goes against the mission given by God: to sacrifice his only son, Isaac, the bearer of the promise. In so doing, he would be giving up everything, for, without descendants, the land promised to his descendants has no meaning. At the very last moment, God himself stops Abraham from offering this kind of sacrifice. He is given something else to offer instead of the son of God—a male lamb. And so representative sacrifice is established by divine command. God gives the lamb, which Abraham then offers back to him. Accordingly, we offer sacrifice, as the Roman Canon says, "de tuis donis ac datis" (from your own gracious gifts). Somehow there always has to be a stinging reminder of this story, an expectation of the true Lamb, who comes from God and is for that very reason not a replacement but a true representative, in whom we ourselves are taken to God. The Christian theology of worship—beginning with Saint John the Baptist—sees in Christ the Lamb given by God. The Apocalypse presents this sacrificed Lamb, who lives as sacrificed, as the center of the heavenly liturgy, a liturgy that, through Christ's Sacrifice, is now present in the midst of the world and makes replacement liturgies superfluous (see Rev 5).

My second point concerns the institution of the Passover liturgy in Exodus 12. Here the rules are laid down for the sacrifice of the Passover lamb as the center of the liturgical year and of Israel's memorial of faith, which is at the same time an everlasting foundation of faith. The lamb appears clearly as the ransom through which Israel is delivered from the death of the firstborn. Now this ransom serves also as a reminder. It is ultimately the firstborn itself to which God lays claim: "Consecrate to me all the first-born; whatever is the first to open the womb among the sons of Israel, both of man and of beast, is

mine" (Ex 13:2). The sacrificed lamb speaks of the necessary holiness of man and of creation as a whole. It points
beyond itself. The Passover sacrifice does not, as it were,
stop with itself, but places an obligation on the firstborn
and, in them, on the people as a whole, on creation as a
whole. This fact should help us appreciate the emphatic
way in which Saint Luke in his infancy narratives describes Jesus as the "first-born" (cf. Lk 2:7). It also helps
us understand why the Captivity Epistles present Christ
as the "first-born of creation", in whom takes place a
sanctification of the firstborn that embraces us all.

But we are still in the Old Testament. Its sacrificial
system is constantly accompanied by prophetic disquiet
and questioning. Already in 1 Samuel 15:22 we meet a
primordial word of prophecy that, with some variations,
runs through the Old Testament before being taken up
anew by Christ: "To obey is better than sacrifice, and
to listen than the fat of rams!" In Hosea the prophecy
appears in this form: "For I desire mercy and not sacrifice, the knowledge of God, rather than burnt offerings" (6:6). In the mouth of Jesus, it assumes a very
simple and elementary form: "I desire mercy, and not
sacrifice" (Mt 9:13; 12:7). Thus Temple worship was always accompanied by a vivid sense of its insufficiency.
"If I were hungry, I would not tell you; for the world
and all that is in it is mine. Do I eat the flesh of bulls,
or drink the blood of goats? Offer to God a sacrifice of
thanksgiving, and pay your vows to the Most High" (Ps
50[49]:12–14). The radical critique of the Temple, which,
according to the account in Acts chapter 7, Stephen delivered in a fiery speech, is certainly unusual in its form,
marked as it is with the new passion of Christian faith,
but it is not without precedent in the history of Israel.

At the end, Stephen takes the key sentence of his critique from the prophet Amos: "I hate, I despise your feasts, and I take no delight in your solemn assemblies. Even though you offer me your burnt offerings and cereal offerings, I will not accept them, and the peace offerings of your fatted beasts I will not look upon. Take away from me the noise of your songs; to the melody of your harps I will not listen" (Amos 5:21–23; cf. Acts 7:42f., citing Amos 5:25–27).

The whole of Saint Stephen's speech is triggered by the accusation that he had said "Jesus of Nazareth will destroy this place [that is, the Temple], and will change the customs which Moses delivered to us" (Acts 6:14). Stephen responds to this allegation only indirectly, by invoking the line of criticism of Temple and sacrifice that runs through the Old Testament. He quotes the controversial criticism of cult to be found in Amos 5:25–27, the original meaning of which is very hard to decipher. He uses the version in the Greek Bible, in which all the worship of the forty years in the wilderness is aligned with the worship of the golden calf. This makes Israel's liturgy during the whole of this foundational period seem like a continuation of the first apostasy. "Did you offer to me slain beasts and sacrifices, forty years in the wilderness, O house of Israel? And you took up the tent of Moloch, and the star of the god Rephan, the figures which you made to worship; and I will remove you beyond Babylon" (Acts 7:42f.; cf. Amos 5:25–27). The very beasts of sacrifice seem here to be a perversion of worship of the one God. The words of the prophet, used by Stephen in the version of the Alexandrian translators, must have come as a violent shock to his hearers. In fact, he could have added to them the dramatic words of the prophet Jeremiah: "[I]n

the day that I brought them out of the land of Egypt, I
did not speak to your fathers or command them concerning burnt offerings and sacrifices" (Jer 7:22). Stephen re-
frains from exploiting such texts, which give us a sense
of the difficult internal debates in Israel before the Exile.
Instead, he adds three other trains of thought to get across
his exposition of the message of Christ.

Moses, he says, made the tent of meeting, in obedience to God's command, according to the pattern he had
seen on the mountain (cf. Acts 7:44; Ex 25:40). This
means that the earthly Temple is only a replica, not the
true Temple. It is an image and likeness, which points
beyond itself. David, who found favor with God, prayed
God to let him build a tabernacle. "But it was Solomon
who built a house for him" (Acts 7:47). The transition
from the tent with all its impermanence to the house intended to lodge God in an edifice of stone is seen as a de-
viance, for "the Most High does not dwell in houses made
with hands" (7:48). Finally, Stephen adds something to
the idea of impermanence, which was conspicuous in the
tent but obscured in the house. He brings out the inner dynamism of the Old Testament, which inevitably
strove to get beyond the impermanence. He quotes the
Messianic prophecy that in a certain sense forms the climax of Deuteronomy (cf. 18:15) and, for Stephen, provides the key for the interpretation of the whole Pentateuch: "God will raise up for you a prophet from your
brethren as he raised me up" (7:37). The essential work of
Moses was the construction of the tabernacle and the ordering of worship, which was also the very heart of the
order of law and moral instruction. If this is so, then it is
clear that the new Prophet, the definitive Prophet, will
lead the people out of the age of the tabernacle and its

impermanence, out of all the inadequacy of sacrificial animals. He will "destroy" the Temple and indeed "change the customs" that Moses had delivered. The prophets who followed Moses were the great witnesses to the impermanence of all these customs. Raising their voices, they pushed history forward toward the New Moses. This is the prophetic line that reached its destination in the Righteous One on the Cross (cf. Acts 7:51f.).

Stephen does not contest the words he is accused of having spoken. Instead, he tries to prove that they contain a deeper fidelity to the message of the Old Testament and, indeed, to the message of Moses. It is important also to note that the charge brought against the first martyrs of the Church is identical, almost to the letter, with the accusation that plays such a central role in the trial of Jesus. For Jesus was accused of having said: "I will destroy this temple that is made with hands, and in three days I will build another, not made with hands" (Mk 14:58). Of course, the witnesses could not agree about the exact meaning of Jesus' prophecy (cf. 14:59), but it is clear that such words played a central role in the dispute about Jesus. Here we reach the heart of the christological question, the question of who Jesus is, and at the same time we reach the heart of the question of what the true worship of God is. The prophecy of the Temple's destruction, which Jesus is accused of having made, points beyond itself to the incident recorded by all four Evangelists: the cleansing of the Temple. This could not be regarded as just an angry outburst against the abuses that happen in all holy places. No, in the final analysis, this had to be seen as an attack on the Temple cult, of which the sacrificial animals and the special Temple moneys collected there were a part. True, none of the

Synoptic Gospels reports any such words of Jesus in this context, but Saint John presents them as a prophetic utterance that Jesus makes in explanation of his action: "Destroy this temple, and in three days I will raise it up" (Jn 2:19). Jesus does not say that *he* will demolish the Temple —that version was the false witness borne against him. But he does prophesy that his accusers will do exactly that. This is a prophecy of the Cross: he shows that the destruction of his earthly body will be at the same time the end of the Temple. With his Resurrection, the new Temple will begin: the living body of Jesus Christ, which will now stand in the sight of God and be the place of all worship. Into this body he incorporates men. It is the tabernacle that no human hands have made, the place of true worship of God, which casts out the shadow and replaces it with reality. Interpreted at its deepest level, the prophecy of the Resurrection is also a prophecy of the Eucharist. The body of Christ is sacrificed and precisely as sacrificed is living. This is the mystery made known in the Mass. Christ communicates himself to us and thus brings us into a real bond with the living God. We should mention in this connection another detail, which is found in all three of the Synoptic Gospels. They all report that, at the moment of Jesus' death, the veil of the Temple was torn in two, from top to bottom (cf. Mk 15:38; Mt 27:51; Lk 23:45). What they mean to say is this: at the moment of Jesus' death, the function of the old Temple comes to an end. It is dissolved. It is no longer the place of God's presence, his "footstool", into which he has caused his glory to descend. Theologically, the visible destruction of the Temple, which will follow in a few decades, has already been anticipated. Worship through types and shadows, worship with replacements, ends at the very moment when the real worship takes place: the self-offering of the Son, who has become man and "Lamb", the "Firstborn", who gathers up and into himself all worship of God, takes it from the types and shadows into the reality of man's union with the living God. The prophetic gesture of cleansing the Temple, of renewing divine worship and preparing it for its new form, has reached its goal. The prophecy connected with it is fulfilled: "[Z]eal for your house has consumed me" (Ps 69[68]:9; Jn 2:17). At the end, it was Jesus' "zeal" for right worship that took him to the Cross. This is precisely what opened the way for the true house of God, the "one not made with human hands"—the risen body of Christ. And the interpretation that the Synoptic Gospels give to Jesus' symbolic act of prophecy is also fulfilled: "My house shall be called a house of prayer for all the nations" (Mk 11:17). The abolition of the Temple inaugurates a new universality of worship, "in spirit and truth" (cf. Jn 4:23), which Jesus foretold in his conversation with the Samaritan woman. Needless to say, the words "spirit and truth" must not be taken in a subjectivist sense, as they were in the Enlightenment. No, they must be seen in the light of him who could say of himself: "I am . . . the truth" (Jn 14:6).

We have so far presented a sketch of the inner dynamism of the idea of worship in the Old Testament and have shown that there was an intense awareness of the impermanence of the Temple sacrifices together with a desire for something greater, something indescribably new. Before trying to pull everything together and draw some conclusions, we must try to hear the voices in which there is already a presentiment of this new thing that is to come. I am thinking of the tendency, that had already become apparent, of taking up an essentially critical attitude toward the previous forms of worship. In pre-exilic Israel, one constantly hears voices warning about the rigidifying of the sacrificial system and its degeneration into externalism and syncretism. The Exile came as a challenging opportunity to formulate clearly a positive doctrine about worship and the new thing that was to come. There was no Temple anymore, no public and communal form of divine worship as decreed in the law. Deprived as it was of worship, Israel was bound to feel immeasurably poor and pathetic. It stood before God with empty hands. There was no expiation anymore, no "holocausts" ascending to God. In this crisis, the conviction became ever clearer that Israel's sufferings, through God and for God, the cry of its broken heart, its persistent pleading before the silent God, had to count in his sight as "fatted sacrifices" and whole burnt offerings. It was the very emptiness of Israel's hands, the heaviness of its heart, that was now to be worship, to serve as a spiritual equivalent of the missing Temple oblations. During the new oppression of Jewish worship under Antiochus IV Epiphanes (175–163 B.C.), these ideas, as set forth in the book of Daniel, acquired a new power and profundity. They remained alive even after the restoration of the Temple by the Maccabees. The Qumran community formed an opposition to the priestly monarchy of the Maccabees: it did not recognize the new Temple and saw itself instead as dedicated to "spiritual worship". In Alexandria, the Jews eventually made contact with the Greek critique of cult, and from then on the concept of *logikē latreia* (*thusia*) [worship and sacrifice with spirit and mind], which we encounter in the epistle to the Romans (cf. Rom 12:1), grew increasingly important. This was the Christian response to the cultic crisis of the whole ancient world. The sacrifice is the "word", the word of prayer, which goes up from man to God, embodying the whole of man's existence and enabling him to become "word" (*logos*) in himself. It is man, conforming himself to *logos* and becoming *logos* through faith, who is the true sacrifice, the true glory of God in the world. Israel's experience of suffering during the Exile and the Hellenistic period first brought the word of prayer into prominence as the equivalent of exterior sacrifice. Now, through the word *logos*, the whole philosophy of *logos* in the Greek world is incorporated into the concept. The Greek mind elevates it eventually to the idea of a mystical union with the Logos, the very meaning of all things.

The Fathers of the Church took up this spiritual development. They saw the Eucharist as essentially *oratio*, sacrifice in the Word, and in this way they also showed how Christian worship stood in relation to the spiritual struggle of antiquity, to its quest for man's true path and for his encounter with God. The Fathers call the Eucharist simply "prayer", that is, the sacrifice of the Word, but in so doing, they go beyond the Greek idea of the sacrifice of the *logos* and provide an answer to the question left open by Old Testament theology, which made prayer the equivalent of sacrifice. A striking conflict is evident in the great Old Testament movement toward worship in the "Word". On the one hand, the way is open to a new, positive form of divine worship. On the other hand, there is still an insufficiency. The Word alone is not enough. There is an expectation of a restoration of the Temple in purified form. This explains the apparent contradictions that we find in Psalm 51(50). On the one hand, there is a magnificent unfolding of the new idea of worship: "For you take no delight in sacrifice. . . . The sacrifice acceptable to God is a broken spirit" (v. 17). On the other hand, the whole psalm ends with a stirring vision of a fulfillment to come: "[T]hen will you delight in right sacrifices, in burnt offerings and whole burnt offerings; then bulls will be offered on your altar" (v. 19). For its part, the Hellenistic Logos-mysticism, however grand and beautiful, allows the body to fall into insubstantiality. The hope for spiritual ascent and universal reunion conforms to the Gnostic pattern of which we spoke earlier. Something is missing.

The idea of the sacrifice of the Logos becomes a full reality only in the *Logos incarnatus*, the Word who is made flesh and draws "all flesh" into the glorification of God. When that happens, the Logos is more than just the "Meaning" behind and above things. Now he himself has entered into flesh, has become bodily. He takes up into himself our sufferings and hopes, all the yearning of creation, and bears it to God. The two themes that Psalm 51(50) could not reconcile, the two themes that throughout the Old Testament keep running toward one another, now really converge. The Word is no longer just the representation of something else, of what is bodily. In Jesus' self-surrender on the Cross, the Word is united with the entire reality of human life and suffering. There is no longer a replacement cult. Now the vicarious sacrifice of Jesus takes us up and leads us into that likeness with God, that transformation into love, which is the only true adoration. In virtue of Jesus' Cross and Resurrection, the Eucharist is the meeting point of all the lines that lead from the Old Covenant, indeed, from the whole of man's religious history. Here at last is right worship, ever longed for and yet surpassing our powers: adoration "in spirit and truth". The torn curtain of the Temple is the curtain torn between the world and the countenance of God. In the pierced heart of the Crucified, God's own heart is opened up—here we see who God is and what he is like. Heaven is no longer locked up. God has stepped out of his hiddenness. That is why Saint John sums up both the meaning of the Cross and the nature of the new worship of God in the mysterious promise made through the prophet Zechariah (cf. 12:10). "They shall look on him whom they have pierced" (Jn 19:37). We shall meet this text again, with a new significance, in Revelation 1:7. For the moment, we must try to sum up some of the conclusions that emerge from what we have said so far.

1. Christian worship, or rather the liturgy of the Christian faith, cannot be viewed simply as a Christianized form of the synagogue service, however much its actual development owes to the synagogue service. The synagogue was always ordered toward the Temple and remained so, even after the Temple's destruction. The synagogue's liturgy of the Word, which is celebrated with magnificent profundity, regards itself as incomplete, and for that reason it is very different from the liturgy of the Word in Islam, which, together with pilgrimage and fasting, constitutes the whole of divine worship as decreed by the Qur'an. By contrast, the synagogue service is the divine worship that takes place in the absence of the Temple and in expectation of its restoration. Christian worship, for its part, regards the destruction of the Temple in Jerusalem as final and as theologically necessary. Its place has been taken by the universal Temple of the risen Christ, whose outstretched arms on the Cross span the world in order to draw all men into the embrace of eternal love. The new Temple already exists, and so too does the new, the definitive sacrifice: the humanity

of Christ opened up in his Cross and Resurrection. The prayer of the man Jesus is now united with the dialogue of eternal love within the Trinity. Jesus draws men into this prayer through the Eucharist, which is thus the ever-open door of adoration and the true Sacrifice, the Sacrifice of the New Covenant, the "reasonable service of God". In modern theological discussion, the exclusive model for the liturgy of the New Covenant has been thought to be the synagogue—in strict opposition to the Temple, which is regarded as an expression of the law and there-fore as an utterly obsolete "stage" in religion. The effects of this theory have been disastrous. Priesthood and sacri-fice are no longer intelligible. The comprehensive "ful-fillment" of pre-Christian salvation history and the inner unity of the two Testaments disappear from view. Deeper understanding of the matter is bound to recognize that the Temple, as well as the synagogue, entered into Chris-tian liturgy.

2. This means that universality is an essential feature of Christian worship. It is the worship of an open heaven. It is never just an event in the life of a community that finds itself in a particular place. No, to celebrate the Eucharist means to enter into the openness of a glorification of God that embraces both heaven and earth, an openness effected by the Cross and Resurrection. Christian liturgy is never just an event organized by a particular group or set of peo-ple or even by a particular local Church. Mankind's move-ment toward Christ meets Christ's movement toward men. He wants to unite mankind and bring about the one Church, the one divine assembly, of all men. Every-thing, then, comes together: the horizontal and the ver-tical, the uniqueness of God and the unity of mankind, the communion of all who worship in spirit and in truth.

3. Accordingly, we must regard Saint Paul's concept of *logikē latreia*, of divine worship in accordance with *logos*, as the most appropriate way of expressing the essential form of Christian liturgy. This concept is the confluence of several different streams: the spiritual movement of the Old Testament, the process of inner purification within the history of religion, human quest, and divine response. The *logos* of creation, the *logos* in man, and the true and eternal Logos made flesh, the Son, come together. All other definitions fall short. For example, one could describe the Eucharist, in terms of the liturgical phenomenon, as an "assembly", or, in terms of Jesus' act of institution at the Last Supper, as a "meal". But this seizes on individual elements while failing to grasp the great historical and theological connections. By contrast, the word "Eucharist" points to the universal form of worship that took place in the Incarnation, Cross, and Resurrection of Christ, and so it can happily serve as a summary of the idea of *logikē latreia* and may legitimately serve as an appropriate designation for Christian worship.

4. Finally, all these insights open up an essential dimension of Christian liturgy that we must consider more concretely in the next chapter. As we have seen, Christian liturgy is a liturgy of promise fulfilled, of a quest, the religious quest of human history, reaching its goal. But it remains a liturgy of hope. It, too, bears within it the mark of impermanence. The new Temple, not made by human hands, does exist, but it is also still under construction. The great gesture of embrace emanating from the Crucified has not yet reached its goal; it has only just begun. Christian liturgy is liturgy on the way, a liturgy of pilgrimage toward the transfiguration of the world, which will only take place when God is "all in all".

PART TWO

TIME AND SPACE IN THE LITURGY

CHAPTER ONE

The Relationship of the Liturgy to Time and Space: Some Preliminary Questions

C AN THERE REALLY be special holy places and holy times in the world of Christian faith? Christian worship is surely a cosmic liturgy, which embraces both heaven and earth. The epistle to the Hebrews stresses that Christ suffered "outside the gate" and adds this exhortation: "Therefore let us go forth to him outside the camp, bearing abuse for him" (13:12). Is the whole world not now his sanctuary? Is sanctity not to be practiced by living one's daily life in the right way? Is our divine worship not a matter of being loving people in our daily life? Is *that* not how we become like God and so draw near to the true sacrifice? Can the sacral be anything other than imitating Christ in the simple patience of daily life? Can there be any other holy time than the time for practicing love of neighbor, whenever and wherever the circumstances of our life demand it?

Whoever asks questions like these touches on a crucial dimension of the Christian understanding of worship but overlooks something essential about the permanent limits of human existence in this world, overlooks the "not yet" that is part of Christian existence and talks as if the New Heaven and New Earth had already come.

The Christ-event and the growth of the Church out of all the nations, the transition from Temple sacrifice to universal worship "in spirit and truth", is the first important step across the frontier, a step toward the fulfillment of the promises of the Old Testament. But it is obvious that hope has not yet fully attained its goal. The New Jerusalem needs no Temple because Almighty God and the Lamb are themselves its Temple. In this City, instead of sun and moon, it is the glory of God and its lamp, the Lamb, that shed their brilliance (cf. Rev 21:22f.). But this City is not yet here. That is why the Church Fathers described the various stages of fulfillment, not just as a contrast between Old and New Testaments, but as the three steps of shadow, image, and reality. In the Church of the New Testament, the shadow has been scattered by the image: "[T]he night is far gone, the day is at hand" (Rom 13:12). But, as Saint Gregory the Great puts it, it is still only the time of dawn, when darkness and light are intermingled. The sun is rising, but it has still not reached its zenith. Thus the time of the New Testament is a peculiar kind of "in-between", a mixture of "already and not yet". The empirical conditions of life in this world are still in force, but they have been burst open, and must be more and more burst open, in preparation for the final fulfillment already inaugurated in Christ.

This idea of the New Testament as the between-time, as image between shadow and reality, gives liturgical theology its specific form. It becomes even clearer when we bear in mind the three levels on which Christian worship operates, the three levels that make it what it is. There is the middle level, the strictly liturgical level, which is familiar to us all and is revealed in the words and actions of Jesus at the Last Supper. These words and actions form the core of Christian liturgical celebration, which was further constructed out of the synthesis of the synagogue and Temple liturgies. The sacrificial actions of the Temple have been replaced by the Eucharistic Prayer, which enters into what Jesus did at the Last Supper, and by the distribution of the consecrated gifts. But this properly liturgical level does not stand on its own. It has meaning only in relation to something that really happens, to a reality that is substantially present. Otherwise, it would lack real content, like bank notes without funds to cover them. The Lord could say that his Body was "given" only because he *had* in fact given it; he could present his Blood in the new chalice as shed for many only because he really *had* shed it. This Body is not the ever-dead corpse of a dead man, nor is the Blood the life-element rendered lifeless. No, sacrifice has become gift, for the Body given in love and the Blood given in love have entered, through the Resurrection, into the eternity of love, which is stronger than death. Without the Cross and Resurrection, Christian worship is null and void, and a theology of liturgy that omitted any reference to them would really just be talking about an empty game.

In considering this foundation of reality that undergirds Christian liturgy, we need to take account of another important matter. The Crucifixion of Christ, his death on the Cross, and, in another way, the act of his Resurrection from the grave, which bestows incorruptibility on the corruptible, are historical events that happen just once and as such belong to the past. The word *semel* (*ephapax*), "once for all", which the epistle to the Hebrews emphasizes so vigorously in contrast to the multitude of repeated sacrifices in the Old Covenant, is strictly applicable to them. But if they were no more than facts in the past, like all the dates we learn in history books, then there could be nothing contemporary about them. In the end, they would remain beyond our reach. However, the exterior act of being crucified is accompanied by an interior act of self-giving (the Body is "given for you"). "No one takes [my life] from me," says the Lord in Saint John's Gospel, "but I lay it down of my own accord" (10:18). This act of giving is in no way just a spiritual occurrence. It is a spiritual act that takes up the bodily into itself, that embraces the whole man; indeed, it is at the same time an act of the Son. As Saint Maximus the Confessor showed so splendidly, the obedience of Jesus' human will is inserted into the everlasting Yes of the Son to the Father. This "giving" on the part of the Lord, in the passivity of his being crucified, draws the passion of human existence into the action of love, and so it embraces all the dimensions of reality—Body, Soul, Spirit, Logos. Just as the pain of the body is drawn into the pathos of the mind and becomes the Yes of obedience, so time is drawn into what reaches beyond time. The real interior act, though it does not exist without the exterior, transcends time, but since it comes from time, time can again and again be brought into it. That is how we can become contemporary with the past events of salvation. Saint Bernard of Clairvaux has this in mind when he says that the true *semel* ("once") bears within itself the *semper* ("always"). What is perpetual takes place in what happens only once. In the Bible, the Once for All is emphasized most vigorously in the epistle to the Hebrews, but the careful reader will discover that the point made by Saint Bernard expresses its true meaning. The *ephapax* ("once for all") is bound up with the *aiōnios* ("everlasting").

"Today" embraces the whole time of the Church. And so in the Christian liturgy, we not only receive something from the past but become contemporaries with what lies at the foundation of that liturgy. Here is the real heart and true grandeur of the celebration of the Eucharist, which is more, much more than a meal. In the Eucharist, we are caught up and made contemporary with the Paschal Mystery of Christ, in his passing from the tabernacle of the transitory to the presence and sight of God.

Let us go back to where we started. We said that there is, first, the level of the event of institution and, secondly, the liturgical making present, the real liturgical level. I have tried to show how the two levels are interconnected. Now if past and present penetrate one another in this way, if the essence of the past is not simply a thing of the past but the far-reaching power of what follows in the present, then the future, too, is present in what happens in the liturgy: it ought to be called, in its essence, an anticipation of what is to come. But we must not be overhasty. The idea of the *eschaton*, of the Second Coming of Christ, immediately comes to mind, and rightly so. But there is yet another dimension to be considered. This liturgy is, as we have seen, not about replacement, but about representation, vicarious sacrifice [*Stellvertretung*]. Now we can see what this distinction means. The liturgy is not about the sacrificing of animals, of a "something" that is ultimately alien to me. This liturgy is founded on the Passion endured by a man who with his "I" reaches into the mystery of the living God himself, by the man who is the Son. So it can never be a mere *actio liturgica*. Its origin also bears within it its future in the sense that representation, vicarious sacrifice, takes up into itself those whom it represents; it is not external to them, but a shaping influence on them. Becoming contemporary with the Pasch of Christ in the liturgy of the Church is also, in fact, an anthropological reality. The celebration is not just a rite, not just a liturgical "game". It is meant to be indeed a *logikē latreia*, the "logicizing" of my existence, my interior contemporaneity with the self-giving of Christ. His self-giving is meant to become mine, so that I become contemporary with the Pasch of Christ and assimilated unto God. That is why in the early Church martyrdom was regarded as a real eucharistic celebration, the most extreme actualization of the Christian's being a contemporary with Christ, of being united with him. The liturgy does indeed have a bearing on everyday life, on me in my personal existence. Its aim, as Saint Paul says in the text already referred to, is that "our bodies" (that is, our bodily existence on earth) become "a living sacrifice", united to the Sacrifice of Christ (cf. Rom 12:1). That is the only explanation of the urgency of the petitions for acceptance that characterize every Christian liturgy. A theology that is blind to the connections we have been considering can only regard this as a contradiction or a lapse into pre-Christian ways, for, so it will be said, Christ's Sacrifice was accepted long ago. True, but in the form of representation it has not come to an end. The *semel* ("once for all") wants to attain its *semper* ("always"). This Sacrifice is only complete when the world has become the place of love, as Saint Augustine saw in his *City of God*. Only then, as we said at the beginning, is worship perfected and what happened on Golgotha completed. That is why, in the petitions for acceptance, we pray that representation become a reality and take hold of us. That is why, in the prayers of the Roman Canon, we unite ourselves with the great men who offered sacrifice at the dawn of history: Abel, Melchizedek, and Abraham. They set out toward the Christ who was to come. They were anticipations of Christ, or, as the Fathers say, "types" of Christ. Even his predecessors were able to enter into the contemporaneousness with him that we beg for ourselves.

It is tempting to say that this third dimension of liturgy, its suspension between the Cross of Christ and our living entry into him who suffered vicariously for us and wants to become "one" with us (cf. Gal 3:28), expresses its moral demands. And without doubt, Christian worship does contain a moral demand, but it goes much farther than mere moralism. The Lord has gone before us. He has already done what we have to do. He has opened a way that we ourselves could not have pioneered, because our powers do not extend to building a bridge to God. He himself became that bridge. And now the challenge is to allow ourselves to be taken up into his being "for" mankind, to let ourselves be embraced by his opened arms, which draw us to himself. He, the Holy One, hallows us with the holiness that none of us could ever give ourselves. We are incorporated into the great historical process by which the world moves toward the fulfillment of God being "all in all". In this sense, what at first seems like the moral dimension is at the same time the eschatological dynamism of the liturgy. The fullness of Christ, of which the Captivity Epistles of Saint Paul speak, becomes a reality, and only thus is the Paschal event completed throughout history. The "today" of Christ lasts right to the end (cf. Heb 4:7ff.).

When we look back on our reflections hitherto in this chapter, we see that we twice encountered—in different contexts—a three-step process. The liturgy, as we saw, is characterized by a tension that is inherent in the historical Pasch of Jesus (his Cross and Resurrection) as the foundation of its reality. The ever-abiding form of the liturgy has been shaped in what is once and for all; and what is everlasting—the second step—enters into our present moment in the liturgical action and—the third step— wants to take hold of the worshipper's life. The immediate event—the liturgy—makes sense and has a meaning for our lives only because it contains the other two dimensions. Past, present, and future interpenetrate and touch upon eternity. Earlier we became acquainted with the three stages of salvation history, which progresses, as the Church Fathers say, from shadow to image to reality. We saw that in our own time, the time of the Church, we were in the middle stage of the movement of history. The curtain of the Temple has been torn. Heaven has been opened up by the union of the man Jesus, and thus of all human existence, with the living God. But this new openness is only mediated by the signs of salvation. We need mediation. As yet we do not see the Lord "as he is". Now if we put the two three-part processes together —the historical and the liturgical—it becomes clear that the liturgy gives precise expression to this historical situation. It expresses the "between-ness" of the time of images, in which we now find ourselves. The theology of the liturgy is in a special way "symbolic theology", a theology of symbols, which connects us to what is present but hidden.

In so saying, we finally discover the answer to the question with which we started. After the tearing of the Temple curtain and the opening up of the heart of God in the pierced heart of the Crucified, do we still need sacred space, sacred time, mediating symbols? Yes, we do need them, precisely so that, through the "image", through the sign, we learn to see the openness of heaven. We need them to give us the capacity to know the mystery of God in the pierced heart of the Crucified. Christian liturgy is no longer replacement worship but the coming of the representative Redeemer to us, an entry into his representation that is an entry into reality itself. We do indeed participate in the heavenly liturgy, but this participation is mediated to us through earthly signs, which the Redeemer has shown to us as the place where his reality is to be found. In liturgical celebration there is a kind of turning around of *exitus* to *reditus*, of departure to return, of God's descent to our ascent. The liturgy is the means by which earthly time is inserted into the time of Jesus Christ and into its present. It is the turning point in the process of redemption. The Shepherd takes the lost sheep onto his shoulders and carries it home.

CHAPTER TWO

Sacred Places—
The Significance of the Church Building

E VEN THE STAUNCHEST opponents of sacred things, of sacred space in this case, accept that the Christian community needs a place to meet, and on that basis they define the purpose of church buildings in a non-sacral, strictly functional sense. Church buildings, they say, make it possible for people to get together for the liturgy. This is without question an essential function of church buildings and distinguishes them from the classical form of the temple in most religions. In the Old Covenant, the high priest performed the rite of atonement in the Holy of Holies. None but he was allowed to enter, and even he could do so only once a year. Similarly, the temples of all the other religions are usually not meeting places for worshippers but cultic spaces reserved to the deity. The Christian church building soon acquired the name *domus ecclesiae* (the house of the Church, the assembly of the People of God), and then, as an abbreviation, the word *ecclesia* ("assembly", "church") came to be used, not just of the living community, but also of the building that housed it. This development is accompanied by another idea: Christ himself offers worship as he stands before the Father. He becomes his members' worship as they come together

with him and around him. This essential difference between the Christian place of worship and the temples of
the other religions must not, of course, be exaggerated
into a false opposition. We must not suggest a break in
the inner continuity of mankind's religious history, a continuity that, for all the differences, the Old and New Testaments never abolish. In his eighteenth catechesis (23–
25), Saint Cyril of Jerusalem makes an interesting point
about the word *convocatio* (*synagogē-ekklēsia*, the assembly
of the people called together and made his own by God).
He rightly points out that in the Pentateuch, when the
word first makes its appearance with the appointment of
Aaron, it is ordered toward worship. Cyril shows that this
applies to all the later passages in the Torah, and, even in
the transition to the New Testament, this ordering is not
forgotten. The calling together, the assembly, has a purpose, and that purpose is worship. The call comes from
worship and leads back to worship. It is worship that
unites the people called together and gives their being
together its meaning and worth: they are united in that
"peace" which the world cannot give. This also becomes
clear in relation to that great Old and New Testament
archetype of the *ekklēsia*, the community on Sinai. They
come together to hear God's Word and to seal everything
with sacrifice. That is how a "covenant" is established between God and man.

But instead of continuing with these theoretical considerations, let us look more closely at the process by
which church buildings took concrete form. Using the
research of E. L. Sukenik, Louis Bouyer has shown how
the Christian house of God comes into being in complete continuity with the synagogue and thus acquires
a specifically Christian newness, without any dramatic

break, through communion with Jesus Christ, the crucified and risen Lord. This close connection with the synagogue, with its architectural structure and liturgical form,
does not in any way contradict what we said above about
the Christian liturgy not just continuing the synagogue
but also incorporating the Temple. For the Jews saw the
synagogue in relation to the Temple. The synagogue was
never just a place for instruction, a kind of religious class-
room, as Bouyer puts it. No, its orientation was always
toward the presence of God. Now, for the Jews, this presence of God was (and is) indissolubly connected with the
Temple. Consequently, the synagogue was characterized
by two focal points. The first is the "seat of Moses", of
which the Lord speaks in the Gospel (cf. Mt 23:2). The
rabbi does not speak from his own resources. He is not
a professor, analyzing and reflecting on the Word of God
in an intellectual way. No, he makes present the Word
that God addressed and addresses to Israel. God speaks
through Moses today. What the seat of Moses stands for
is this: Sinai is not just a thing of the past. It is not mere
human speech that is happening here. God is speaking.

The seat of Moses, then, does not stand for itself and
by itself, nor is it simply turned toward the people. No,
the rabbi looks—as does everyone else in the synagogue
—toward the Ark of the Covenant, or rather the shrine of
the Torah, which represents the lost Ark. Up to the Exile,
the Ark of the Covenant was the only "object" allowed
inside the Holy of Holies. That is what gave the Holy of
Holies its special dignity. The Ark was seen as an empty
throne, upon which the Shekinah—the cloud of God's
presence—came down. The cherubim—representing, as
it were, the elements of the world—served as "assistants
at the throne". They were not self-subsistent deities, but

an expression of the created powers that worship the only God. God is addressed as "thou who art enthroned between the cherubim". The heavens cannot contain him, but he has chosen the Ark as the "footstool" of his presence. In this sense, the Ark embodies something like the real presence of God among his own. At the same time, it is an impressive sign of the absence of images from the liturgy of the Old Testament, which maintains God in his sovereignty and holds out to him, so to speak, only the footstool of his throne. During the Exile, the Ark of the Covenant was lost, and from then on the Holy of Holies was empty. That is what Pompeius found when he strode through the Temple and pulled back the curtain. He entered the Holy of Holies full of curiosity and there, in the very emptiness of the place, discovered what is special about biblical religion. The empty Holy of Holies had now become an act of expectation, of hope, that God himself would one day restore his throne.

The synagogue, in its shrine of the Torah, contains a kind of Ark of the Covenant, which means it is the place of a kind of "real presence". Here are kept the scrolls of the Torah, the living Word of God, through which he sits on his throne in Israel among his own people. The shrine is surrounded, therefore, with signs of reverence befitting the mysterious presence of God. It is protected by a curtain, before which burn the seven lights of the menorah, the seven-branch candlestick. Now the furnishing of the synagogue with an "Ark of the Covenant" does not in any way signify that the local community has become, so to speak, independent, self-sufficient. No, it is the place where the local community reaches out beyond itself to the Temple, to the commonality of the one People of God as defined by the one God. The Torah is in all places one and the same. And so the Ark points beyond itself to the one place of its presence that God chose for himself—the Holy of Holies in the Temple in Jerusalem. This Holy of Holies, as Bouyer puts it, remained "the ultimate focus of the synagogal worship".[1] "Thus have all the synagogues, at the time of Our Lord and since that time, been oriented."[2] The rabbi and the people gaze at the "Ark of the Covenant", and in so doing, they orient themselves toward Jerusalem, turn themselves toward the Holy of Holies in the Temple as the place of God's presence for his people. This remained the case even after the destruction of the Temple. The empty Holy of Holies had already been an expression of hope, and so, too, now is the destroyed Temple, which waits for the return of the Shekinah, for its restoration by the Messiah when he comes.

This orientation toward the Temple, and thus the connection of the synagogue's liturgy of the Word with the sacrificial liturgy of the Temple, can be seen in its form of prayer. The prayers said at the unrolling and reading of the scrolls of Scripture developed out of the ritual prayers originally linked to the sacrificial actions in the Temple and now regarded, in accord with the tradition of the time without the Temple, as an equivalent of sacrifice. The first of the two great prayers of the synagogue rite comes to a climax in the common recitation of the *Kiddush*, of which the hymn of the seraphim in Isaiah chapter 6 and the hymn of the cherubim in Ezekiel chapter 3 are a part. Bouyer makes this comment: "But the truth must be that the association of men with these heavenly canticles, in the worship of the Temple, had probably been a central

[1] Louis Bouyer, *Liturgy and Architecture* (Notre Dame, Ind.: Univ. of Notre Dame Press, 1967), 15.
[2] Ibid.

feature of the offering of the sacrifice of incense, morning and evening of every day."[3] Who would not be reminded of the Trisagion of the Christian liturgy, the "thrice holy" hymn at the beginning of the Canon? Here the congregation does not offer its own thoughts or poetry but is taken out of itself and given the privilege of sharing in the cosmic song of praise of the cherubim and seraphim. The other great prayer of the synagogue culminates in "the recitation of the *Abodah* which, according to the rabbis, was formerly the consecration prayer of the daily burnt offering in the Temple".[4] The petition added to it about the coming of the Messiah and the final restoration of Israel may be seen, according to Bouyer, "as the expression of the essence of the sacrificial worship".[5] Let us remind ourselves here of that transition from animal sacrifices to "worship in harmony with *logos*" which characterizes the path from the Old Testament into the New. Finally, we must mention the fact that no special architectural form was created for the synagogue. The "typical Greek building for public meetings: the basilica", was used.[6] Its aisles, divided off by rows of columns, enabled people entering the building to circulate around it.

I have lingered over this description of the synagogue because it exhibits already the essential and constant features of Christian places of worship. Once again we see clearly the essential unity of the two Testaments. Not surprisingly, in Semitic, non-Greek Christianity, the original form of church buildings generally retains the close connection of church with synagogue, a pattern of religious continuity and innovation. (I am thinking here of the

[3] Ibid., 22.
[4] Ibid.
[5] Ibid.
[6] Ibid., 17.

Monophysite and Nestorian Churches of the Near East, which broke away from the Church of the Byzantine Empire during the christological debates of the fifth century.) Christian faith produced three innovations in the form of the synagogue as we have just sketched it. These give Christian liturgy its new and proper profile. First of all, the worshipper no longer looks toward Jerusalem. The destroyed Temple is no longer regarded as the place of God's earthly presence. The Temple built of stone has ceased to express the hope of Christians; its curtain is torn forever. Christians look toward the east, the rising sun. This is not a case of Christians worshipping the sun but of the cosmos speaking of Christ. The song of the sun in Psalm 19(18) is interpreted as a song about Christ when it says: "[The sun] comes forth like a bridegroom leaving his chamber. . . . Its rising is from the end of the heavens, and its circuit to the end of them" (vv. 5f.). This psalm proceeds directly from applauding creation to praising the law. Christians interpret it in terms of Christ, who is the living Word, the eternal Logos, and thus the true light of history, who came forth in Bethlehem from the bridal chamber of the Virgin Mother and now pours out his light on all the world. The east supersedes the Jerusalem Temple as a symbol. Christ, represented by the sun, is the place of the Shekinah, the true throne of the living God. In the Incarnation, human nature truly becomes the throne and seat of God, who is thus forever bound to the earth and accessible to our prayers. In the early Church, prayer toward the east was regarded as an apostolic tradition. We cannot date exactly when this turn to the east, the diverting of the gaze from the Temple, took place, but it is certain that it goes back to the earliest times and was always regarded as an essential characteristic of Christian liturgy (and, indeed, of private prayer). This "orientation"[7] of Christian prayer has several different meanings. Orientation is, first and foremost, a simple expression of looking to Christ as the meeting place between God and man. It expresses the basic christological form of our prayer.

The fact that we find Christ in the symbol of the rising sun is the indication of a Christology defined eschatologically. Praying toward the east means going to meet the coming Christ. The liturgy, turned toward the east, effects entry, so to speak, into the procession of history toward the future, the New Heaven and the New Earth, which we encounter in Christ. It is a prayer of hope, the prayer of the pilgrim as he walks in the direction shown us by the life, Passion, and Resurrection of Christ. Thus very early on, in parts of Christendom, the eastward direction for prayer was given added emphasis by a reference to the Cross. This may have come from linking Revelation 1:7 with Matthew 24:30. In the first of these, the Revelation of Saint John, it says: "Behold, he is coming with the clouds, and every eye will see him, every one who pierced him; and all tribes of the earth will wail on account of him. Even so. Amen." Here the seer of the Apocalypse depends on John 19:37, where, at the end of the account of the Crucifixion, the mysterious text of the prophet Zechariah (12:10) is quoted, a text that suddenly acquires a wholly new meaning: "They shall look on him whom they have pierced." Finally, in Matthew 24:30 we are given these words of the Lord: "[T]hen [on the Last Day] will appear the sign of the Son of man in heaven, and then all the tribes of the earth will mourn [cf. Zech 12:10], and they will see the Son of man coming on the clouds of heaven [cf. Dan 7:13] with power and

[7] The word "orientation" comes from *oriens*, "the East". "Orientation" means "east-ing", turning toward the east.

great glory." The sign of the Son of Man, of the Pierced One, is the Cross, which has now become the sign of victory of the Risen One. Thus the symbolism of the Cross merges with that of the east. Both are an expression of one and the same faith, in which the remembrance of the Pasch of Jesus makes it present and gives dynamism to the hope that goes out to meet the One who is to come. But, finally, this turning toward the east also signifies that cosmos and saving history belong together. The cosmos is praying with us. It, too, is waiting for redemption. It is precisely this cosmic dimension that is essential to Christian liturgy. It is never performed solely in the self-made world of man. It is always a cosmic liturgy. The theme of creation is embedded in Christian prayer. It loses its grandeur when it forgets this connection. That is why, wherever possible, we should definitely take up again the apostolic tradition of facing the east, both in the building of churches and in the celebration of the liturgy. We shall come back to this later, when we say something about the ordering of liturgical prayer.

The second innovation in regard to the synagogue is as follows. A new element has appeared that could not exist in the synagogue. At the east wall, or in the apse, there now stands an altar on which the Eucharistic Sacrifice is celebrated. As we saw, the Eucharist is an entry into the liturgy of heaven; by it we become contemporaries with Jesus Christ's own act of worship, into which, through his Body, he takes up worldly time and straightway leads it beyond itself, snatching it out of its own sphere and enfolding it into the communion of eternal love. Thus the altar signifies the entry of him who is the Orient into the assembled community and the going out of the community from the prison of this world through the curtain now torn open, a participation in the Pasch, the "passing

over" from the world to God, which Christ has opened
up. It is clear that the altar in the apse both looks toward
the *Oriens* and forms part of it. In the synagogue the worshippers looked beyond the "Ark of the Covenant", the
shrine of the Word, toward Jerusalem. Now, with the
Christian altar, comes a new focal point. Let us say it
again: on the altar, what the Temple had in the past foreshadowed is now present in a new way. Yes, it enables us
to become the contemporaries of the Sacrifice of the Logos. Thus it brings heaven into the community assembled
on earth, or rather it takes that community beyond itself
into the communion of saints of all times and places. We
might put it this way: the altar is the place where heaven
is opened up. It does not close off the church, but opens
it up—and leads it into the eternal liturgy. We shall have
more to say about the practical consequences of the significance of the Christian altar, because the question of
the correct position for the altar is at the center of the
postconciliar debate.

   But first we must finish what we were saying about the
different ways in which Christian faith transformed the
synagogue. The third point to be noted is that the shrine
of the Word remained, even with regard to its position
in the church building. However, of necessity, there is a
fundamental innovation here. The Torah is replaced by
the Gospels, which alone can open up the meaning of the
Torah. "Moses", says Christ, "wrote of me" (Jn 5:46).
The shrine of the Word, the "Ark of the Covenant", now
becomes the throne of the Gospel. The Gospel does not,
of course, abolish the "Scriptures" or push them to one
side but, rather, interprets them, so that henceforth and
forever they form the Scriptures of Christians, without
which the Gospel would have no foundation. The practice in the synagogue of covering the shrine with a curtain,

in order to express the sacredness of the Word, is retained. Quite spontaneously, the new, second holy place, the altar, is surrounded by a curtain, from which, in the Eastern Church, the Iconostasis develops. The fact that there are two holy places had significance for the celebration of the liturgy. During the Liturgy of the Word, the congregation gathered around the shrine of the Sacred Books or around the seat associated with it, which evolved quite spontaneously from the seat of Moses to the bishop's throne. Just as the rabbi did not speak by his own authority, so the bishop expounds the Bible in the name, and by the mandate, of Christ. Thus, from being a written word from the past, it again becomes what it is: God's addressing us here and now. At the end of the Liturgy of the Word, during which the faithful stand around the bishop's seat, everyone walks together with the bishop to the altar, and now the cry resounds: "Conversi ad Dominum", Turn toward the Lord! In other words, look toward the east with the bishop, in the sense of the words from the epistle to the Hebrews: "[Look] . . . to Jesus the pioneer and perfecter of our faith" (12:2). The Liturgy of the Eucharist is celebrated as we look up to Jesus. It *is* our looking up to Jesus. Thus, in early church buildings, the liturgy has two places. First, the Liturgy of the Word takes place at the center of the building. The faithful are grouped around the *bema*, the elevated area where the throne of the Gospel, the seat of the bishop, and the lectern are located. The Eucharistic celebration proper takes place in the apse, at the altar, which the faithful "stand around". Everyone joins with the celebrant in facing east, toward the Lord who is to come.

Finally, we must mention one last difference between the synagogue and the earliest church buildings. In Israel only the presence of men was deemed to be necessary for divine worship. The common priesthood described in Exodus chapter 19 was ascribed to them alone. Consequently, in the synagogue, women were only allowed into the tribunes or galleries. As far as the apostles were concerned, as far as Jesus himself is concerned, there was no such discrimination in the Church of Christ. Even though the public Liturgy of the Word was not entrusted to women, they were included in the liturgy as a whole in exactly the same way as men. And so now they had a place—albeit in separation from men—in the sacred space itself, around both the *bema* and the altar.

CHAPTER THREE

The Altar and the Direction of Liturgical Prayer

T HE RESHAPING so far described, of the Jewish synagogue for the purpose of Christian worship, clearly
shows—as we have already said—how, even in architecture, there is both continuity and newness in the relationship of the Old Testament to the New. As a consequence,
expression in space had to be given to the properly Christian act of worship, the celebration of the Eucharist, together with the ministry of the Word, which is ordered
toward that celebration. Plainly, further developments became not only possible but necessary. A place set aside for
Baptism had to be found. The Sacrament of Penance went
through a long process of development, which resulted in
changes to the form of the church building. Popular piety
in its many different forms inevitably found expression
in the place dedicated to divine worship. The question of
sacred images had to be resolved. Church music had to
be fitted into the spatial structure. We saw that the architectural canon for the liturgy of Word and sacrament is
not a rigid one, though with every new development and
reordering the question has to be posed: What is in harmony with the essence of the liturgy, and what detracts
from it? In the very form of its places of divine worship,
which we have just been considering, Christianity, speak-

ing and thinking in a Semitic way, has laid down principles by which this question can be answered. Despite all the variations in practice that have taken place far into the second millennium, one thing has remained clear for the whole of Christendom: praying toward the east is a tradition that goes back to the beginning. Moreover, it is a fundamental expression of the Christian synthesis of cosmos and history, of being rooted in the once-for-all events of salvation history while going out to meet the Lord who is to come again. Here both the fidelity to the gift already bestowed and the dynamism of going forward are given equal expression.

Modern man has little understanding of this "orientation". Judaism and Islam, now as in the past, take it for granted that we should pray toward the central place of revelation, to the God who has revealed himself to us, in the manner and in the place in which he revealed himself. By contrast, in the Western world, an abstract way of thinking, which in a certain way is the fruit of Christian influence, has become dominant. God is spiritual, and God is everywhere: Does that not mean that prayer is not tied to a particular place or direction? Now, we can indeed pray everywhere, and God is accessible to us everywhere. This idea of the universality of God is a consequence of Christian universality, of the Christian's looking up to God above all gods, the God who embraces the cosmos and is more intimate to us than we are to ourselves. But our knowledge of this universality is the fruit of revelation: God has shown himself to us. Only for this reason do we know him; only for this reason can we confidently pray to him everywhere. And precisely for this reason is it appropriate, now as in the past, that we should express in Christian prayer our turning to the God who has revealed himself to us. Just as God assumed a body and entered the time and space of this world, so it is appropriate to prayer—at least to communal liturgical prayer—that our speaking to God should be "incarnational", that it should be christological, turned through the incarnate Word to the triune God. The cosmic symbol of the rising sun expresses the universality of God above all particular places and yet maintains the concreteness of divine revelation. Our praying is thus inserted into the procession of the nations to God.

But what about the altar? In what direction should we pray during the Eucharistic liturgy? In Byzantine church buildings, the structure just described was by and large retained, but in Rome a somewhat different arrangement developed. The bishop's chair was shifted to the center of the apse, and so the altar was moved into the nave. This seems to have been the case in the Lateran basilica and in Saint Mary Major's well into the ninth century. However, in Saint Peter's, during the pontificate of Saint Gregory the Great (590–604), the altar was moved nearer to the bishop's chair, probably for the simple reason that he was supposed to stand as much as possible above the tomb of Saint Peter. This was an outward and visible expression of the truth that we celebrate the Sacrifice of the Lord in the communion of saints, a communion spanning all times and ages. The custom of erecting an altar above the tombs of the martyrs probably goes back a long way and is an outcome of the same motivation. Throughout history the martyrs continue Christ's self-oblation; they are like the Church's living altar, made not of stones but of men, who have become members of the Body of Christ and thus express a new kind of cultus: sacrifice is humanity becoming love with Christ.

The ordering of Saint Peter's was then copied, so it would seem, in many other stational churches in Rome. For the purposes of this discussion, we do not need to go into the disputed details of this process. The controversy in our own century was triggered by another innovation. Because of topographical circumstances, it turned out that Saint Peter's faced west. Thus, if the celebrating priest wanted—as the Christian tradition of prayer demands—to face east, he had to stand behind the people and look—this is the logical conclusion—toward the people. For whatever reason it was done, one can also see this arrangement in a whole series of church buildings within Saint Peter's direct sphere of influence. The liturgical renewal in our own century took up this alleged model and developed from it a new idea for the form of the liturgy. The Eucharist—so it was said—had to be celebrated *versus populum* (toward the people). The altar—as can be seen in the normative model of Saint Peter's—had to be positioned in such a way that priest and people looked at each other and formed together the circle of the celebrating community. This alone—so it was said—was compatible with the meaning of the Christian liturgy, with the requirement of active participation. This alone conformed to the primordial model of the Last Supper. These arguments seemed in the end so persuasive that after the council (which says nothing about "turning toward the people") new altars were set up everywhere, and today celebration *versus populum* really does look like the characteristic fruit of Vatican II's liturgical renewal. In fact, it is the most conspicuous consequence of a reordering that not only signifies a new external arrangement of the places dedicated to the liturgy, but also brings with it a new idea of the essence of the liturgy—the liturgy as a communal meal.

This is, of course, a misunderstanding of the significance of the Roman basilica and of the positioning of its
altar, and the representation of the Last Supper is also,
to say the least, inaccurate. Consider, for example, what
Louis Bouyer has to say on the subject:

> The idea that a celebration facing the people must have
> been the primitive one, and that especially of the last sup-
> per, has no other foundation than a mistaken view of
> what a meal could be in antiquity, Christian or not. In
> no meal of the early Christian era, did the president of
> the banqueting assembly ever face the other participants.
> They were all sitting, or reclining, on the convex side of
> a sigma-shaped table, or of a table having approximately
> the shape of a horse shoe. The other side was always left
> empty for the service. Nowhere in Christian antiquity,
> could have arisen the idea of having to "face the people"
> to preside at a meal. The communal character of a meal
> was emphasized just by the opposite disposition: the fact
> that all the participants were on the same side of the table.[1]

In any case, there is a further point that we must add to
this discussion of the "shape" of meals: the Eucharist that
Christians celebrate really cannot adequately be described
by the term "meal". True, the Lord established the new
reality of Christian worship within the framework of a
Jewish (Passover) meal, but it was precisely this new reality, not the meal as such, that he commanded us to repeat. Very soon the new reality was separated from its
ancient context and found its proper and suitable form,
a form already predetermined by the fact that the Eucharist refers back to the Cross and thus to the transformation of Temple sacrifice into worship of God that is
in harmony with *logos*. Thus it came to pass that the syn-

[1] Louis Bouyer, *Liturgy and Architecture* (Notre Dame, Ind.: Univ. of
Notre Dame Press, 1967), 53–54.

agogue liturgy of the Word, renewed and deepened in a Christian way, merged with the remembrance of Christ's death and Resurrection to become the "Eucharist", and precisely thus was fidelity to the command "Do this" fulfilled. This new and all-encompassing form of worship could not be derived simply from the meal but had to be defined through the interconnection of Temple and synagogue, Word and sacrament, cosmos and history. It expresses itself in the very form that we discovered in the liturgical structure of the early Churches in the world of Semitic Christianity. It also, of course, remained fundamental for Rome. Once again let me quote Bouyer:

> Never, and nowhere, before that [that is, before the sixteenth century] have we any indication that any importance, or even attention, was given to whether the priest celebrated with the people before him or behind him. As Professor Cyrille Vogel has recently demonstrated it, the only thing ever insisted upon, or even mentioned, was that he should say the eucharistic prayer, as all the other prayers, facing East. . . . Even when the orientation of the church enabled the celebrant to pray turned toward the people, when at the altar, we must not forget that it was not the priest alone who, then, turned East: it was the whole congregation, together with him.[2]

Admittedly, these connections were obscured or fell into total oblivion in the church buildings and liturgical practice of the modern age. This is the only explanation for the fact that the common direction of prayer of priest and people was labeled as "celebrating toward the wall" or "turning your back on the people" and came to seem absurd and totally unacceptable. And this alone explains why the meal—even in modern pictures—became the normative

[2] Ibid., 55–56.

idea of liturgical celebration for Christians. In reality, what happened was that an unprecedented clericalization came on the scene. Now the priest—the "presider", as they now prefer to call him—becomes the real point of reference for the whole liturgy. Everything depends on him. We have to see him, to respond to him, to be involved in what he is doing. His creativity sustains the whole thing. Not surprisingly, people try to reduce this newly created role by assigning all kinds of liturgical functions to different individuals and entrusting the "creative" planning of the liturgy to groups of people who like to, and are supposed to, "make their own contribution". Less and less is God in the picture. More and more important is what is done by the human beings who meet here and do not like to subject themselves to a "pre-determined pattern". The turning of the priest toward the people has turned the community into a self-enclosed circle. In its outward form, it no longer opens out on what lies ahead and above, but is closed in on itself. The common turning toward the east was not a "celebration toward the wall"; it did not mean that the priest "had his back to the people": the priest himself was not regarded as so important. For just as the congregation in the synagogue looked together toward Jerusalem, so in the Christian liturgy the congregation looked together "toward the Lord". As one of the fathers of Vatican II's Constitution on the Liturgy, J. A. Jungmann, put it, it was much more a question of priest and people facing in the same direction, knowing that together they were in a procession toward the Lord. They did not close themselves into a circle; they did not gaze at one another; but as the pilgrim People of God they set off for the *Oriens*, for the Christ who comes to meet us.

But is this not all romanticism and nostalgia for the

past? Can the original form of Christian prayer still say something to us today, or should we try to find our own form, a form for our own times? Of course, we cannot simply replicate the past. Every age must discover and express the essence of the liturgy anew. The point is to discover this essence amid all the changing appearances. It would surely be a mistake to reject all the reforms of our century wholesale. When the altar was very remote from the faithful, it was right to move it back to the people. In cathedrals, this made it possible to recover the tradition of having the altar at the crossing, the meeting point of the nave and the presbyterium. It was also important clearly to distinguish the place for the Liturgy of the Word from the place for the properly Eucharistic liturgy. For the Liturgy of the Word is about speaking and responding, and so a face-to-face exchange between proclaimer and hearer does make sense. In the psalm, the hearer internalizes what he has heard, takes it into himself, and transforms it into prayer, so that it becomes a response. On the other hand, a common turning to the east during the Eucharistic Prayer remains essential. This is a case, not of something accidental, but of what is essential. Looking at the priest has no importance. What matters is looking together at the Lord. It is now a question, not of dialogue, but of common worship, of setting off toward the One who is to come. What corresponds with the reality of what is happening is not the closed circle but the common movement forward, expressed in a common direction for prayer.

Häussling has leveled several objections at these ideas of mine, which I have presented before. The first I have just touched on. These ideas are alleged to be a romanticism for the old ways, a misguided longing for the past. It is said to be odd that I should speak only of Christian antiquity and pass over the succeeding centuries. Coming as it does from a liturgical scholar, this objection is quite remarkable. As I see it, the problem with a large part of modern liturgiology is that it tends to recognize only antiquity as a source, and therefore normative, and to regard everything developed later, in the Middle Ages and through the Council of Trent, as decadent. And so one ends up with dubious reconstructions of the most ancient practice, fluctuating criteria, and never-ending suggestions for reform, which lead ultimately to the disintegration of the liturgy that has evolved in a living way. On the other hand, it is important and necessary to see that we cannot take as our norm the ancient in itself and as such, nor must we automatically write off later developments as alien to the original form of the liturgy. There can be a thoroughly living kind of development in which a seed at the origin of something ripens and bears fruit. We shall have to come back to this idea in a moment. But in our case, as we have said, what is at issue is not a romantic escape into antiquity, but a rediscovery of something essential, in which Christian liturgy expresses its permanent orientation. Of course, Häussling thinks that turning to the east, toward the rising sun, is something that nowadays we just cannot bring into the liturgy. Is that really the case? Are we not interested in the cosmos anymore? Are we today really hopelessly huddled in our own little circle? Is it not important, precisely today, to pray with the whole of creation? Is it not important, precisely today, to find room for the dimension of the future, for hope in the Lord who is to come again, to recognize again, indeed to live, the dynamism of the new creation as an essential form of the liturgy?

Another objection is that we do not need to look

toward the east, toward the crucifix—that, when priest and faithful look at one another, they are looking at the image of God in man, and so facing one another is the right direction for prayer. I find it hard to believe that the famous critic thought this was a serious argument. For we do not see the image of God in man in such a simplistic way. The "image of God" in man is not, of course, something that we can photograph or see with a merely photographic kind of perception. We can indeed see it, but only with the new seeing of faith. We can see it, just as we can see the goodness in a man, his honesty, interior truth, humility, love—everything, in fact, that gives him a certain likeness to God. But if we are to do this, we must learn a new kind of seeing, and that is what the Eucharist is for.

A more important objection is of the practical order. Ought we really to be rearranging everything all over again? Nothing is more harmful to the liturgy than a constant activism, even if it seems to be for the sake of genuine renewal. I see a solution in a suggestion that comes from the insights of Erik Peterson. Facing east, as we heard, was linked with the "sign of the Son of Man", with the Cross, which announces the Lord's Second Coming. That is why very early on the east was linked with the sign of the Cross. Where a direct common turning toward the east is not possible, the cross can serve as the interior "east" of faith. It should stand in the middle of the altar and be the common point of focus for both priest and praying community. In this way we obey the ancient call to prayer: "Conversi ad Dominum", Turn toward the Lord! In this way we look together at the One whose death tore the veil of the Temple—the One who stands before the Father for us and encloses us in his arms in order to make us the new and living Temple. Moving the altar cross to the side to give an uninterrupted view of the priest is something I regard as one of the truly absurd phenomena of recent decades. Is the cross disruptive during Mass? Is the priest more important than the Lord? This mistake should be corrected as quickly as possible; it can be done without further rebuilding. The Lord is the point of reference. He is the rising sun of history. That is why there could be a cross of the Passion, which represents the suffering Lord who for us let his side be pierced, from which flowed blood and water (Eucharist and Baptism), as well as a cross of triumph, which expresses the idea of the Second Coming and guides our eyes toward it. For it is always the one Lord: Christ yesterday, today, and forever (Heb 13:8).

CHAPTER FOUR

The Reservation of the Blessed Sacrament

T HE CHURCH of the first millennium knew nothing
of tabernacles. Instead, first the shrine of the Word
and, then, even more so the altar served as sacred "tent".
Approached by steps, it was sheltered, and its sacredness
underscored, by a "ciborium", or marble baldacchino,
with burning lamps hanging from it. A curtain was hung
between the columns of the ciborium.[1] The tabernacle
as sacred tent, as place of the Shekinah, the presence of
the living Lord, developed only in the second millennium. It was the fruit of passionate theological struggles
and their resulting clarifications, in which the permanent
presence of Christ in the consecrated Host emerged with
greater clarity. Now here we run up against the decadence
theory, the canonization of the early days and romanticism about the first century. Transubstantiation (the substantial change of the bread and wine), the adoration of
the Lord in the Blessed Sacrament, eucharistic devotions
with monstrance and processions—all these things, it is
alleged, are medieval errors, errors from which we must
once and for all take our leave. "The Eucharistic Gifts are
for eating, not for looking at"—these and similar slogans
are all too familiar. The glib way such statements are made

[1] Louis Bouyer, *Liturgy and Architecture* (Notre Dame, Ind.: Univ. of
Notre Dame Press, 1967), 46–48.

is quite astonishing when we consider the intense debates in the history of dogma, theology, and ecumenism undertaken by the great theologians in the nineteenth century and the first half of the twentieth. All that seems now to be forgotten.

It is not the intention of this little book to enter into these theological discussions in detail. It is plain for all to see that already for Saint Paul bread and wine become the Body and Blood of Christ, that it is the risen Lord himself who is present and gives himself to us to eat. The vigor with which the Real Presence is emphasized in John chapter 6 could hardly be surpassed. For the Church Fathers, too, from the earliest witnesses onward—just think of Saint Justin Martyr or Saint Ignatius of Antioch—there is no doubt about the great mystery of the Presence bestowed upon us, about the change of the gifts during the Eucharistic Prayer. Even a theologian of such a spiritualizing tendency as Saint Augustine never had a doubt about it. Indeed, he shows just how far confession of faith in the Incarnation and Resurrection, which is so closely bound up with eucharistic faith in the bodily presence of the risen Lord, has transformed Platonism. "Flesh and blood" have received a new dignity and entered into the Christian's hope for eternal life. An important finding of Henri de Lubac has often been misunderstood. It has always been clear that the goal of the Eucharist is our own transformation, so that we become "one body and spirit" with Christ (cf. 1 Cor 6:17). This correlation of ideas—the insight that the Eucharist is meant to transform *us*, to change humanity itself into the living temple of God, into the Body of Christ—was expressed, up to the early Middle Ages, by the twin concepts of *corpus mysticum* and *corpus verum*. In the vocabulary of the Fathers, *mysticum* meant, not "mystical" in the modern sense, but, rather, "pertaining to the mystery, the sphere of the sacrament". Thus the phrase *corpus mysticum* was used to express the sacramental Body, the corporeal presence of Christ in the Sacrament. According to the Fathers, that Body is given to us so that we may become the *corpus verum*, the real Body of Christ. Changes in the use of language and the forms of thought resulted in the reversal of these meanings. The Sacrament was now addressed as the *corpus verum*, the "true Body", while the Church was called the *corpus mysticum*, the "Mystical Body", "mystical" here meaning no longer "sacramental" but "mysterious". Many people have drawn the conclusion from de Lubac's careful description of the linguistic change that a hitherto unknown realism, indeed naturalism, was now forcing its way into eucharistic doctrine and that the large views of the Fathers were giving way to a static and one-sided idea of the Real Presence.

It is true that this linguistic change also represented a spiritual development, but we should not describe it in the slanted way just mentioned. We can agree that something of the eschatological dynamism and corporate character (the sense of "we") of eucharistic faith was lost or at least diminished. As we saw above, the Blessed Sacrament contains a dynamism, which has the goal of transforming mankind and the world into the New Heaven and New Earth, into the unity of the risen Body. This truth was not seen so vividly as before. Again, the Eucharist is not aimed primarily at the individual. Eucharistic personalism is a drive toward union, the overcoming of the barriers between God and man, between "I" and "thou" in the new "we" of the communion of saints. People did not exactly forget this truth, but they were not so clearly aware of it as before. There were, therefore, losses in Christian awareness, and in our time we must try to make up for them, but still there were gains overall. True, the Eucharistic Body of the Lord is meant to bring us together, so that we become his "true Body". But the gift of the Eucharist can do this only because in it the Lord gives us *his true Body*. Only the true Body in the Sacrament can build up the true Body of the new City of God. This insight connects the two periods and provides our starting point.

The early Church was already well aware that the bread once changed remains changed. That is why they reserved it for the sick, and that is why they showed it such reverence, as is still the case today in the Eastern Church. But now, in the Middle Ages, this awareness is deepened: the gift *is* changed. The Lord has definitively drawn this piece of matter to himself. It does not contain just a matter-of-fact kind of gift. No, the Lord himself is present, the Indivisible One, the risen Lord, with Flesh and Blood, with Body and Soul, with Divinity and Humanity. The whole Christ is there. In the early days of the Liturgical Movement, people sometimes argued for a distinction between the "thing-centered" view of the Eucharist in the patristic age and the personalistic view of the post-medieval period. The Eucharistic Presence, they said, was understood, not as the presence of a Person, but as the presence of a gift distinct from the Person. This is nonsense. Anyone reading the texts will find that there is no support anywhere for these ideas. How is the Body of Christ supposed to become a "thing"? The only presence is the presence of the whole Christ. Receiving the Eucharist does not mean eating a "thing-like" gift (Body and Blood?). No, there is a person-to-person exchange, a coming of the one into the other. The living Lord gives himself to me, enters into me, and invites me to surrender myself to him, so that the apostle's words come true: "[I]t is no longer I who live, but Christ who lives in me" (Gal 2:20). Only thus is the reception of Holy Communion an act that elevates and transforms a man.

"He is here, he himself, the whole of himself, and he remains here." This realization came upon the Middle Ages with a wholly new intensity. It was caused in part by the deepening of theological reflection, but still more important was the new experience of the saints, especially in the Franciscan movement and in the new evangelization undertaken by the Order of Preachers. What happens in the Middle Ages is not a misunderstanding due to losing sight of what is central, but a new dimension of the reality of Christianity opening up through the experience of the saints, supported and illuminated by the reflection of the theologians. At the same time, this new development is in complete continuity with what had always been believed hitherto. Let me say it again: This deepened awareness of faith is impelled by the knowledge that in the consecrated species *he* is there and remains there. When a man experiences this with every fiber of his heart and mind and senses, the consequence is inescapable: "We must make a proper place for this Presence." And so little by little the tabernacle takes shape, and more and more, always in a spontaneous way, it takes the place previously occupied by the now disappeared "Ark of the Covenant". In fact, the tabernacle is the complete fulfillment of what the Ark of the Covenant represented. It is the place of the "Holy of Holies". It is the tent of God, his throne. Here he is among us. His presence (Shekinah) really does now dwell among us—in the humblest parish church no less than in the grandest cathedral. Even though the definitive Temple will only come to be when the world has become the New Jerusalem, still what the Temple in Jerusalem pointed to is here present in a supreme way. The New Jerusalem is anticipated in the humble species of bread.

So let no one say, "The Eucharist is for eating, not looking at." It is not "ordinary bread", as the most ancient traditions constantly emphasize. Eating it—as we have just said—is a spiritual process, involving the whole man. "Eating" it means worshipping it. Eating it means letting it come into me, so that my "I" is transformed and opens up into the great "we", so that we become "one" in him (cf. Gal 3:16). Thus adoration is not opposed to Communion, nor is it merely added to it. No, Communion only reaches its true depths when it is supported and surrounded by adoration. The Eucharistic Presence in the tabernacle does not set another view of the Eucharist alongside or against the Eucharistic celebration, but simply signifies its complete fulfillment. For this Presence has the effect, of course, of keeping the Eucharist forever in church. The church never becomes a lifeless space but is always filled with the presence of the Lord, which comes out of the celebration, leads us into it, and always makes us participants in the cosmic Eucharist. What man of faith has not experienced this? A church without the Eucharistic Presence is somehow dead, even when it invites people to pray. But a church in which the eternal light is burning before the tabernacle is always alive, is always something more than a building made of stones. In this place, the Lord is always waiting for me, calling me, wanting to make me "eucharistic". In this way, he prepares me for the Eucharist, sets me in motion toward his return.

The changes in the Middle Ages brought losses, but they also provided a wonderful spiritual deepening. They unfolded the magnitude of the mystery instituted at the Last Supper and enabled it to be experienced with a new fullness. How many saints—yes, including saints of the love of neighbor—were nourished and led to the Lord by this experience! We must not lose this richness. If the presence of the Lord is to touch us in a concrete way, the tabernacle must also find its proper place in the architecture of our church buildings.

CHAPTER FIVE

Sacred Time

A S WE BEGIN to consider the significance of sacred time in the structure of Christian liturgy, we must remember all that we said in the first chapter of this second part about the significance of time and space in Christian worship. All time is God's time. When the eternal Word assumed human existence at his Incarnation, he also assumed temporality. He drew time into the sphere of eternity. Christ is himself the bridge between time and eternity. At first it seems as if there can be no connection between the "always" of eternity and the "flowing away" of time. But now the Eternal One himself has taken time to himself. In the Son, time co-exists with eternity. God's eternity is not mere time-lessness, the negation of time, but a power over time that is really present with time and in time. In the Word incarnate, who remains man forever, the presence of eternity with time becomes bodily and concrete.

All time is God's time. On the other hand, as we saw above, the time of the Church is a "between" time, between the shadow and the reality, and so its special structure demands a sign, a time specially chosen and designated to draw time as a whole into the hands of God. This, of course, is one of the marks of the Bible's universalism: it is not based on some general, transcendental character of mankind, but strives to attain the whole through an election. But now there can be no escaping the question: What *is* time? Needless to say, this is not the place to plumb the depths of this question, which has exercised the minds of all the great thinkers of history. However, a few hints at an answer are imperative if the contact of the liturgy with time is to be properly understood. The first thing to say is that time is a cosmic reality. The orbiting of the sun by the earth (or, as the ancients thought, of the earth by the sun) gives existence the rhythm that we call time—from hour to hour, from morning to evening and evening to morning, from spring through summer and autumn to winter. In addition to this rhythm of the sun, there is the shorter rhythm of the moon—from its slow growth to its disappearance with the new moon and the new beginning. The two rhythms have created two measures, which appear in the history of culture in various combinations. Both show how much man is woven into the fabric of the universe. Time is first of all a cosmic phenomenon. Man lives with the stars. The course of the sun and the moon leaves its mark on his life.

But beside and beneath this there are other rhythms, each with its own measure, at the various levels of being. Plants have their time. For example, the rings in the trunk of a tree display the tree's own internal time, which is, of course, inseparably intertwined with cosmic time. Again, man, as he matures and declines, has his own time. We could say that his heartbeat is like the internal rhythm of his own time. In the time of man, the different levels of life, the organic and the spiritual-intellectual, enter into a mysterious synthesis, which is inserted into the immensity of the universe but also into a common history. The path of man that we call history is a specific form of time.

All of this is present in the liturgy and in the liturgy's own particular way of relating to time. The sacred space of the Christian worship of God is itself already opened toward time. Facing east means that when one prays, one is turned toward the rising sun, which has now become a subject of historical significance. It points to the Paschal Mystery of Jesus Christ, to his death and new rising. It points to the future of the world and the consummation of all history in the final coming of the Redeemer. Thus time and space are interconnected in Christian prayer. Space itself has become time, and time has, so to speak, become spatial, has entered into space. And just as time and space intertwine, so, too, do history and cosmos. Cosmic time, which is determined by the sun, becomes a representation of human time and of historical time, which moves toward the union of God and world, of history and the universe, of matter and spirit—in a word, toward the New City whose light is God himself. Thus time becomes eternity, and eternity is imparted to time.

In the piety of the Old Testament, we find a double division of time: one determined by the weekly rhythm, which moves toward the Sabbath, and the other by the feast days, which are determined partly by the theme of creation (seed-time and harvest in addition to feasts of the nomadic tradition) and partly by the remembrance of God's actions in history. These two sources are frequently interconnected. This basic arrangement still applies in Christianity. Even in its ordering of time, Christianity retains a profound, interior continuity with its Jewish heritage, in which, in turn, the heritage of the world's religions is taken up and dedicated to the one God, albeit purified and illuminated by him.

Let us begin with the weekly rhythm. We have already seen that the Sabbath brought the sign of the covenant into time, tied creation and covenant together. This fundamental ordering of things, which was also incorporated into the Decalogue, was still taken for granted in Christianity. But now the covenant was raised up to a new level through the Incarnation, Cross, and Resurrection, so that henceforth we must speak of a "New Covenant". God has acted once more in a new way in order to give the covenant its universal breadth and definitive form. But this divine action had something to do with the rhythm of the week. Its climax, toward which everything else was ordered, was the Resurrection of Jesus "on the third day". In our reflections on the Last Supper, we saw that Supper, Cross, and Resurrection belong together. Jesus' giving of himself unto death gives the words he speaks at the Supper their realism. On the other hand, his self-giving would be meaningless were death to have the last word. Thus only through the Resurrection does the covenant come fully into being. Now man is forever united with God. Now the two are really bound together indissolubly. Thus the Day of Resurrection is the new Sabbath. It is the day on which the Lord comes among his own and invites them into his "liturgy", into his glorification of God, and communicates himself to them. The morning of the "third day" becomes the hour of Christian worship of God. Saint Augustine showed—in regard to the connection of Supper, Cross, and Resurrection—how through their inner unity the Supper has become quite spontaneously the morning sacrifice, and precisely thus is the task entrusted to the apostles at the time of the Last Supper fulfilled. The transition from Old to New Testament is plainly revealed in the transition from Sabbath to Day of Resurrection as the new sign of the covenant, and in the process Sunday takes over the significance of the Sabbath. There are three different names for this day. Seen from the Cross, it is the third day—in the Old Testament, the third day was regarded as the day of theophany, the day when God entered into the world after the time of expectation. In terms of the weekly schedule, it is the first day of the week. Finally, the Fathers added another consideration: seen in relation to the whole preceding week, Sunday is the eighth day.

Thus the three symbolisms are interlocked. Of the three, the most important is that of its being the first day of the week. In the Mediterranean world in which Christianity came into being, the first day of the week was regarded as the day of the sun, while the other days were allotted to the various planets then known. The Christians' day of worship was determined by the remembrance of God's action, the date of the Resurrection of Jesus. But now this date came to carry the same cosmic symbolism that also determined the Christian direction of prayer. The sun proclaims Christ. Cosmos and history together speak of him. And to this a third factor was added: the first day is the beginning of creation. The new creation takes up the old creation. The Christian Sunday is also a festival of creation: thanksgiving for the gift of creation, for the "Let there be . . ." with which God established the being of the world. It is thanksgiving for the fact that God does not let creation be destroyed but restores it after all of man's attempts to destroy it. The "first day" contains Saint Paul's idea of the whole creation waiting for the revelation of the sons of God (cf. Rom 8:19). Just as sin wrecks creation (as we can see!), so it is restored when the "sons of God" make their appearance. Sunday thus explains the commission given to man in the account of creation: "Subdue [the earth]!" (Gen 1:28). This does not mean: Enslave it! Exploit it! Do with it what you will! No, what it does mean is: Recognize it as God's gift! Guard it and look after it, as sons look after what they have inherited from their father. Look after it, so that it becomes a true garden for God and its meaning is fulfilled, so that for it, too, God is "all in all". This is the orientation that the Fathers wanted to express by calling the Day of the Resurrection the "eighth day". Sunday looks not only backward but forward. Looking toward the Resurrection means looking toward the final consummation. With the Day of the Resurrection coming after the Sabbath, Christ, as it were, strode across time and lifted it up above itself. The Fathers connected with this the idea that the history of the world as a whole can be seen as one great week of seven days corresponding to the ages of a man's life. The eighth day, therefore, signifies the new time that has dawned with the Resurrection. It is now, so to speak, concurrent with history. In the liturgy, we already reach out to lay hold of it. But, at the same time, it is ahead of us. It is the sign of God's definitive world, in which shadow and image are superseded in the final mutual indwelling of God and his creatures. It was to reflect this symbolism of the eighth day that people liked to build baptisteries, baptismal churches, with eight sides. This was meant to show that Baptism is birth into the eighth day, into the Resurrection of Christ, and into the new time that opened up with the Resurrection.

Sunday is thus, for the Christian, time's proper measure, the temporal measure of his life. It is not based on an arbitrary convention that could be exchanged for another, but contains a unique synthesis of the remembrance of history, the recalling of creation, and the theology of hope. For Christians, it is the weekly returning feast of the Resurrection, though it is one that does not render a specific remembrance of Christ's Passover superfluous. It is quite clear from reading the New Testament that Jesus approached his "hour" with full awareness. The phrase emphasized in Saint John's Gospel, the "hour of Jesus", certainly has many layers of meaning. But first and foremost it refers to a date: Jesus did not want to die on just any date. His death had a significance for history, for mankind, for the world. That is why it had to be woven into a very particular cosmic and historical hour. It coincides with the Passover of the Jews as set out and regulated in Exodus chapter 12. Saint John and the epistle to the Hebrews show in a special way how it incorporates the content of other feasts, especially the Day of Atonement, but its proper date is Passover. The Lord's death is not any kind of accident. It is a "feast". It brings to an end what is symbolically opened up in the Passover. He takes it—as we have seen—from replacement to reality, to the vicarious ministry of his self-oblation.

The Passover is the "hour" of Jesus. It is precisely in connection with this date that we see the universal significance of Jesus' death for human history. At first, Passover was the feast of nomads. From Abel to the Apocalypse, the sacrificed lamb is a type of the Redeemer, of his pure self-giving. We do not need to go farther into the importance of nomadic culture in the origins of biblical religion. What is significant is this, that monotheism was not able to develop in the great cities and fertile countryside of Mesopotamia. No, it was in the wilderness, where heaven and earth face each other in stark solitude, that monotheism was able to grow—in the homelessness of the wanderer, who does not deify places but has constantly to put his trust in the God who wanders with him. It has recently been pointed out that the date of Passover coincides with the constellation of Aries the Ram—the Lamb. This was of no more than marginal importance for the fixing of the date of Easter. What was essential was the connection with the date of the death and Resurrection of Jesus, which was of its very nature linked with the Jewish liturgical calendar. Now this link, raising as it does the question of the relation of New Testament to Old and of the newness of Christianity, was to have explosive potential. In the second century A.D., it led to the Easter controversy, which was not to be settled, at least for the Great Church, until the Council of Nicaea (325). On the one hand, there was the custom in Asia Minor of conforming to the Jewish calendar and always celebrating the Christian Easter on 14 Nisan, the date of the Jewish Passover. On the other hand, there was the custom, especially in Rome, of regarding Sunday, the day of the Resurrection, as the determining factor: the Christian Easter should, therefore, be celebrated on the Sunday after the first full moon of spring. The Council of Nicaea promulgated this decision. Through its ruling, the solar and lunar calendars were interconnected, and the two great cosmic forms of ordering time were linked to each other in association with the history of Israel and the life of Jesus. But let us return to the image of the lamb (or ram). In the fifth century, there was a controversy between Rome and Alexandria about what the latest possible date for Easter could be. According to Alexandrian tradition, it was April 25. Pope Saint Leo the

Great (440–461) criticized this very late date by pointing out that, according to the Bible, Easter should fall in the first month, and the first month did not mean April but the time when the sun is passing through the first part of the Zodiac—the sign of Aries. The constellation in the heavens seemed to speak, in advance and for all time, of the Lamb of God, who takes away the sins of the world (Jn 1:29), the one who sums up in himself all the sacrifices of the innocent and gives them their meaning. The mysterious story of the ram, caught in the thicket and taking the place of Isaac as the sacrifice decreed by God himself, was now seen as the pre-history of Christ. The fork of the tree in which the ram was hanging was seen as a replica of the sign of Aries, which in turn was the celestial foreshadowing of the crucified Christ. We should also say that Jewish tradition gave the date of March 25 to Abraham's sacrifice. Now, as we shall see presently, this day was also regarded as the day of creation, the day when God's Word decreed: "Let there be light." It was also considered, very early on, as the day of Christ's death and eventually as the day of his conception. We may see a reflection of these connections in the first epistle of Saint Peter, which describes Christ as the lamb "without blemish" demanded by Exodus 12:5 and "destined before the foundation of the world" (1 Pet 1:20). The mysterious words in Revelation 13:8 about the "Lamb slain from the beginning of the world" [translated from the German] could also perhaps be interpreted in the same way —though other translations are possible that tone down the paradox. These cosmic images enabled Christians to see, in an unprecedented way, the world-embracing meaning of Christ and so to understand the grandeur of the hope inscribed in Christian faith. This is most illuminating. It seems clear to me that we have to recapture this cosmic vision if we want once again to understand and live Christianity in its full breadth.

I should like to make two further remarks about the celebration of Easter. In our reflections so far, we have seen how deeply Christianity is marked by the symbolism of the sun. The dating of Easter, finally fixed at Nicaea, incorporated the feast into the solar calendar, but it did not break its link with the lunar calendar. In the world of religion, the moon, with its alternating phases, is frequently seen as the symbol of the feminine, but especially as a symbol of transitoriness. Thus the cosmic symbolism of the moon corresponds to the mystery of death and resurrection, which is celebrated in the Christian Passover. When the Sunday after the first full moon of spring comes to be the date of Easter, the symbolism of sun and moon are linked together. Transitoriness is taken up into what never passes away. Death becomes resurrection and passes into eternal life.

Finally, we should add that, for Israel, Passover was not simply a cosmic festival but essentially aimed at historical remembrance. It is the feast of the Exodus out of Egypt, the feast of Israel's liberation, with which it begins its own journey in history as the People of God. Israel's Passover is the recalling of an act of God that was liberation and thus the foundation of the community. This content of the feast also entered into Christianity and helped it understand the depth of meaning in the Resurrection of Christ. Jesus had consciously connected his final journey with Israel's Passover. He defined it as his "hour". There must, therefore, be an inner connection between Israel's remembrance and the new event of Christendom's sacred triduum. Man's last enemy is death. Man is fully set free only when he is set free from death. The oppression of Israel in Egypt was indeed a kind of death, which threatened to, and was intended to, destroy the people as such. Death was imposed on all male progeny. But on the night of Passover, the angel of death now passes over Egypt and strikes down its firstborn. Liberation is liberation for life. Christ, the Firstborn from the dead, takes death upon himself and, by his Resurrection, shatters death's power. Death no longer has the last word. The love of the Son proves to be stronger than death because it unites man with God's love, which is God's very being. Thus, in the Resurrection of Christ, it is not just the destiny of an individual that is called to mind. He is now perpetually present, because he lives, and he gathers us up, so that we may live: "[B]ecause I live, you will live also" (Jn 14:19). In the light of Easter, Christians see themselves as people who truly *live*. They have found their way out of an existence that is more death than life. They have discovered real life: "And this is eternal life, that they know you the only true God, and Jesus Christ whom you have sent" (Jn 17:3). Deliverance from death is at the same time deliverance from the captivity of individualism, from the prison of self, from the incapacity to love and make a gift of oneself. Thus Easter becomes the great feast of Baptism, in which man, as it were, enacts the passage through the Red Sea, emerges from his own existence into communion with Christ and so into communion with all who belong to Christ. Resurrection builds communion. It creates the new People of God. The grain of wheat that dies all alone does not remain alone but brings much fruit with it. The risen Lord does not remain alone. He draws all mankind to himself and so creates a new universal communion of men. The whole meaning of the Jewish Passover is made present in the Christian Easter. At the same time, it is not about remembering a past and unrepeatable event, but, as we have seen, "once for all" here becomes "forever". The risen Lord lives and gives life. He lives and brings about communion. He lives and opens up the future. He lives and shows the way. But we must also not forget that this feast of salvation history, open as it is to the future, to what lies ahead, has its roots in a cosmic celebration, roots that it does not relinquish. The dying and rising moon becomes the sign in the cosmos for death and resurrection. The sun of the first day becomes the messenger of Christ, who "comes forth like a bridegroom leaving his chamber, and like a strong man runs its course with joy" (Ps 19:5f.). That is why the calendar of the Christian feasts is not to be manipulated at will. The "hour" of Jesus makes its appearance, again and again, within the unity of cosmic and historical time. Through the feast we enter into the rhythm of creation and into God's plan for human history.

A question comes up at this point that I should like to discuss briefly before moving to the Christmas season. The cosmic symbolism that I have been describing has its precise setting in the area of the Mediterranean and the Near East in which the Jewish and Christian religions came into being. By and large it applies to the Northern Hemisphere of the globe. Now in the Southern Hemisphere, everything is reversed. The Christian Easter falls, not in the spring, but in the autumn. Christmas coincides, not with the winter solstice, but with high summer. This raises the question of "inculturation" with great urgency. If the cosmic symbolism is so important, ought we not to adjust the liturgical calendar for the Southern

Hemisphere? G. Voss has rightly responded by pointing out that, if we did this, we would reduce the mystery of Christ to the level of a merely cosmic religion; we would be subordinating history to the cosmos. But the historical does not serve the cosmic; no, the cosmic serves the historical. Only in history is the cosmos given its center and goal. To believe in the Incarnation means to be bound to Christianity's origins, their particularity, and, in human terms, their contingency. Here is the guarantee that we are not chasing myths; that God really has acted in our history and taken our time into his hands. Only over the bridge of this "once for all" can we come into the "forever" of God's mercy. At the same time, we must take account of the full breadth of the symbol and of God's action in history. Voss has very beautifully pointed to the "autumnal" aspects of the Easter mystery, which deepen and broaden our understanding of the feast and give it a special profile appropriate to the Southern Hemisphere. Incidentally, the Scriptures and the liturgy offer their own suggestions for a transferral of the symbols. I have already pointed out that, in interpreting the Passion of Jesus, Saint John's Gospel and the epistle to the Hebrews do not just refer to the feast of Passover, which is the Lord's "hour", in terms of date. No, they also interpret it in light of the ritual of the Day of Atonement celebrated on the tenth day of the seventh month (September-October). In the Passover of Jesus, there is, so to speak, a coincidence of Easter (spring) and the Day of Atonement (autumn). Christ connects the world's spring and autumn. The autumn of declining time becomes a new beginning, while the spring, as the time of the Lord's death, now points to the end of time, to the autumn of the world, in which, according to the Fathers, Christ came among us.

The liturgical calendar used before the postconciliar reforms contained a strange transferral of the seasons, a use that, of course, had long eluded people's understanding and was interpreted in a much too superficial way. Depending on how late or early Easter fell, the time after Epiphany had to be shortened or lengthened. The Sundays left out after Epiphany had to be moved to the end of the Church's year. If one looks carefully at the readings then in use, one finds that the texts are largely taken up with the theme of sowing the seed, which is a metaphor for the seed of the Gospel to be scattered throughout the world. Now these texts and their respective Sundays can be accommodated just as well in the spring as in the autumn. Both seasons are seed-time. In the spring, the farmer sows seed for autumn, in autumn for the coming year. Sowing seed always points to the future. It belongs to the waxing year but also to the waning year, for the waning year also points to a new future. In both seasons, the mystery of hope is at work and reaches its proper depth in the waning year, which leads beyond decline to a new beginning. It would be a great work of inculturation to develop this approach and to bring it into the common consciousness of Christians in the two hemispheres, southern and northern. The South could help the North to discover a new breadth and depth in the mystery, thus enabling us all to draw afresh on its richness.

Let us turn—albeit very briefly—to the second focal point of the Church's year, the Christmas season, which developed somewhat later than the cycle that leads to and comes from Easter. Sunday, like the eastward stance for Christian prayer, is a primordial *datum* of Christianity. It had a fixed place from the beginning and shaped

Christian existence so profoundly that Saint Ignatius of Antioch said that we "no longer observe the Sabbath, but live in the observance of the Lord's Day" (*Mag.* 9, 1). But already in the New Testament, Christians look back from the Easter mystery to the Incarnation of Christ from the Virgin Mary. In the Gospel of Saint John, which is the concluding synthesis of New Testament faith, the theology of the Incarnation stands on equal footing alongside the theology of Easter. Or rather, the theology of the Incarnation and the theology of Easter do not simply stand alongside each other. No, these are the two inseparable focal points of the one faith in Jesus Christ, the incarnate Son of God and Redeemer. The Cross and Resurrection presuppose the Incarnation. It is only because the Son, and in him God himself, "came down from heaven" and "became incarnate from the Virgin Mary" that Jesus' death and Resurrection are events that are contemporary with us all and touch us all, delivering us from a past marked by death and opening up the present and future. On the other hand, the Incarnation has as its goal the attainment by the "flesh", by corruptible earthly existence, of an incorruptible form, in other words, an entry into Paschal transformation. Having been recognized as a focal point of faith in Christ, the Incarnation had to be given some expression in liturgical celebration, some place in the rhythm of sacred time. It is hard to say how far back the beginnings of the Christmas feast go. It assumed its definitive form in the third century. At about the same time, the feast of the Epiphany emerged in the East on January 6 and the feast of Christmas in the West on December 25. The two feasts had different emphases because of the different religious and cultural contexts in which they arose, but essentially their meaning was the same:

the celebration of the birth of Christ as the dawning of the new light, the true sun, of history. The complicated and somewhat disputed details of the development of the two feasts need not detain us in this little book. Here I should simply like to indicate what seems to me to be helpful to understanding the two days. Astonishingly, the starting point for dating the birth of Christ was March 25. As far as I know, the most ancient reference to it is in the writings of the African ecclesiastical author Tertullian (ca. 150–ca. 207), who evidently assumes as a well-known tradition that Christ suffered death on March 25. In Gaul, right up to the sixth century, this was kept as the immovable date of Easter. In a work on the calculation of the date of Easter, written in A.D. 243, and also emanating from Africa, we find March 25 interpreted as the day of the world's creation, and, in connection with that, we find a very peculiar dating for the birth of Christ. According to the account of creation in Genesis 1, the sun was created on the fourth day, that is, on March 28. This day should, therefore, be regarded as the day of Christ's birth, as the rising of the true sun of history. This idea was altered during the third century, so that the day of Christ's Passion and the day of his conception were regarded as identical. On March 25, the Church honored both the Annunciation by the angel and the Lord's conception by the Holy Spirit in the womb of the Virgin. The feast of Christ's birth on December 25—nine months after March 25—developed in the West in the course of the third century, while the East—probably because of a difference of calendar—at first celebrated January 6 as the birthday of Christ. It may also have been the response to a feast of the birth of the mythical gods observed on this day in Alexandria. The claim used to be made that

December 25 developed in opposition to the Mithras myth, or as a Christian response to the cult of the unconquered sun promoted by Roman emperors in the third century in their efforts to establish a new imperial religion. However, these old theories can no longer be sustained. The decisive factor was the connection of creation and Cross, of creation and Christ's conception. In the light of the "hour of Jesus", these dates brought the cosmos into the picture. The cosmos was now thought of as the pre-annunciation of Christ, the Firstborn of creation (cf. Col 1:15). It is he of whom creation speaks, and it is by him that its mute message is deciphered. The cosmos finds its true meaning in the Firstborn of creation, who has now entered history. From him comes the assurance that the adventure of creation, of a world with its own free existence distinct from God, does not end up in absurdity and tragedy but, throughout all its calamities and upheavals, remains something positive. God's blessing of the seventh day is truly and definitively confirmed. The fact that the dates of the Lord's conception and birth originally had a cosmic significance means that Christians can take on the challenge of the sun cult and incorporate it positively into the theology of the Christmas feast. There are magnificent texts in the writings of the Fathers that express this synthesis. For example, Saint Jerome in a Christmas sermon says this: "Even creation approves our preaching. The universe itself bears witness to the truth of our words. Up to this day the dark days increase, but from this day the darkness decreases. . . . The light advances, while the night retreats." Likewise, Saint Augustine, preaching at Christmas to his flock in Hippo: "Brethren, let us rejoice. The heathen, too, may still make merry, for this day consecrates for us, not the visible sun, but the sun's invisible Creator." Again and again, the Fathers take up the verse about the sun that we have already quoted from Psalm 18(19). For the early Church, this became the real Christmas psalm: the sun, that is, Christ, is like a bridegroom coming forth from his chamber. An echo of the Marian mystery was also heard in this psalm, which was interpreted as a prophecy of Christ. Between the two dates of March 25 and December 25 comes the feast of the Forerunner, Saint John the Baptist, on June 24, at the time of the summer solstice. The link between the dates can now be seen as a liturgical and cosmic expression of the Baptist's words: "He [Christ] must increase, but I must decrease" (Jn 3:30). The birthday of Saint John the Baptist takes place on the date when the days begin to shorten, just as the birthday of Christ takes place when they begin again to lengthen. The fabric of this feast is of an entirely Christian weave, without direct precedent in the Old Testament. However, it stands in continuity with the synthesis of cosmos and history, of remembrance and hope, that was already characteristic of the Old Testament feasts and took on a new form in the Christian calendar. The close interweaving of incarnation and resurrection can be seen precisely in the relation, both proper and common, that each has to the rhythm of the sun and its symbolism.

I should like briefly to mention the feast of the Epiphany, celebrated on January 6, which is closely connected with Christmas. Let us leave on one side all the historical details and the many glorious patristic texts on the subject. Let us try to understand it very simply in the form that we have here in the West. It interprets the Incarnation of the Logos in terms of the ancient category of "epiphany", that is, of the self-revelation of God, the

God who manifests himself to his creatures. In this perspective, the feast links together several different epiphanies: the adoration of the Magi as the beginning of the Church of the Gentiles, the procession of the nations to the God of Israel (cf. Is 60); the Baptism of Jesus in the Jordan, in which the voice from above publicly proclaims Jesus as the Son of God; and the wedding at Cana, where he reveals his glory. The narrative of the adoration of the Magi became important for Christian thought because it shows the inner connection between the wisdom of the nations and the Word of promise in Scripture; because it shows how the language of the cosmos and the truth-seeking thought of man lead to Christ. The mysterious star could become the symbol for these connections and once again emphasize that the language of the cosmos and the language of the human heart trace their descent from the Word of the Father, who in Bethlehem came forth from the silence of God and assembled the fragments of our human knowledge into a complete whole.

The great feasts that structure the year of faith are feasts of Christ and precisely as such are ordered toward the one God who revealed himself to Moses in the burning bush and chose Israel as the confessor of faith in his uniqueness. In addition to the sun, which is the image of Christ, there is the moon, which has no light of its own but shines with a brightness that comes from the sun. This is a sign to us that we men are in constant need of a "little" light, whose hidden light helps us to know and love the light of the Creator, God one and triune. That is why the feasts of the saints from earliest times have formed part of the Christian year. We have already encountered Mary, whose person is so closely interwoven with the mystery of Christ that the development of the Christmas cycle inevitably introduced a Marian note into the Church's year. The Marian dimension of the christological feasts was made visible. Then, in addition, come the commemorations of the apostles and martyrs and, finally, the memorials of the saints of every century. One might say that the saints are, so to speak, new Christian constellations, in which the richness of God's goodness is reflected. Their light, coming from God, enables us to know better the interior richness of God's great light, which we cannot comprehend in the refulgence of its glory.

PART THREE

ART AND LITURGY

CHAPTER ONE

The Question of Images

I N THE FIRST commandment of the Decalogue, which underscores the uniqueness of the God to whom alone adoration is due, we read this admonition: "You shall not make for yourself a graven image, or any likeness of anything that is in heaven above, or that is in the earth beneath, or that is in the water under the earth" (Ex 20:4; cf. Deut 5:8). There is a notable exception to this prohibition of images at the very center of the Old Testament, one that concerns the most sacred of places, the gold covering of the Ark of the Covenant, which was regarded as the place of expiation. "There I will meet with you", says God to Moses, "I will speak with you of all that I will give you in commandment for the sons of Israel" (Ex 25:22). With regard to the fashioning of the covering, Moses receives the following instructions: "And you shall make two cherubim of gold; of hammered work shall you make them, on the two ends of the mercy seat. . . . The cherubim shall spread out their wings above. . . . [T]heir faces [shall be turned] one to another; toward the mercy seat shall the faces of the cherubim be" (Ex 25:18–20). The mysterious beings that cover and protect the place of divine revelation can be represented, precisely to conceal the mystery of the presence of God himself. As we have already seen, Saint Paul saw the crucified Christ as the true and living "place of expiation", of whom the "mercy seat", the *kapporeth* lost during the Exile, was but a foreshadowing. In him God has now, so to speak, lifted the veil from his face. The Eastern Church's icon of the Resurrection of Christ takes up this link between the Ark of the Covenant and the Paschal Mystery of Christ when it shows Christ standing on cross-shaped slabs, which symbolize the grave but also suggest a reference to the *kapporeth* of the Old Covenant. Christ is flanked by the cherubim and approached by the women who came to the tomb to anoint him. The fundamental image of the Old Testament is retained, but it is reshaped in the light of the Resurrection and given a new center: the God who no longer completely conceals himself but now shows himself in the form of the Son. This transformation of the narrative of the Ark of the Covenant into an image of the Resurrection reveals the very heart of the development from Old Testament to New. However, if we are to understand it correctly in its totality, we must follow the main lines of the development a little more closely.

The prohibition of images in Islam and in Judaism since about the third or fourth century A.D. has been interpreted in a radical way, so that only non-figurative, geometrical designs are permitted in the ornamentation of the sanctuary. However, in the Judaism at the time of Jesus and well into the third century, a much more generous interpretation of the image-question developed. Paradoxically, in the images of salvation we see exactly the same continuity between synagogue and church that we have already noticed in our discussion of liturgical space. As a result of archaeological discoveries, we now know that the ancient synagogues were richly decorated with representations of scenes from the Bible. They were by no means regarded as mere images of past events, as a kind of pictorial history lesson, but as a narrative (*haggadah*), which, while calling something to mind, makes it present. On liturgical feasts, the deeds of God in the past are made present. The feasts are a participation in God's action in time, and the images themselves, as remembrance in visible form, are involved in the liturgical re-presentation. The Christian images, as we find them in the catacombs, simply take up and develop the canon of images already established by the synagogue, while giving it a new modality of presence. The individual events are now ordered toward the Christian sacraments and to Christ himself. Noah's ark and the crossing of the Red Sea now point to Baptism. The sacrifice of Isaac and the meal of the three angels with Abraham speak of Christ's Sacrifice and the Eucharist. Shining through the rescue of the three young men from the fiery furnace and of Daniel from the lions' den we see Christ's Resurrection and our own. Still more than in the synagogue, the point of the images is not to tell a story about something in the past, but to incorporate the events of history into the sacrament. In past history, Christ with his sacraments is on his way through the ages. We are taken into the events. The events themselves transcend the passing of time and become present in our midst through the sacramental action of the Church.

The centering of all history in Christ is both the liturgical transmission of that history and the expression of a new experience of time, in which past, present, and future make contact because they have been inserted into the presence of the risen Lord. As we have seen already and now find confirmed anew, liturgical presence contains eschatological hope within it. All sacred images are, without exception, in a certain sense images of the Resurrection, history read in the light of the Resurrection, and for that very reason they are images of hope, giving us the assurance of the world to come, of the final coming of Christ. However inferior the first images of the Christian tradition may often be in their artistic qualities, an extraordinary spiritual process has taken place in them, though one that is in close and deep unity with the iconography of the synagogue. The Resurrection sheds a new light on history. It is seen as a path of hope, into which the images draw us. Thus the images of the early Church have a thoroughly sacramental significance. They have the character of mysteries, going far beyond the didactic function of telling the stories of the Bible.

None of the early images attempts to give us anything like a portrait of Christ. Instead, Christ is shown in his significance, in "allegorical" images—for example, as the true philosopher instructing us in the art of living and dying. He appears as the great teacher, but above all in the form of the shepherd. The reason why this image, which is derived from Sacred Scripture, became so precious to early Christianity is that the shepherd was regarded as an allegory of the Logos. The Logos, through whom all things were made, who bears within himself, so to speak, the archetypes of all existing things, is the guardian of creation. In the Incarnation, he takes the lost sheep, human nature, humanity as a whole, onto his shoulders and carries it home. The image of the shepherd thus sums up the whole of salvation history: God's entry into history, the Incarnation, the pursuit of the lost sheep, and the homeward path into the Church of the Jews and Gentiles.

One development of far-reaching importance in the history of the images of faith was the emergence for the first time of a so-called *acheiropoietos*, an image which has not been made by human hands and portrays the very face of Christ. Two of these images appeared in the East at about the same time in the middle of the sixth century. The first of these was the so-called *camulianium*, the imprint of the image of Christ on a woman's gown. The second was the *mandylion*, as it was called later, which was brought from Edessa in Syria to Constantinople and is thought by many scholars today to be identical with the Shroud of Turin. In each case, as with the Turin Shroud, it must have been a question of a truly mysterious image, which no human artistry was capable of producing. In some inexplicable way, it appeared imprinted upon cloth and claimed to show the true face of Christ, the crucified and risen Lord. The first appearance of this image must have provoked immense fascination. Now at last could the true face of the Lord, hitherto hidden, be seen and thus the promise be fulfilled: "He who has seen me has seen the Father" (Jn 14:9). The sight of the God-Man and, through him, of God himself seemed to have been opened up; the Greek longing for the vision of the Eternal seemed to be fulfilled. Thus the icon inevitably assumed in its form the status of a sacrament. It was regarded as bestowing a communion no less than that of the Eucharist. People began to think that there was virtually a kind of real presence of the Person imaged in the image. The image in this case, the image not made by human hands, was an image in the full sense, a participation in the reality concerned, the refulgence and thus the presence of the One who gives himself in the image. It is not hard to see why the images modeled on the *acheiropoietos* became the center of the whole canon of iconography, which meanwhile had made progress and was understood better in its wider implications.

Clearly, though, there was a danger lurking here: a false sacramentalizing of the image, which seemed to lead beyond the sacraments and their hiddenness into a direct vision of the divine presence. And so it is also clear that this new development was bound to lead to violent counter-movements, to that radical rejection of the image which we call "iconoclasm", the destruction of images. Iconoclasm derived its passion in part from truly religious motives, from the undeniable dangers of a kind of adoration of the image, but also from a cluster of political factors. It was important for the Byzantine emperors not to give any unnecessary provocation to Muslims and Jews. The suppression of images could be beneficial to the unity of the empire and to relations with the empire's Muslim neighbors. And so the thesis was proposed that Christ must not be represented in an image. Only the sign of the Cross (without a *corpus*) could be, as it were, his seal. Cross or image—that was the choice. In the course of this struggle, the true theology of icons matured and bequeathed us a message that has a profound relevance to us today in the iconographic crisis of the West.

The icon of Christ is the icon of the risen Lord. That truth, with all its implications, now dawned on the Christian mind. There is no *portrait* of the risen Lord. At first the disciples do not recognize him. They have to be led toward a new kind of seeing, in which their eyes are gradually opened from within to the point where they recognize him afresh and cry out: "It is the Lord!" Perhaps the most telling episode of all is that of the disciples on the road to Emmaus. Their hearts are transformed, so that, through the outward events of Scripture, they can discern its inward center, from which everything comes and to which everything tends: the Cross and Resurrection of Jesus Christ. They then detain their mysterious companion and give him their hospitality, and at the breaking of bread they experience in reverse fashion what happened to Adam and Eve when they ate the fruit of the tree of the knowledge of good and evil: their eyes are opened. Now they see no longer just the externals but the reality that is not apparent to their senses yet shines through their senses: it is the Lord, now alive in a new way. In the icon, it is not the facial features that count (though icons essentially adhere to the appearance of the *acheiropoietos*). No, what matters is the new kind of seeing. The icon is supposed to originate from an opening up of the inner senses, from a facilitation of sight that gets beyond the surface of the empirical and perceives Christ, as the later theology of icons puts it, in the light of Tabor. It thus leads the man who contemplates it to the point where, through the interior vision that the icon embodies, he beholds in the sensible that which, though above the sensible, has entered into the sphere of the senses. As Evdokimov says so beautifully, the icon requires a "fast from the eyes". Icon painters, he says, must learn how to fast with their eyes and prepare themselves by a long path of prayerful asceticism. This is what marks the transition from art to sacred art.[1] The icon comes from prayer and leads to prayer. It delivers

[1] Paul Evdokimov, *The Art of the Icon: A Theology of Beauty*, trans. Steven Bigham (Redondo Beach, Calif.: Oakwood, 1996), 188.

a man from that closure of the senses which perceives only the externals, the material surface of things, and is blind to the transparency of the spirit, the transparency of the Logos. At the most fundamental level, what we are dealing with here is nothing other than the transcendence of faith. The whole problem of knowledge in the modern world is present. If an interior opening-up does not occur in man that enables him to see more than what can be measured and weighed, to perceive the reflection of divine glory in creation, then God remains excluded from our field of vision. The icon, rightly understood, leads us away from false questions about portraits, portraits comprehensible at the level of the senses, and thus enables us to discern the face of Christ and, in him, of the Father. Thus in the icon we find the same spiritual orientations that we discovered previously when emphasizing the eastward direction of the liturgy. The icon is intended to draw us onto an inner path, the eastward path, toward the Christ who is to return. Its dynamism is identical with the dynamism of the liturgy as a whole. Its Christology is trinitarian. It is the Holy Spirit who makes us capable of seeing, he whose work is always to move us toward Christ. "We have drunk deeply of the Spirit," says Saint Athanasius, "and we drink Christ."[2] This seeing, which teaches us to see Christ, not "according to the flesh", but according to the Spirit (cf. 2 Cor 5:16), grants us also a glimpse of the Father himself.

Only when we have understood this interior orientation of the icon can we rightly understand why the Second Council of Nicaea and all the following councils concerned with icons regard it as a confession of faith in the Incarnation and iconoclasm as a denial of the Incar-

[2] Ibid., 204.

nation, as the summation of all heresies. The Incarnation means, in the first place, that the invisible God enters into the visible world, so that we, who are bound to matter, can know him. In this sense, the way to the Incarnation was already being prepared in all that God said and did in history for man's salvation. But this descent of God is intended to draw us into a movement of ascent. The Incarnation is aimed at man's transformation through the Cross and to the new corporeality of the Resurrection. God seeks us where we are, not so that we stay there, but so that we may come to be where he is, so that we may get beyond ourselves. That is why to reduce the visible appearance of Christ to a "historical Jesus" belonging to the past misses the point of his visible appearance, misses the point of the Incarnation.

The senses are not to be discarded, but they should be expanded to their widest capacity. We see Christ rightly only when we say with Thomas: "My Lord and my God!" We have just established that the icon has a trinitarian scope, and now we must come to terms with its ontological proportions. The Son could only become incarnate as man because man was already planned in advance in relation to him, as the image of him who is in himself the image of God. As Evdokimov again says so strikingly, the light of the first day and the light of the eighth day meet in the icon. Present already in creation is the light that will shine with its full brightness on the eighth day in the Resurrection of the Lord and in the new world, the light that enables us to see the splendor of God. The Incarnation is rightly understood only when it is seen within the broad context of creation, history, and the new world. Only then does it become clear that the senses belong to faith, that the new seeing does not abolish them but leads them to their original purpose. Iconoclasm rests ultimately on a one-sided apophatic theology, which recognizes only the Wholly Other-ness of the God beyond all images and words, a theology that in the final analysis regards revelation as the inadequate human reflection of what is eternally imperceptible. But if this is the case, faith collapses. Our current form of sensibility, which can no longer apprehend the transparency of the spirit in the senses, almost inevitably brings with it a flight into a purely "negative" (apophatic) theology. God is beyond all thought, and therefore all propositions about him and every kind of image of God are in equal proportions valid and invalid. What seems like the highest humility toward God turns into pride, allowing God no word and permitting him no real entry into history. On the one hand, matter is absolutized and thought of as completely impervious to God, as mere matter, and thus deprived of its dignity. But, as Evdokimov says, there is also an apophatic Yes, not just an apophatic No, the denial of all likeness. Following Gregory Palamas, he emphasizes that in his essence God is radically transcendent, but in his existence he can be, and wants to be, represented as the Living One. God is the Wholly Other, but he is powerful enough to be able to show himself. And he has so fashioned his creature that it is capable of "seeing" him and loving him.

With these reflections we once again make contact with our own times and therefore also the development of liturgy, art, and faith in the Western world. Is this theology of the icon, as developed in the East, true? Is it valid for us? Or is it just a peculiarity of the Christian East? Let us start with the historical facts. In early Christian art, right up to the end of the Romanesque period, in other words, up to the threshold of the thirteenth century, there is no *essential* difference between East and

West with regard to the question of images. True, if we think of Saint Augustine or Saint Gregory the Great, the West emphasized, almost exclusively, the pedagogical function of the image. The so-called *Libri Carolini*, as well as the synods of Frankfurt (794) and Paris (824), came out against the poorly understood Seventh Ecumenical Council, Nicaea II, which canonized the defeat of iconoclasm and the rooting of the icon in the Incarnation. By contrast, the Western synods insist on the purely educative role of the images: "Christ", they said, "did not save us by paintings."[3]

But the themes and fundamental orientation of iconography remained the same, even though now, in the Romanesque style, plastic art emerges, something that never had a foothold in the East. It is always the risen Christ, even on the Cross, to whom the community looks as the true *Oriens*. And art is always characterized by the unity of creation, Christology, and eschatology: the first day is on its way toward the eighth, which in turn takes up the first. Art is still ordered to the mystery that becomes present in the liturgy. It is still oriented to the heavenly liturgy. The figures of the angels in Romanesque art are essentially no different from those in Byzantine painting. They show that we are joining with the cherubim and seraphim, with all the heavenly powers, in praise of the Lamb. In the liturgy, the curtain between heaven and earth is torn open, and we are taken up into a liturgy that spans the whole cosmos.

With the emergence of Gothic, a change slowly takes place. Much remains the same, especially the fundamental inner correspondence between the Old Testament and the New, which for its part always has a reference to what

[3] Ibid., 167.

is still to come. But the central image becomes different. The depiction is no longer of the *Pantocrator*, the Lord of all, leading us into the eighth day. It has been superseded by the image of the crucified Lord in the agony of his Passion and death. The story is told of the historical events of the Passion, but the Resurrection is not made visible. The historical and narrative aspect of art comes to the fore. It has been said that the mysterial image has been replaced by the devotional image. Many factors may have been involved in this change of perspective. Evdokimov thinks that the turn from Platonism to Aristotelianism during the thirteenth century played a part. Platonism sees sensible things as shadows of the eternal archetypes. In the sensible we can and should know the archetypes and rise up through the former to the latter. Aristotelianism rejects the doctrine of Ideas. The thing, composed of matter and form, exists in its own right. Through abstraction I discern the species to which it belongs. In place of seeing, by which the super-sensible becomes visible in the sensible, comes abstraction. The relationship of the spiritual and the material has changed and with it man's attitude to reality as it appears to him. For Plato, the category of the beautiful had been definitive. The beautiful and the good, ultimately the beautiful and God, coincide. Through the appearance of the beautiful, we are wounded in our innermost being, and that wound grips us and takes us beyond ourselves; it stirs longing into flight and moves us toward the truly Beautiful, to the Good in itself. Something of this Platonic foundation lives on in the theology of icons, even though the Platonic ideas of the beautiful and of vision have been transformed by the light of Tabor. Moreover, Plato's conception has been profoundly reshaped by the interconnection of creation, Christology, and eschatology, and the material order as such has been given a new dignity and a new value. This kind of Platonism, transformed as it is by the Incarnation, largely disappears from the West after the thirteenth century, so that now the art of painting strives first and foremost to depict events that have taken place. Salvation history is seen less as a sacrament than as a narrative unfolded in time. Thus the relationship to the liturgy also changes. It is seen as a kind of symbolic reproduction of the event of the Cross. Piety responds by turning chiefly to meditation on the mysteries of the life of Jesus. Art finds its inspiration less in the liturgy than in popular piety, and popular piety is in turn nourished by the historical images in which it can contemplate the way to Christ, the way of Jesus himself, and its continuation in the saints. The separation in iconography between East and West, which took place at the latest by the thirteenth century, doubtless goes very deep: very different themes, different spiritual paths, open up. A devotion to the Cross of a more historicizing kind replaces orientation to the *Oriens*, to the risen Lord who has gone ahead of us.

Nevertheless, we should not exaggerate the differences that developed. True, the depiction of Christ dying in pain on the Cross is something new, but it still depicts him who bore *our* pains, by whose stripes we are healed. In the extremes of pain, it represents the redemptive love of God. Though Grünewald's altarpiece takes the realism of the Passion to a radical extreme, the fact remains that it was an image of consolation. It enabled the plague victims cared for by the Antonians to recognize that God identified with them in their fate, to see that he had descended into their suffering and that their suffering lay hidden in his. There is a decisive turn to what is human, historical, in Christ, but it is animated by a sense that these human afflictions of his belong to the mystery. The images are consoling, because they make visible the overcoming of our anguish in the incarnate God's sharing of our suffering, and so they bear within them the message of the Resurrection. These images, too, come from prayer, from interior meditation on the way of Christ. They are identifications with Christ, which are based in turn on God's identification with us in Christ. They open up the realism of the mystery without diverging from it. As for the Mass, as the making present of the Cross, do these images not enable us to understand that mystery with a new vividness? The mystery is unfolded in an extremity of concreteness, and popular piety is enabled thereby to reach the heart of the liturgy in a new way. These images, too, do not show just the "surface of the skin", the external sensible world; they, too, are intended to lead us through mere outward appearance and open our eyes to the heart of God. What we are suggesting here about the images of the Cross applies also to all the rest of the "narrative" art of the Gothic style. What power of inward devotion lies in the images of the Mother of God! They manifest the new humanity of the faith. Such images are an invitation to prayer, because they are permeated with prayer from within. They show us the true image of man as planned by the Creator and renewed by Christ. They guide us into man's authentic being. And finally, let us not forget the glorious art of Gothic stained glass! The windows of the Gothic cathedrals keep out the garishness of the light outside, while concentrating that light and using it so that the whole history of God in relation to man, from creation to the Second Coming, shines through. The walls of the church, in interplay with the sun, become an image in their own right, the iconostasis of the West, lending the place a sense of the sacred that can touch the hearts even of agnostics.

The Renaissance did something quite new. It "emancipated" man. Now we see the development of the "aesthetic" in the modern sense, the vision of a beauty that no longer points beyond itself but is content in the end with itself, the beauty of the appearing thing. Man experiences himself in his autonomy, in all his grandeur. Art speaks of this grandeur of man almost as if it were surprised by it; it needs no other beauty to seek. There is often scarcely a difference between the depictions of pagan myths and those of Christian history. The tragic burden of antiquity has been forgotten; only its divine beauty is seen. A nostalgia for the gods emerges, for myth, for a world without fear of sin and without the pain of the Cross, which had perhaps been too overpowering in the images of the late Middle Ages. True, Christian subjects are still being depicted, but such "religious art" is no longer sacred art in the proper sense. It does not enter into the humility of the sacraments and their time-transcending dynamism. It wants to enjoy today and to bring redemption through beauty itself. Perhaps the iconoclasm of the Reformation should be understood against this background, though doubtless its roots were extensive.

Baroque art, which follows the Renaissance, has many different aspects and modes of expression. In its best form, it is based on the reform of the Church set in motion by the Council of Trent. In line with the tradition of the West, the council again emphasized the didactic and pedagogical character of art, but, as a fresh start toward

interior renewal, it led once more to a new kind of seeing that comes from and returns within. The altarpiece is
like a window through which the world of God comes
out to us. The curtain of temporality is raised, and we
are allowed a glimpse into the inner life of the world of
God. This art is intended to insert us into the liturgy
of heaven. Again and again, we experience a Baroque
church as a unique kind of *fortissimo* of joy, an Alleluia
in visual form. "The joy of the LORD is your strength"
(Neh 8:10). These words from the Old Testament express the basic emotion that animates this iconography.
The Enlightenment pushed faith into a kind of intellectual and even social ghetto. Contemporary culture turned
away from the faith and trod another path, so that faith
took flight in historicism, the copying of the past, or else
attempted compromise or lost itself in resignation and
cultural abstinence. The last of these led to a new iconoclasm, which has frequently been regarded as virtually
mandated by the Second Vatican Council. The destruction of images, the first signs of which reach back to
the 1920s, eliminated a lot of *kitsch* and unworthy art,
but ultimately it left behind a void, the wretchedness of
which we are now experiencing in a truly acute way.

Where do we go from here? Today we are experienc-
ing, not just a crisis of sacred art, but a crisis of art in general of unprecedented proportions. The crisis of art for
its part is a symptom of the crisis of man's very existence.
The immense growth in man's mastery of the material
world has left him blind to the questions of life's meaning
that transcend the material world. We might almost call it
a blindness of the spirit. The questions of how we ought
to live, how we can overcome death, whether existence
has a purpose and what it is—to all these questions there

is no longer a common answer. Positivism, formulated in the name of scientific seriousness, narrows the horizon to what is verifiable, to what can be proved by experiment; it renders the world opaque. True, it still contains mathematics, but the *logos* that is the presupposition of this mathematics and its applicability is no longer evident. Thus our world of images no longer surpasses the bounds of sense and appearance, and the flood of images that surrounds us really means the end of the image. If something cannot be photographed, it cannot be seen. In this situation, the art of the icon, sacred art, depending as it does on a wider kind of seeing, becomes impossible. What is more, art itself, which in impressionism and expressionism explored the extreme possibilities of the sense of sight, becomes literally object-less. Art turns into experimenting with self-created worlds, empty "creativity", which no longer perceives the *Creator Spiritus*, the Creator Spirit. It attempts to take his place, and yet, in so doing, it manages to produce only what is arbitrary and vacuous, bringing home to man the absurdity of his role as creator.

Again we must ask: Where do we go from here? Let us try to sum up what we have said so far and to identify the fundamental principles of an art ordered to divine worship.

1. The complete absence of images is incompatible with faith in the Incarnation of God. God has acted in history and entered into our sensible world so that it may become transparent to him. Images of beauty, in which the mystery of the invisible God becomes visible, are an essential part of Christian worship. There will always be ups and downs in the history of iconography, upsurge and decline, and therefore periods when images

are somewhat sparse. But they can never be totally lacking. Iconoclasm is not a Christian option.

2. Sacred art finds its subjects in the images of salvation history, beginning with creation and continuing all the way from the first day to the eighth day, the day of the resurrection and Second Coming, in which the line of human history will come full circle. The images of biblical history have pride of place in sacred art, but the latter also includes the history of the saints, which is an unfolding of the history of Jesus Christ, the fruit borne throughout history by the dead grain of wheat. "You are not struggling against icons", said Saint John Damascene to the iconoclastic emperor Leo III, "but against the saints." In the same period, and with the same view in mind, Pope Saint Gregory III instituted in Rome the feast of All Saints.[4]

3. The images of the history of God in relation to man do not merely illustrate the succession of past events but display the inner unity of God's action. In this way, they have a reference to the sacraments, above all, to Baptism and the Eucharist, and, in pointing to the sacraments, they are contained within them. Images thus point to a presence; they are essentially connected with what happens in the liturgy. Now history becomes sacrament in Christ, who is the source of the sacraments. Therefore, the icon of Christ is the center of sacred iconography. The center of the icon of Christ is the Paschal Mystery: Christ is presented as the Crucified, the risen Lord, the One who will come again and who here and now hiddenly reigns over all. Every image of Christ must contain these three essential aspects of the mystery of Christ and, in this sense, must be an image of Easter. At the same

[4] Ibid., 164.

time, it goes without saying that different emphases are possible. The image may give more prominence to the Cross, the Passion, and in the Passion to the anguish of our own life today, or again it may bring the Resurrection or the Second Coming to the fore. But whatever happens, one aspect can never be completely isolated from another, and in the different emphases the Paschal Mystery as a whole must be plainly evident. An image of the Crucifixion no longer transparent to Easter would be just as deficient as an Easter image forgetful of the wounds and the suffering of the present moment. And, centered as it is on the Paschal Mystery, the image of Christ is always an icon of the Eucharist, that is, it points to the sacramental presence of the Easter mystery.

4. The image of Christ and the images of the saints are not photographs. Their whole point is to lead us beyond what can be apprehended at the merely material level, to awaken new senses in us, and to teach us a new kind of seeing, which perceives the Invisible in the visible. The sacredness of the image consists precisely in the fact that it comes from an interior vision and thus leads us to such an interior vision. It must be a fruit of contemplation, of an encounter in faith with the new reality of the risen Christ, and so it leads us in turn into an interior gazing, an encounter in prayer with the Lord. The image is at the service of the liturgy. The prayer and contemplation in which the images are formed must, therefore, be a praying and seeing undertaken in communion with the seeing faith of the Church. The ecclesial dimension is essential to sacred art and thus has an essential connection with the history of the faith, with Scripture and tradition.

5. The Church in the West does not need to disown the specific path she has followed since about the thirteenth

century. But she must achieve a real reception of the Seventh Ecumenical Council, Nicaea II, which affirmed the fundamental importance and theological status of the image in the Church. The Western Church does not need to subject herself to all the individual norms concerning images that were developed at the councils and synods of the East, coming to some kind of conclusion in 1551 at the Council of Moscow, the Council of the Hundred Canons. Nevertheless, she should regard the fundamental lines of this theology of the image in the Church as normative for her. There must, of course, be no rigid norms. Freshly received intuitions and the ever-new experiences of piety must find a place in the Church. But still there is a difference between sacred art (which is related to the liturgy and belongs to the ecclesial sphere) and religious art in general. There cannot be completely free expression in sacred art. Forms of art that deny the *logos* of things and imprison man within what appears to the senses are incompatible with the Church's understanding of the image. No sacred art can come from an isolated subjectivity. No, it presupposes that there is a subject who has been inwardly formed by the Church and opened up to the "we". Only thus does art make the Church's common faith visible and speak again to the believing heart. The freedom of art, which is also necessary in the more narrowly circumscribed realm of sacred art, is not a matter of do-as-you-please. It unfolds according to the measure indicated by the first four points in these concluding reflections, which are an attempt to sum up what is constant in the iconographic tradition of faith. Without faith, there is no art commensurate with the liturgy. Sacred art stands beneath the imperative stated in the second epistle to the Corinthians. Gazing at the Lord, we are "changed into his likeness from one degree of glory to another; for this comes from the Lord who is the Spirit" (3:18).

But what does all this mean practically? Art cannot be "produced", as one contracts out and produces technical equipment. It is always a gift. Inspiration is not something one can choose for oneself. It has to be received, otherwise it is not there. One cannot bring about a renewal of art in faith by money or through commissions. Before all things, it requires the gift of a new kind of seeing. And so it would be worth our while to regain a faith that sees. Wherever that exists, art finds its proper expression.

CHAPTER TWO

Music and Liturgy

T HE IMPORTANCE of music in biblical religion is shown very simply by the fact that the verb "to sing" (with related words such as "song", and so forth) is one of the most commonly used words in the Bible. It occurs 309 times in the Old Testament and thirty-six in the New. When man comes into contact with God, mere speech is not enough. Areas of his existence are awakened that spontaneously turn into song. Indeed, man's own being is insufficient for what he has to express, and so he invites the whole of creation to become a song with him: "Awake, my soul! Awake, O harp and lyre! I will awake the dawn! I will give thanks to you, O Lord, among the peoples; I will sing praises to you among the nations. For your mercy is great to the heavens, your faithfulness to the clouds" (Ps 57:8–10). We find the first mention of singing in the Bible after the crossing of the Red Sea. Israel has now been definitively delivered from slavery. In a desperate situation, it has had an overwhelming experience of God's saving power. Just as Moses as a baby was taken from the Nile and only then really received the gift of life, so Israel now feels as if it has been, so to speak, taken out of the water: it is free, newly endowed with the gift of itself from God's own hands. In the biblical account, the people's reaction to the foundational event of salvation is described in this sentence: "[T]hey believed in the LORD and in his servant Moses" (Ex 14:31). But then follows a second reaction, which soars up from the first with elemental force: "Then Moses and the sons of Israel sang this song to the LORD" (15:1). Year by year, at the Easter Vigil, Christians join in the singing of this song. They sing it in a new way as their song, because they know that they have been "taken out of the water" by God's power, set free by God for authentic life. The Apocalypse of Saint John draws the bow back even farther. The final enemies of the People of God have stepped onto the stage of history: the satanic trinity, consisting of the beast, its image, and the number of its name. Everything seems lost for the holy Israel of God in the face of such overwhelming odds. But then the Seer is given the vision of the conquerors, "standing beside the sea of glass with harps of God in their hands. And they sing the song of Moses, the servant of God, and the song of the Lamb" (Rev 15:2–3). The paradox now becomes even more powerful. It is not the gigantic beasts of prey, with their power over the media and their technical strength, who win the victory. No, it is the sacrificed Lamb that conquers. And so once again, definitively, there resounds the song of God's servant Moses, which has now become the song of the Lamb.

Liturgical singing is established in the midst of this great historical tension. For Israel, the event of salvation in the Red Sea will always be the main reason for praising God, the basic theme of the songs it sings before God. For Christians, the Resurrection of Christ is the true Exodus. He has stridden through the Red Sea of death itself, descended into the world of shadows, and smashed open the prison door. In Baptism, this Exodus is made ever present. To be baptized is to be made a partaker, a contemporary, of Christ's descent into hell and of his rising up therefrom, in which he takes us up into the fellowship of new life. On the very next day after the joy of the Exodus, the Israelites had to accept that they were now exposed to the wilderness and its terrors, and even entry into the Promised Land did not put a stop to the threats to their life. But there were also the mighty deeds of God, which were new every day. These were cause for singing Moses' song anew and proved that God is not a God of the past, but a God of the present and future. Of course, while singing the song, they realized it was only provisional, and so they longed for the definitive new song, for the salvation that would no longer be followed by a moment of anguish but would be a song only of praise. The man who believes in the Resurrection of Christ really does know what definitive salvation is. He realizes that Christians, who find themselves in the "New Covenant", now sing an altogether new song, which is truly and definitively new in view of the wholly new thing that has taken place in the Resurrection of Christ. What we discovered in the first part about the "in-between" state of Christian reality (no longer a shadow, but still not full reality, only an "image") applies again here. The definitively new song has been intoned, but still all the sufferings of history must be endured, all pain gathered in and brought into the sacrifice of praise, in order to be transformed there into a song of praise.

Here, then, is the theological basis for liturgical singing. We need now to look more closely at its practical reality. In addition to the various witnesses that are found throughout Scripture to the singing of the individual and of the community, as well as to the music of the Temple, the book of Psalms is the proper source for us to rely on here. Because it lacks musical notation, we are unable to reconstruct the "sacred music" of Israel, but it does give us an idea of the richness of both the instruments and the different kinds of singing used in Israel. In their prayed poetry, the Psalms display the whole range of human experiences, which become prayer and song in the presence of God. Lamentation, complaint, indeed accusation, fear, hope, trust, gratitude, joy—the whole of human life is reflected here, as it is unfolded in dialogue with God. It is striking that even complaints made in desperate affliction almost always end with words of trust, with an anticipation, as it were, of God's saving act. In a certain sense, one might describe all these "new songs" as variations on the song of Moses. Singing before God rises up, on the one hand, out of an affliction from which no earthly power can save man—his only refuge is God. But at the same time, it emerges out of a trust that, even in utter darkness, knows that the crossing of the Red Sea is a promise that will have the last word in life and in history. Finally, it is important to say that the Psalms frequently come from very personal experiences of suffering and answered prayer, and yet they always flow into the common prayer of Israel. They are nourished out of the common store of God's saving deeds in the past.

With regard to the singing of the Church, we notice the same pattern of continuity and renewal that we have seen in the nature of the liturgy in general, in church architecture, and in sacred images. Quite spontaneously, the Psalter becomes the prayer book of the infant Church, which, with equal spontaneity, has become a Church that sings her prayers. That applies first of all to the

Psalter, which Christians, of course, now pray together with Christ. In its canon of Scripture, Israel had ascribed most of the Psalms to King David and had given them a definite interpretation in terms of theology and the history of salvation. For Christians, it is clear that Christ is the true David, that David in the Holy Spirit prays through and with the One who is to be his Son and who is the only begotten Son of God. With this new key, Christians entered into the prayer of Israel and came to realize that, precisely through them, that prayer was to become the new song. The Holy Spirit, who had inspired David to sing and to pray, moves him to speak of Christ, indeed, causes him to become the very mouth of Christ, thus enabling us in the Psalms to speak through Christ, in the Holy Spirit, to the Father. Now this exegesis of the Psalms, at once christological and pneumatological, not only concerns the text but also includes the element of music. It is the Holy Spirit who teaches us to sing—first David and then, through him, Israel and the Church. Yes, singing, the surpassing of ordinary speech, is a "pneumatic" event. Church music comes into being as a "charism", a gift of the Spirit. It is the true *glossolalia*, the new tongue that comes from the Holy Spirit. It is above all in Church music that the "sober inebriation" of faith takes place—an inebriation surpassing all the possibilities of mere rationality. But this intoxication remains sober, because Christ and the Holy Spirit belong together, because this drunken speech stays totally within the discipline of the Logos, in a new rationality that, beyond all words, serves the primordial Word, the ground of all reason. This is a matter to which we must return.

We have already seen how in the Apocalypse the horizon is widened by the confession of faith in Christ: the song of the conquerors is described as the song of God's servant Moses and of the Lamb. Now this opens up a further dimension of singing before God. In Israel's Bible, we have so far discovered two principal motivations of this singing before God: affliction and joy, distress and deliverance. Man's relationship with God was doubtless too strongly marked by reverential fear of the Creator's eternal might for anyone to dare to see these songs to God as love songs. Ultimately, love lies hidden in the trust that deeply marks all these texts, but the love remains diffident, precisely hidden. The alliance of love and song came into the Old Testament in a rather curious way, namely, through the acceptance of the Song of Songs. This was a collection of thoroughly human love songs, but almost certainly its acceptance involved a far deeper interpretation. These very beautiful love poems of Israel could be seen as the inspired words of Sacred Scripture because of the conviction that, in this serenading of human love, the mystery of the love of God and Israel shines through. The prophets described the worship of foreign gods as harlotry, a term that in this case has an exact meaning, because fertility rites and temple prostitution were part of the fertility cults. Conversely, the election of Israel now appears as the love story of God and his people. The covenant is expounded through the analogy of betrothal and marriage, as the binding of God's love to man and of man to God. Thus human love was able to serve as a profoundly real analogy for God's action in Israel. Jesus took up this line in Israel's tradition and presented himself, in an early parable, as the Bridegroom. When asked why his disciples, unlike John's and the Pharisees, did not fast, he replied: "Can the wedding guests fast while the bridegroom is with them? As long as they have the bridegroom with them, they cannot fast. The days will come, when the bridegroom is taken away from them, and then they will fast in that day" (Mk 2:19f.). This is a prophecy of the Passion but also an announcement of the marriage that constantly appears in Jesus' parables of the wedding banquet and that, in the Apocalypse, the last book of the New Testament, becomes the central theme. Everything moves through the Passion toward the wedding of the Lamb. Since, in the visions of the heavenly liturgy, that wedding seems always to be already anticipated, Christians came to see the Eucharist as the presence of the Bridegroom and thus as a foretaste of the wedding feast of God. In the Eucharist a communion takes place that corresponds to the union of man and woman in marriage. Just as they become "one flesh", so in Communion we all become "one spirit", one person, with Christ. The spousal mystery, announced in the Old Testament, of the intimate union of God and man takes place in the Sacrament of the Body and Blood of Christ, precisely through his Passion and in a very real way (cf. Eph 5:29–32; 1 Cor 6:17; Gal 3:28). The singing of the Church comes ultimately out of love. It is the utter depth of love that produces the singing. "Cantare amantis est", says Saint Augustine, singing is a lover's thing. In so saying, we come again to the trinitarian interpretation of Church music. The Holy Spirit is love, and it is he who produces the singing. He is the Spirit of Christ, the Spirit who draws us into love for Christ and so leads to the Father.

We must turn once more from these inner driving forces of liturgical music to more practical questions. The expression used in the Psalms for "singing" has its etymological roots in the common stock of ancient oriental languages and denotes an instrumentally supported singing, the instruments probably being stringed. The singing was clearly related to a text and always, with regard to content, directed to a particular statement. It presumably involved a kind of speech-song that allowed changes of note in the melody only at the beginning and end. The Greek Bible translated the Hebrew *zamir* by the word *psallein*, which in Greek meant "to pluck" (especially in the sense of a stringed instrument) but now became the word for the special kind of instrumental playing used in Jewish worship and later described the singing of Christians. Several times there is an additional expression, the meaning of which is obscure, but in any case it refers in some way to ordered artistic singing. Thus, in the musical sphere, biblical faith created its own form of culture, an expression appropriate to its inward essence, one that provides a standard for all later forms of inculturation.

The question of how far inculturation can go soon became a very practical one for early Christianity, especially in the area of music. The Christian communities had grown out of the synagogue and, along with the christologically interpreted Psalter, had also taken over the synagogue's way of singing. Very soon new Christian hymns and canticles came into being: first, with a wholly Old Testament foundation, the Benedictus and Magnificat, but then christologically focused texts, preeminently the prologue of Saint John's Gospel (1:1–18), the hymn of Christ in the epistle to the Philippians (2:6–11), and the song of Christ in the first epistle to Timothy (3:16). In his first epistle to the Corinthians, Saint Paul provides us with some very interesting information about the order of service in early Christian liturgy: "When you come together, each one has a hymn, a lesson, a revelation, a tongue, or an interpretation. Let all things be done for edification" (14:26). Through the Roman author Pliny, who informed the emperor about the religious services of the Christians, we know that, at the beginning of the second century A.D., singing to the glory of Christ in his divinity was at the very heart of Christian liturgy. One can well imagine that with these new Christian texts came a more varied use of the singing than hitherto and the composition of new melodies. It would seem that one of the ways in which Christian faith was developed was precisely in the writing of canticles, which arose at this time in the Church as "gifts of the Spirit". Herein lay hope but also danger. As the Church was uprooted from her Semitic soil and moved into the Greek world, a spontaneous and far-reaching fusion took place with Greek *logos* mysticism, with its poetry and music, that eventually threatened to dissolve Christianity into a generalized mysticism. It was precisely hymns and their music that provided the point of entry for Gnosticism, that deadly temptation which began to subvert Christianity from within. And so it is understandable that, in their struggle for the identity of the faith and its rooting in the historical figure of Jesus Christ, the Church authorities resorted to a radical decision. The fifty-ninth canon of the Council of Laodicea forbids the use of privately composed psalms and non-canonical writings in divine worship. The fifteenth canon restricts the singing of psalms to the choir of psalm-singers, while "other people in church should not sing." That is how post-biblical hymns were almost entirely lost. There was a rigorous return to the restrained, purely vocal style of singing taken over from the synagogue. We may regret the cultural impoverishment this entailed, but it was necessary for the sake of a greater good. A return to apparent cultural poverty saved the identity of biblical faith, and the very rejection of false inculturation opened up the cultural breadth of Christianity for the future.

When we look at the history of liturgical music, we can see extensive parallels with the evolution of the image question. The East, at least in the Byzantine world, kept to purely vocal music. True, among the Slavs, probably under Western influence, it has been extended into polyphony. The male-voice choirs of this tradition, through their sacral dignity and restrained power, touch the heart and make the Eucharist a true feast of faith. In the West, in the form of Gregorian chant, the inherited tradition of psalm-singing was developed to a new sublimity and purity, which set a permanent standard for sacred music, music for the liturgy of the Church. Polyphony developed in the late Middle Ages, and then instruments came back into divine worship—quite rightly, too, because, as we have seen, the Church not only continues the synagogue, but also takes up, in the light of Christ's Pasch, the reality represented by the Temple. Two new factors are thus at work in Church music. Artistic freedom increasingly asserts its rights, even in the liturgy. Church music and secular music are now each influenced by the other. This is particularly clear in the case of the so-called "parody Masses", in which the text of the Mass was set to a theme or melody that came from secular music, with the result that anyone hearing it might think he was listening to the latest "hit". It is clear that these opportunities for artistic creativity and the adoption of secular tunes brought danger with them. Music was no longer developing out of prayer, but, with the new demand for artistic autonomy, was now heading away from the liturgy; it was becoming an end in itself, opening the door to new, very different ways of feeling and of experiencing the world. Music was alienating the liturgy from its true nature.

At this point, the Council of Trent intervened in the culture war that had broken out. It was made a norm that liturgical music should be at the service of the Word; the use of instruments was substantially reduced; and the difference between secular and sacred music was clearly affirmed. At the beginning of the last century, Pope Saint Pius X made a similar intervention. The age of the Baroque, albeit in different forms in the Catholic and Protestant worlds, achieved an astounding unity of secular music-making with the music of the liturgy. It succeeded in dedicating the whole luminous power of music, which reached such a high point in this period of cultural history, to the glorifying of God. Whether it is Bach or Mozart that we hear in church, we have a sense in either case of what *gloria Dei*, the glory of God, means. The mystery of infinite beauty is there and enables us to experience the presence of God more truly and vividly than in many sermons. But there are already signs of danger to come. Subjective experience and passion are still held in check by the order of the musical universe, reflecting as it does the order of the divine creation itself. But there is already the threat of invasion by the virtuoso mentality, the vanity of technique, which is no longer the servant of the whole but wants to push itself to the fore. During the nineteenth century, the century of self-emancipating subjectivity, this led in many places to the obscuring of the sacred by the operatic. The dangers that had forced the Council of Trent to intervene were back again. In similar fashion, Pope Pius X tried to remove the operatic element from the liturgy and declared Gregorian chant and the great polyphony of the age of the Catholic Reformation (of which Palestrina was the outstanding representative) to be the standard for liturgical music. A clear distinction was made between liturgical music and religious music in general, just as visual art in the liturgy has to conform to different standards from those employed in religious art in general. Art in the liturgy has a very specific responsibility, and precisely as such does it serve as a wellspring of culture, which in the final analysis owes its existence to cult.

After the cultural revolution of recent decades, we are faced with a challenge no less great than that of the three moments of crisis that we have encountered in our historical sketch: the Gnostic temptation, the crisis at the end of the Middle Ages and the beginning of modernity, and the crisis at the beginning of the twentieth century, which formed the prelude to the still more radical questions of the present day. Three developments in recent music epitomize the problems that the Church has to face when she is considering liturgical music. First of all, there is the cultural universalization that the Church has to undertake if she wants to get beyond the boundaries of the European mind. This is the question of what inculturation should look like in the realm of sacred music if, on the one hand, the identity of Christianity is to be preserved and, on the other, its universality is to be expressed in local forms. Then there are two developments in music itself that have their origins primarily in the West but that for a long time have affected the whole of mankind in the world culture that is being formed. Modern so-called "classical" music has maneuvered itself, with some exceptions, into an elitist ghetto, which only specialists may enter—and even they do so with what may sometimes be mixed feelings. The music of the masses has broken loose from this and treads a very different path. On the one hand, there is pop music, which is certainly no longer supported by the people in the ancient sense (pop*ulus*). It is aimed at the phenomenon of the masses, is industrially produced, and ultimately has to be described as a cult of the banal. "Rock", on the other hand, is the expression of elemental passions, and at rock festivals it assumes a cultic character, a form of worship, in fact, in opposition to Christian worship. People are, so to speak, released from themselves by the experience of being part of a crowd and by the emotional shock of rhythm, noise, and special lighting effects. However, in the ecstasy of having all their defenses torn down, the participants sink, as it were, beneath the elemental force of the universe. The music of the Holy Spirit's sober inebriation seems to have little chance when self has become a prison, the mind is a shackle, and breaking out from both appears as a true promise of redemption that can be tasted at least for a few moments.

What is to be done? Theoretical solutions are perhaps even less helpful here. There has to be renewal from within. Nevertheless, by way of conclusion, I am going to try to sum up the principles that have emerged from our look at the inner foundations of Christian sacred music.

The music of Christian worship is related to *logos* in three senses:

1. It is related to the events of God's saving action to which the Bible bears witness and which the liturgy makes present. God's action continues in the history of the Church, but it has its unshakeable center in the Paschal Mystery of Jesus Christ, his Cross, Resurrection, and Ascension. This takes up, interprets, and brings to fulfill-

ment the history of salvation in the Old Testament as well as the hopes and experiences of deliverance in the religious history of mankind. In liturgical music, based as it is on biblical faith, there is, therefore, a clear dominance of the Word; this music is a higher form of proclamation. Ultimately, it rises up out of the love that responds to God's love made flesh in Christ, the love that for us went unto death. After the Resurrection, the Cross is by no means a thing of the past, and so this love is always marked by pain at the hiddenness of God, by the cry that rises up from the depths of anguish, *Kyrie eleison*, by hope and by supplication. But it also has the privilege, by anticipation, of experiencing the reality of the Resurrection, and so it brings with it the joy of being loved, that gladness of heart which Haydn said came upon him when he set liturgical texts to music. Thus the relation of liturgical music to *logos* means, first of all, simply its relation to words. That is why singing in the liturgy has priority over instrumental music, though it does not in any way exclude it. It goes without saying that the biblical and liturgical texts are the normative words from which liturgical music has to take its bearings. This does not rule out the continuing creation of "new songs" but, instead, inspires them and assures them of a firm grounding in God's love for mankind and his work of redemption.

2. Saint Paul tells us that of ourselves we do not know how to pray as we ought but that the Spirit himself intercedes for us "with sighs too deep for words" (Rom 8:26). Prayer is a gift of the Holy Spirit, both prayer in general and that particular kind of prayer which is the gift of singing and playing before God. The Holy Spirit is love. He enkindles love in us and thus moves us to sing. Now the Spirit of Christ "takes what is [Christ's]" (cf.

Jn 16:14), and so the gift that comes from him, the gift that surpasses all words, is always related to Christ, *the* Word, the great Meaning that creates and sustains all life. Words are superseded, but not the Word, the Logos. This is the second, deeper sense in which liturgical music is related to *logos*. The Church's tradition has this in mind when it talks about the sober inebriation caused in us by the Holy Spirit. There is always an ultimate sobriety, a deeper rationality, resisting any decline into irrationality and immoderation. We can see what this means in practice if we look at the history of music. The writings of Plato and Aristotle on music show that the Greek world in their time was faced with a choice between two kinds of worship, two different images of God and man. Now what this choice came down to concretely was a choice between two fundamental types of music. On the one hand, there is the music that Plato ascribes, in line with mythology, to Apollo, the god of light and reason. This is the music that draws senses into spirit and so brings man to wholeness. It does not abolish the senses, but inserts them into the unity of this creature that is man. It elevates the spirit precisely by wedding it to the senses, and it elevates the senses by uniting them with the spirit. Thus this kind of music is an expression of man's special place in the general structure of being. But then there is the music that Plato ascribes to Marsyas, which we might describe, in terms of cultic history, as "Dionysian". It drags man into the intoxication of the senses, crushes rationality, and subjects the spirit to the senses. The way Plato (and more moderately, Aristotle) allots instruments and keys to one or other of these two kinds of music is now obsolete and may in many respects surprise us. But the Apollonian/Dionysian alternative runs through the whole history of religion and confronts us again today. Not every kind of music can have a place in Christian worship. It has its standards, and that standard is the Logos. If we want to know with whom we are dealing, the Holy Spirit or the unholy spirit, we have to remember that it is the Holy Spirit who moves us to say, "Jesus is Lord" (1 Cor 12:3). The Holy Spirit leads us to the Logos, and he leads us to a music that serves the Logos as a sign of the *sursum corda*, the lifting up of the human heart. Does it integrate man by drawing him to what is above, or does it cause his disintegration into formless intoxication or mere sensuality? That is the criterion for a music in harmony with *logos*, a form of that *logikē latreia* (reason-able, *logos*-worthy worship) of which we spoke in the first part of this book.

3. The Word incarnate in Christ, the Logos, is not just the power that gives meaning to the individual, not even just the power that gives meaning to history. No, he is the creative Meaning from which the universe comes and which the universe, the cosmos, reflects. That is why this Word leads us out of individualism into the communion of saints spanning all times and places. This is the "broad place" (Ps 31:8), the redemptive breadth into which the Lord places us. But its span stretches still farther. As we have seen, Christian liturgy is always a cosmic liturgy. What does this mean for our question? The Preface, the first part of the Eucharistic Prayer, always ends with the affirmation that we are singing "Holy, Holy, Holy" together with the cherubim and seraphim and with all the choirs of heaven. The liturgy is echoing here the vision of God in Isaiah chapter 6. In the Holy of Holies in the Temple, the prophet sees the throne of God, protected by the seraphim, who call to one another: "Holy, holy,

holy is the LORD of hosts; the whole earth is full of his glory" (Is 6:1–3). In the celebration of Holy Mass, we insert ourselves into this liturgy that always goes before us. All our singing is a singing and praying with the great liturgy that spans the whole of creation.

Among the Fathers, it was especially Saint Augustine who tried to connect this characteristic view of the Christian liturgy with the world view of Greco-Roman antiquity. In his early work "On Music", he is still completely dependent on the Pythagorean theory of music. According to Pythagoras, the cosmos was constructed mathematically, a great edifice of numbers. Modern physics, beginning with Kepler, Galileo, and Newton, has gone back to this vision and, through the mathematical interpretation of the universe, has made possible the technological use of its powers. For the Pythagoreans, this mathematical order of the universe ("cosmos" means "order"!) was identical with the essence of beauty itself. Beauty comes from meaningful inner order. And for them this beauty was not only optical but also musical. Goethe alludes to this idea when he speaks of the singing contest of the fraternity of the spheres: the mathematical order of the planets and their revolutions contains a secret timbre, which is the primal form of music. The courses of the revolving planets are like melodies, the numerical order is the rhythm, and the concurrence of the individual courses is the harmony. The music made by man must, according to this view, be taken from the inner music and order of the universe, be inserted into the "fraternal song" of the "fraternity of the spheres". The beauty of music depends on its conformity to the rhythmic and harmonic laws of the universe. The more that human music adapts itself to the musical laws of the universe, the more beautiful will it be.

Saint Augustine first took up this theory and then deepened it. In the course of history, transplanting it into the world view of faith was bound to bring with it a twofold personalization. Even the Pythagoreans did not interpret the mathematics of the universe in an entirely abstract way. In the view of the ancients, intelligent actions presupposed an intelligence that caused them. The intelligent, mathematical movements of the heavenly bodies was not explained, therefore, in a purely mechanical way; they could only be understood on the assumption that the heavenly bodies were animated, were themselves "intelligent". For Christians, there was a spontaneous turn at this point from stellar deities to the choirs of angels that surround God and illuminate the universe. Perceiving the "music of the cosmos" thus becomes listening to the song of the angels, and the reference to Isaiah chapter 6 naturally suggests itself. But a further step was taken with the help of trinitarian faith, faith in the Father, the Logos, and the Pneuma. The mathematics of the universe does not exist by itself, nor, as people now came to see, can it be explained by stellar deities. It has a deeper foundation: the mind of the Creator. It comes from the Logos, in whom, so to speak, the archetypes of the world's order are contained. The Logos, through the Spirit, fashions the material world according to these archetypes. In virtue of his work in creation, the Logos is, therefore, called the "art of God" (*ars = technē*!). The Logos himself is the great artist, in whom all works of art—the beauty of the universe—have their origin. To sing with the universe means, then, to follow the track of the Logos and to come close to him. All true human art is an assimilation to *the* artist, to Christ, to the mind of the Creator. The idea of the music of the cosmos, of singing with the angels, leads back again to the relation of art to *logos*, but now it is broadened and deepened in the context of the cosmos. Yes, it is the cosmic context that gives art in the liturgy both its measure and its scope. A merely subjective "creativity" is no match for the vast compass of the cosmos and for the message of its beauty. When a man conforms to the measure of the universe, his freedom is not diminished but expanded to a new horizon.

One final point follows from this. The cosmic interpretation remained alive, with some variations, well into the early modern age. Only in the nineteenth century was there a move away from it, because "metaphysics" seemed so outdated. Hegel now tried to interpret music as just an expression of the subject and of subjectivity. But whereas Hegel still adhered to the fundamental idea of reason as the starting point and destination of the whole enterprise, a change of direction took place with Schopenhauer that was to have momentous consequences. For him, the world is no longer grounded in reason but in "will and idea" (*Wille und Vorstellung*). The will precedes reason. And music is the primordial expression of being human as such, the pure expression of the will—anterior to reason—that creates the world. Music should not, therefore, be subjected to the word, and only in exceptional cases should it have any connection with the word. Since music is pure will, its origin precedes that of reason. It takes us back behind reason to the actual foundation of reality. It is reminiscent of Goethe's recasting of the prologue of Saint John: no longer "In the beginning was the Word", but now "In the beginning was the Deed." In our own times, this continues in the attempt to replace "orthodoxy" with "orthopraxy"—there is no common faith anymore (because truth is unattainable), only common praxis. By contrast, for Christian faith, as Guardini shows so penetratingly in his masterly early work, *The Spirit of the Liturgy*, logos has precedence over *ethos*. When this is reversed, Christianity is turned upside down. The cosmic character of liturgical music stands in opposition to the two tendencies of the modern age that we have described: music as pure subjectivity, music as the expression of mere will. We sing with the angels. But this cosmic character is grounded ultimately in the ordering of all Christian worship to *logos*.

Let us have one last brief look at our own times. The dissolution of the subject, which coincides for us today with radical forms of subjectivism, has led to "deconstructionism"—the anarchistic theory of art. Perhaps this will help us to overcome the unbounded inflation of subjectivity and to recognize once more that a relationship with the Logos, who was at the beginning, brings salvation to the subject, that is, to the person. At the same time it puts us into a true relationship of communion that is ultimately grounded in trinitarian love.

As we have seen in both chapters of this part of the book, the problems of the present day pose without doubt a grave challenge to the Church and the culture of the liturgy. Nevertheless, there is no reason at all to be discouraged. The great cultural tradition of the faith is home to a presence of immense power. What in museums is only a monument from the past, an occasion for mere nostalgic admiration, is constantly made present in the liturgy in all its freshness. But the present day, too, is not condemned to silence where the faith is concerned. Anyone who looks carefully will see that, even in our own time, important works of art, inspired by faith, have been produced and are being produced—in visual art as well as in music (and, indeed, literature). Today, too, joy in the Lord and contact with his presence in the liturgy has an inexhaustible power of inspiration. The artists who take this task upon themselves need not regard themselves as the rearguard of culture. They are weary of the empty freedom from which they have emerged. Humble submission to what goes before us releases authentic freedom and leads us to the true summit of our vocation as human beings.

PART FOUR

LITURGICAL FORM

CHAPTER ONE

Rite

F OR MANY PEOPLE today, the word "rite" does not have a very good ring to it. "Rite" suggests rigidity, a restriction to prescribed forms. It is set in opposition to that creativity and dynamism of inculturation by which, so people say, we get a really living liturgy, in which each community can express itself. Before going into the questions raised here, we must first of all see what rite in the Church really means, what rites there are, and how they relate to one another. In the second century, the Roman jurist Pomponius Festus, who was not a Christian, defined *ritus* as an "approved practice in the administration of sacrifice" (*mos comprobatus in administrandis sacrificiis*). He thereby summed up in a precise formula one of the great realities in the history of religion. Man is always looking for the right way of honoring God, for a form of prayer and common worship that pleases God and is appropriate to his nature. In this connection, we must remember that originally the word "orthodoxy" did not mean, as we generally think today, right doctrine. In Greek, the word *doxa* means, on the one hand, opinion or splendor. But then, in Christian usage, it means something on the order of "true splendor", that is, the glory of God. Orthodoxy means, therefore, the right way to glorify God, the right form of adoration. In this sense, orthodoxy is inward "orthopraxy". If we go back to the word's origins, the modern opposition disappears. It is not a question of theories about God but of the right way to encounter him. This, then, was seen as Christian faith's great gift: we know what right worship is. We know how we should truly glorify God—by praying and living in communion with the Paschal journey of Jesus Christ, by accomplishing with him his *Eucharistia*, in which Incarnation leads to Resurrection—along the way of the Cross. To adapt a saying of Kant, liturgy "covers everything" from the Incarnation to the Resurrection, but only on the way of the Cross. For Christians, then, "rite" means the practical arrangements made by the community, in time and space, for the basic type of worship received from God in faith. And, of course, as we saw in the first part, worship always includes the whole conduct of one's life. Thus rite has its primary place in the liturgy, but not only in the liturgy. It is also expressed in a particular way of doing theology, in the form of spiritual life, and in the juridical ordering of ecclesiastical life.

At this point, we must try, as we have just indicated, to get at least a brief overview of the major rites that have left their stamp on the Church. What rites are there? Where do they come from? These are questions that in their details present a multitude of problems, which we cannot discuss here. If we want to get an overview of the whole, then the sixth canon of the First Council of Nicaea may be a helpful starting point. It speaks of three primatial sees: Rome, Alexandria, and Antioch. The fact that all three sees are connected with Petrine traditions need not concern us here. At any rate, all three are points of crystallization in the liturgical tradition. We should also realize that, beginning with the fourth century (soon after Nicaea), Byzantium emerged as an additional regulatory center of ecclesiastical, and thus also of liturgical, life. After the transfer of imperial rule to the Bosphorus, Byzantium regarded itself as the "New Rome" and assumed the prerogatives of Rome. But it also increased its influence through the waning importance of Antioch, and indeed the functions of Antioch to a large extent passed over to Byzantium. Thus we may speak of four great circles of liturgical tradition. At the beginning, the relations of Rome and Alexandria were comparatively close, while Byzantium and Antioch were nearer to each other.

Without going into details outside the scope of this book, we must become a little more specific. Antioch was bound to be a center of liturgical tradition. It was here that Gentile Christianity came into being and the name "Christian" was first used (cf. Acts 11:26). It was the capital of Syria and therefore of the cultural and linguistic world in which divine revelation took place. Syria was also the setting for the great theological debates about how rightly to confess faith in Christ, and so it is not surprising that such a culturally dynamic area should become the birthplace of distinctive traditions in the liturgy. On the one hand, there are the West Syrian rites, prominent among which is the Syro-Malankar rite, which still flourishes in India and goes back to the apostle James. The Maronite rite should also be assigned to the West Syrian family. On the other hand, there are the so-called Chaldean rites (also called East Syrian or "Assyrian"). Their starting point is to be found in the great theological schools of Nisibis and Edessa. These rites were characterized by an extraordinary missionary zeal and spread as far as India, Central Asia, and China. In the early Middle Ages, there were about seventy million of the faithful in this ritual family, which suffered irretrievable losses through Islam and the Mongol invasions. At any rate, the Syro-Malabar Church still continues to exist in India. The Chaldean liturgical family goes back to the apostle Thomas and to Addai and Mari, disciples of the apostles. There is no doubt that it has preserved very ancient traditions, and the tradition that the apostle Thomas was a missionary in India definitely has to be taken seriously at the historical level.

The great ecclesiastical sphere of Alexandria includes above all the Coptic and Ethiopian rites. The Liturgy of Saint Mark, which developed in Alexandria, bears the marks of strong Byzantine influence, to which we shall return. In a category and with a significance all its own is the Armenian rite, which tradition traces back to the apostles Bartholomew and Thaddeus. Saint Gregory the Illuminator (260–323) is to be regarded as its special Father. In its form, it largely follows the Byzantine liturgy.

And so we come finally to the two greatest families of rites: the Byzantine and the Roman. As we saw, Byzantium takes up, first and foremost, the tradition of Antioch. The Liturgy of Saint John Chrysostom carries the Antiochene heritage to Byzantium, but the influences of Asia Minor and Jerusalem are also taken up, so that there is a confluence here of the rich inheritance of the lands evangelized by the apostles. A large part of the Slavic world adopted the Byzantine liturgy and, by this means, entered into communion of prayer with the Fathers and the apostles. In the West, three great ritual groups can at first be discerned. Alongside the Roman liturgy, which was very similar to the Latin liturgy of Africa, stood the old Gaulish or "Gallican" liturgy, to which in turn the Celtic was closely related, as was the old Spanish or "Mozarabic" liturgy. All three ritual domains were at first very similar to one another, but, in contrast to the conservatism of Rome, which in liturgical matters was rather archaic and sober, Spain and Gaul opened themselves to Eastern influences and assimilated them in their own distinctive way. By comparison with the strict brevity of Rome, the Gallican liturgy is characterized by poetic exuberance. From about the end of the first millennium, Rome began to appropriate the Gallican heritage, and the Gallican rite, in its proper grandeur, disappeared, though precious elements of it lived on in the Roman rite. Only with the liturgical reform after the Second Vatican Council, with its concern to restore the Roman tradition in its purity, did the Gallican inheritance more or less completely disappear. For the first time, a radical standardization of the liturgy had been carried out, though in the previous century the surviving rites proper to particular places and religious orders had increasingly been disappearing. Meanwhile, of course, what began as a process of making everything uniform has swung to the opposite extreme: a widespread dissolution of the rite, which must now be replaced by the "creativity" of the community.

Before exploring the fundamental question that this once more raises, the question of the meaning and validity of rite, we must draw some conclusions from our perhaps rather tedious sketch of the existing ritual landscape. First, it is important that the individual rites have a relation to the places where Christianity originated and the apostles preached: they are anchored in the time and place of the event of divine revelation. Here again, "once for all" and "always" belong together. The Christian faith can never be separated from the soil of sacred events, from the choice made by God, who wanted to speak to us, to become man, to die and rise again, in a particular place and at a particular time. "Always" can only come from "once for all". The Church does not pray in some kind of mythical omnitemporality. She cannot forsake her roots. She recognizes the true utterance of God precisely in the concreteness of its history, in time and place: to these God ties us, and by these we are all tied together. The diachronic aspect, praying with the Fathers and the apostles, is part of what we mean by rite, but it also includes a local aspect, extending from Jerusalem to Antioch, Rome, Alexandria, and Constantinople. Rites are not, therefore, just the products of inculturation, however much they may have incorporated elements from different cultures. They are forms of the apostolic tradition and of its unfolding in the great places of the tradition.

We must add a second point. Rites are not rigidly fenced off from each other. There is exchange and cross-fertilization between them. The clearest example is in the case of the two great focal points of ritual development: Byzantium and Rome. In their present form, most of the Eastern rites are very strongly marked by Byzantine influences. For its part, Rome has increasingly united the different rites of the West in the universal Roman rite. While Byzantium gave a large part of the Slavic world its special form of divine worship, Rome left its liturgical imprint on the Germanic and Latin peoples and on a part of the Slavs. In the first millennium, there was still liturgical exchange between East and West. Then, of course, the rites hardened into their definitive forms, which allowed hardly any cross-fertilization. What is important is that the great forms of rite embrace many cultures. They not only incorporate the diachronic aspect, but also create communion among different cultures and languages. They elude control by any individual, local community, or regional Church. Unspontaneity is of their essence. In these rites, I discover that something is approaching me here that I did not produce myself, that I am entering into something greater than myself, which ultimately derives from divine revelation. That is why the Christian East calls the liturgy the "Divine Liturgy", expressing thereby the liturgy's independence from human control. The West, by contrast, has felt ever more strongly the historical element, which is why Jungmann tried to sum up the Western view in the phrase "the liturgy that has come to be". He wanted to show that this coming-to-be still goes on—as an organic growth, not as a specially contrived production. The liturgy can be compared, therefore, not to a piece of technical equipment, something manufactured, but to a plant, something organic that grows and whose laws of growth determine the possibilities of further development. In the West, there was, of course, another factor. With his Petrine authority, the pope more and more clearly took over responsibility for liturgical legislation, thus providing a juridical authority for the continuing formation of the liturgy. The more vigorously the primacy was displayed, the more the question came up about the extent and limits of this authority, which, of course, as such had never been considered. After the Second Vatican Council, the impression arose that the pope really could do anything in liturgical matters, especially if he were acting on the mandate of an ecumenical council. Eventually, the idea of the givenness of the liturgy, the fact that one cannot do with it what one will, faded from the public consciousness of the West. In fact, the First Vatican Council had in no way defined the pope as an absolute monarch. On the contrary, it presented him as the guarantor of obedience to the revealed Word. The pope's authority is bound to the tradition of faith, and that also applies to the liturgy. It is not "manufactured" by the authorities. Even the pope can only be a humble servant of its lawful development and abiding integrity and identity. Here again, as with the questions of icons and sacred music, we come up against the special path trod by the West as opposed to the East. And here again is it true that this special path, which finds space for freedom and historical development, must not be condemned wholesale. However, it would lead to the breaking up of the foundations of Christian identity if the fundamental intuitions of the East, which are the fundamental intuitions of the early Church, were abandoned. The authority of the pope is not unlimited; it is at the service of sacred tradition. Still less is any kind of general "freedom" of manufacture, degenerating into spontaneous improvisation, compatible with the essence of faith and liturgy. The greatness of the liturgy depends—we shall have to repeat this frequently—on its unspontaneity (*Unbeliebigkeit*).

Let us ask the question again: "What does 'rite' mean in the context of Christian liturgy?" The answer is: "It is the expression, which has become form, of ecclesiality and of the Church's identity as a historically transcendent communion of liturgical prayer and action." Rite makes concrete the liturgy's bond with that living subject which is the Church, who for her part is characterized by adherence to the form of faith that has developed in the apostolic tradition. This bond with the subject that is the Church allows for different patterns of liturgy and includes living development, but it equally excludes spontaneous improvisation. This applies to the individual and the community, to the hierarchy and the laity. Because of the historical character of God's action, the "Divine Liturgy" (as they call it in the East) has been fashioned, in a way similar to Scripture, by human beings and their capacities. But it contains an essential exposition of the biblical legacy that goes beyond the limits of the individual rites, and thus it shares in the authority of the Church's faith in its fundamental form. The authority of the liturgy can certainly be compared to that of the great confessions of faith of the early Church. Like these, it developed under the guidance of the Holy Spirit (cf. Jn 16:13). It was the tragedy of Luther's efforts at reform that they occurred at a time when the essential form of the liturgy was not understood and had to a large extent been obscured. Despite the radicalism of his reversion to the principle of "Scripture alone", Luther did not contest the validity of the ancient Christian creeds and thereby left behind an inner tension that became the fundamental problem in the history of the Reformation. The Reformation would surely have run a different course if Luther had been able to see the analogous binding force of the great liturgical tradition and its understanding of sacrificial presence and of man's participation in the vicarious action of the Logos. With the radicalization of the historical-critical method, it has become very clear today that the *sola scriptura* principle cannot provide a foundation for the Church and the commonality of her faith. Scripture is Scripture only when it lives within the living subject that is the Church. This makes it all the more absurd that a not insignificant number of people today are trying to construct the liturgy afresh on the basis of *sola scriptura*. In these reconstructions, they identify Scripture with the prevailing exegetical opinions, thus confusing faith with opinion. Liturgy "manufactured" in this way is based on human words and opinions. It is a house built on sand and remains totally empty, however much human artistry may adorn it. Only respect for the liturgy's fundamental unspontaneity and pre-existing identity can give us what we hope for: the feast in which the great reality comes to us that we ourselves do not manufacture but receive as a gift.

This means that "creativity" cannot be an authentic category for matters liturgical. In any case, this is a word that developed within the Marxist world view. Creativity means that in a universe that in itself is meaningless and came into existence through blind evolution, man can creatively fashion a new and better world. Modern theories of art think in terms of a nihilistic kind of creativity. Art is not meant to copy anything. Artistic creativity is under the free mastery of man, without being bound by norms or goals and subject to no questions of meaning. It may be that in such visions a cry for freedom is to be heard, a cry that in a world totally in the control of technology becomes a cry for help. Seen in this way, art appears as the final refuge of freedom. True, art has something to do with freedom, but freedom understood in the way we have been describing is empty. It is not redemptive, but makes despair sound like the last word of human existence. This kind of creativity has no place within the liturgy. The life of the liturgy does not come from what dawns upon the minds of individuals and planning groups. On the contrary, it is God's descent upon our world, the source of real liberation. He alone can open the door to freedom. The more priests and faithful humbly surrender themselves to this descent of God, the more "new" the liturgy will constantly be and the more true and personal it becomes. Yes, the liturgy becomes personal, true, and new, not through tomfoolery and banal experiments with the words, but through a courageous entry into the great reality that through the rite is always ahead of us and can never quite be overtaken.

Does it still need to be explicitly stated that all this has nothing to do with rigidity? Whereas, for Muslims, the Qur'an is God's speech, pure and simple, without any human mediation, Christians know that God has spoken through man and that the human and historical factor is, therefore, part of the way God acts. That, too, is why the Word of the Bible becomes complete only in that responsive word of the Church which we call tradition. That is why the accounts of the Last Supper in the Bible become a concrete reality only when they are appropriated by the Church in her celebration. That is why there can be development in the "Divine Liturgy", a development, though, that takes place without haste or aggressive production, like the grain produced "of itself" by the earth (cf. Mk 4:28). We saw above that each of the various ritual families grew out of the "apostolic sees", the central places of the apostolic tradition, and that this connection with apostolic origins is essential to what defines them. From this it follows that there can be no question of creating totally new rites. However, there can be variations within the ritual families. The Christian West, in particular, well into modern times, saw such variations taking place within the general framework of a fundamental ritual form. An example of this kind of development seems to me to be the Missal that may be used in Zaire (the Congo). It is the Roman rite "in the Zairean mode". It still belongs within the great fellowship of the apostolically rooted Roman rite, but that rite is now, so to speak, clad in Congolese garments, with the addition—this seems to me to make perfect sense—of certain elements from the Christian East. For example, in line with what is said in Matthew 5:23–25, the sign of peace is exchanged, not before Communion, but before the Presentation of the Gifts, which would be desirable for the whole of the Roman rite, insofar as the sign of peace is something we want to retain.

CHAPTER TWO

The Body and the Liturgy

a. *"Active Participation"*

TO EXPRESS one of its main ideas for the shaping of the liturgy, the Second Vatican Council gave us the phrase *participatio actuosa*, the "active participation" of everyone in the *opus Dei*, in what happens in the worship of God. It was quite right to do so. The *Catechism of the Catholic Church* points out that the word "liturgy" speaks to us of a common service and thus has a reference to the whole holy People of God (cf. *CCC* 1069). But what does this active participation come down to? What does it mean that we have to do? Unfortunately, the word was very quickly misunderstood to mean something external, entailing a need for general activity, as if as many people as possible, as often as possible, should be visibly engaged in action. However, the word "part-icipation" refers to a principal action in which everyone has a "part". And so if we want to discover the kind of doing that active participation involves, we need, first of all, to determine what this central *actio* is in which all the members of the community are supposed to participate. The study of the liturgical sources provides an answer that at first may surprise us, though, in the light of the biblical foundations considered in the first part, it is quite self-evident. By the *actio* of the liturgy, the sources mean the Eucharistic Prayer. The real liturgical action, the true liturgical act, is the *oratio*, the great prayer that forms the core of the Eucharistic celebration, the whole of which was, therefore, called *oratio* by the Fathers. At first, simply in terms of the form of the liturgy, this was quite correct, because the essence of the Christian liturgy is to be found in the *oratio*; this is its center and fundamental form. Calling the Eucharist *oratio* was, then, a quite standard response to the pagans and to questioning intellectuals in general. What the Fathers were saying was this: The sacrificial animals and all those things that you had and have, and which ultimately satisfy no one, are now abolished. In their place has come the Sacrifice of the Word. We are the spiritual religion, in which in truth a Word-based worship takes place. Goats and cattle are no longer slaughtered. Instead, the Word, summing up our existence, is addressed to God and identified with *the* Word, the Word of God, who draws us into true worship. Perhaps it would be useful to note here that the word *oratio* originally means, not "prayer" (for which the word is *prex*), but solemn public speech. Such speech now attains its supreme dignity through its being addressed to God in full awareness that it comes from him and is made possible by him.

But this is only just a hint of the central issue. This *oratio*—the Eucharistic Prayer, the "Canon"—is really more than speech; it is *actio* in the highest sense of the word. For what happens in it is that the human *actio* (as performed hitherto by the priests in the various religions of the world) steps back and makes way for the *actio divina*, the action of God. In this *oratio*, the priest speaks with the I of the Lord—"This is my Body", "This is my Blood." He knows that he is not now speaking from his own resources but in virtue of the Sacrament that he has received, he has become the voice of Someone Else, who is now speaking and acting. This action of God, which takes place through human speech, is the real "action" for which all of creation is in expectation. The elements of the earth are transubstantiated, pulled, so to speak, from their creaturely anchorage, grasped at the deepest ground of their being, and changed into the Body and Blood of the Lord. The New Heaven and the New Earth are anticipated. The real "action" in the liturgy in which we are all supposed to participate is the action of God himself. This is what is new and distinctive about the Christian liturgy: God himself acts and does what is essential. He inaugurates the new creation, makes himself accessible to us, so that, through the things of the earth, through our gifts, we can communicate with him in a personal way. But how can we part-icipate, have a part, in this action? Are not God and man completely incommensurable? Can man, the finite and sinful one, cooperate with God, the Infinite and Holy One? Yes, he can, precisely because God himself has become man, become body, and here, again and again, he comes through his body to us who live in the body. The whole event of the Incarnation, Cross, Resurrection, and Second Coming is present as the way by which God draws man into cooperation with himself. As we have seen, this is expressed in the liturgy in the fact that the petition for acceptance is part of the *oratio*. True, the Sacrifice of the Logos is accepted already and forever. But we must still pray for it to become *our* sacrifice, that we ourselves, as we said, may be transformed into the Logos (*logisiert*), conformed to the Logos, and so be made the true Body of Christ. That is the issue, and that is what we have to pray for. This petition itself is a way into the Incarnation and the Resurrection, the path that we take in the wayfaring state of our existence. In this real "action", in this prayerful approach to participation, there is no difference between priests and laity. True, addressing the *oratio* to the Lord in the name of the Church and, at its core, speaking with the very "I" of Jesus Christ—that is something that can be done only through sacramental empowerment. But participation in that which no human being does, that which the Lord himself and only he can do—that is equally for everyone. In the words of Saint Paul, it is a question of being "united to the Lord" and thus becoming "one spirit with him" (1 Cor 6:17). The point is that, ultimately, the difference between the *actio Christi* and our own action is done away with. There is only *one* action, which is at the same time his and ours—ours because we have become "one body and one spirit" with him. The uniqueness of the Eucharistic liturgy lies precisely in the fact that God himself is acting and that we are drawn into that action of God. Everything else is, therefore, secondary.

Of course, external actions—reading, singing, the bringing up of the gifts—can be distributed in a sensible way. By the same token, participation in the Liturgy of the Word (reading, singing) is to be distinguished from the sacramental celebration proper. We should be clearly aware that external actions are quite secondary here. *Doing* really must stop when we come to the heart of the matter: the *oratio*. It must be plainly evident that the *oratio* is the heart of the matter, but that it is important precisely because it provides a space for the *actio* of God. Anyone who grasps this will easily see that it is now a matter, not of looking at or toward the priest, but of looking together toward the Lord and going out to meet him. The almost theatrical entrance of different players into the liturgy, which is so common today, especially during the Preparation of the Gifts, quite simply misses the point. If the various external actions (as a matter of fact, there are not very many of them, though they are being artificially multiplied) become the essential in the liturgy, if the liturgy degenerates into general activity, then we have radically misunderstood the "theo-drama" of the liturgy and lapsed almost into parody. True liturgical education cannot consist in learning and experimenting with external activities. Instead, one must be led toward the essential *actio* that makes the liturgy what it is, toward the transforming power of God, who wants, through what happens in the liturgy, to transform us and the world. In this respect, liturgical education today, of both priests and laity, is deficient to a deplorable extent. Much remains to be done here.

At this point the reader will perhaps ask: "What about the body? With this idea of a word-based sacrifice (*oratio*), have you not shifted everything over to the spiritual side?" That charge might have applied to the pre-Christian idea of a *logos*-liturgy, but it cannot be true of the liturgy of the Word incarnate, who offers himself to us in his Body and Blood and, thus, in a corporeal way. It is, of course, the new corporeality of the risen Lord, but it remains true corporeality, and it is this that we are given in the material signs of bread and wine. This means that we are laid hold of by the Logos and for the Logos in our very bodies, in the bodily existence of our everyday life. The true liturgical action is the deed of God, and for that very reason the liturgy of faith always reaches beyond the cultic act into everyday life, which must itself become "liturgical", a service for the transformation of the world.

Much more is required of the body than carrying objects around and other such activities. A demand is made on the body in all its involvement in the circumstances of everyday life. The body is required to become "capable of resurrection", to orient itself toward the resurrection, toward the Kingdom of God, in a word: "Thy will be done on earth as it is in heaven." Where God's will is done, there is heaven, there earth becomes heaven. Surrendering ourselves to the action of God, so that we in our turn may cooperate with him—that is what begins in the liturgy and is meant to unfold further beyond it. Incarnation must always lead through Cross (the transforming of our wills in a communion of will with God) to Resurrection—to that rule of love which is the Kingdom of God. The body must be trained, so to speak, for the resurrection. Let us remember incidentally that the unfashionable word *askēsis* can be simply translated into English as "training". Nowadays we train with enthusiasm, perseverance, and great renunciation for many different purposes—why do we not train ourselves for God and his Kingdom? "I train my body", says Saint Paul, "and subdue it" (1 Cor 9:27, RSV adapted). He also uses the discipline of athletes as an image for training in one's own life. This training is an essential part of everyday life, but it has to find its inner support in the liturgy, in the liturgy's "orientation" toward the risen Christ. Let me say once again: it is a way of learning to accept the other in his otherness, a training for love, a training to help us accept the Wholly Other, God, to be shaped and used by him. The body has a place within the divine worship of the Word made flesh, and it is expressed liturgically in a certain discipline of the body, in gestures that have developed out of the liturgy's inner demands and that make the essence of the liturgy, as it were, bodily visible. These gestures may vary in their details from culture to culture, but in their essential forms they are part of that culture of faith which has grown out of Christian cult. They form, therefore, a common language that crosses the borders of the different cultures. Let us have a closer look at them.

b. *The Sign of the Cross*

The most basic Christian gesture in prayer is and always will be the sign of the Cross. It is a way of confessing Christ crucified with one's very body, in accordance with the programmatic words of Saint Paul: "[W]e preach Christ crucified, a stumbling block to Jews and folly to Gentiles, but to those who are called, both Jews and Greeks, Christ the power of God and the wisdom of God" (1 Cor 1:23f.). Again he says: "I decided to know nothing among you except Jesus Christ and him crucified" (2:2). To seal oneself with the sign of the Cross is a visible and public Yes to him who suffered for us; to him who in the body has made God's love visible, even to the utmost; to the God who reigns not by destruction but by the humility of suffering and love, which is stronger than all the power of the world and wiser than all the calculating intelligence of men. The sign of the Cross is a confession of faith: I believe in him who suffered for me and rose again; in him who has transformed the sign of shame into a sign of hope and of the love of God that is present with us. The confession of faith is a confession of hope: I believe in him who in his weakness is the Almighty; in him who can and will save me even in apparent absence and impotence. By signing ourselves with the Cross, we place ourselves under the protection of the Cross, hold it in front of us like a shield that will guard us in all the distress of daily life and give us the courage to go on. We accept it as a signpost that we follow: "If any man would come after me, let him deny himself and take up his cross and follow me" (Mk 8:34). The Cross shows us the road of life—the imitation of Christ.

We connect the sign of the Cross with confession of faith in the triune God—the Father, the Son, and the Holy Spirit. In this way it becomes a remembrance of Baptism, which is particularly clear when we use holy water with it. The Cross is a sign of the Passion, but at the same time it is a sign of the Resurrection. It is, so to speak, the saving staff that God holds out to us, the bridge by which we can pass over the abyss of death, and all the threats of the Evil One, and reach God. It is made present in Baptism, in which we become contemporary with Christ's Cross and Resurrection (cf. Rom 6:1–14). Whenever we make the sign of the Cross, we accept our Baptism anew; Christ from the Cross draws us, so to speak, to himself (cf. Jn 12:32) and thus into communion with the living God. For Baptism and the sign of the Cross, which is a kind of summing up and re-acceptance of Baptism, are above all a divine event: the Holy Spirit leads us to Christ, and Christ opens the door to the Father. God is no longer the "unknown god"; he has a name. We are allowed to call upon him, and he calls us.

Thus we can say that in the sign of the Cross, together with the invocation of the Trinity, the whole essence of Christianity is summed up; it displays what is distinctively Christian. Nevertheless, or rather for this very reason, it also opens the way into the wider history of religion and the divine message of creation. In 1873, on the Mount of Olives, Greek and Hebrew grave inscriptions bearing the sign of a cross were discovered from the time of Jesus. The excavators inevitably assumed that they were dealing with Christians of the earliest times. In about 1945, increasing numbers of Jewish graves with the sign of the cross were being discovered and assigned to more or less the first century after Christ. The discoveries no longer left room for the view that these were first-generation Christians. On the contrary, it had to be recognized that signs of the cross were established in the Jewish *milieu*. How are we to make sense of this? The key is to be found in Ezekiel 9:4ff. In the vision described there, God says to his linen-clad messenger, who carries the writing case at his side: "Go through the city, through Jerusalem, and put a mark [*Tav*] upon the foreheads of the men who sigh and groan over all the abominations that are committed in it." In the terrible catastrophe now imminent, those who do not connive in the sin of the world yet suffer from it for the sake of God, suffering impotently yet at a distance from sin, are sealed with the last letter of the Hebrew alphabet, the *Tav*, which was written in the form of a cross (T or + or X). The *Tav*, which as a matter of fact had the form of a cross, becomes the seal of God's ownership. It corresponds to man's longing for God, his suffering for the sake of God, and so places him under God's special protection. E. Dinkler was able to show that cultic stigmatization—on the hands or forehead—was occasionally practiced in the Old Testament and that this custom was also well known in New Testament times. In the New Testament, Revelation 7:1–8 takes up the basic idea in Ezekiel's vision. The discoveries of the graves, in conjunction with the texts of the time, prove that in certain circles within Judaism the *Tav* was a widespread sacred sign—a sign of confession of faith in the God of Israel and at the same time a sign of hope in his protection. Dinkler summarizes his findings by saying that, in the cross-shaped *Tav*, "a whole confession of faith is summed up in *one* sign." "The realities believed in and hoped for", he says, "are read into a visible image, but the image is more than a mere reflection; it is in fact an image in whose saving power one places one's hopes."[1] As far as we know, Christians did not at first take up this Jewish symbol of the cross, but they found the sign of the Cross from within their faith and were able to see in it the summing up of their whole faith. But was Ezekiel's vision of the salvific *Tav*, with the whole tradition built upon it, not bound to appear to Christians later as a glimpse of the One who was to come? Was the meaning of this mysterious sign not now "unveiled" (cf. 2 Cor 3:18)? Did it not now become clear to whom this sign belonged, from whom it derived its power? Could they fail to see in all this a prophecy of the Cross of Jesus Christ, who has transformed the *Tav* into the power of salvation?

The Fathers belonging to the Greek cultural world were more directly affected by another discovery. In the writings of Plato, they found the remarkable idea of a cross inscribed upon the cosmos.[2] Plato took this from the Pythagorean tradition, which in its turn had a connection with the traditions of the ancient East. First, there is an astronomical statement about the two great movements of the stars with which ancient astronomy was familiar: the ecliptic (the great circle in the heavens along which the sun appears to run its course) and the orbit of the earth. These two intersect and form together the Greek

---

[1] E. Dinkler, *Signum crucis: Aufzätze zum Neuen Testament und zur christlichen Archäologie* (Tübingen: Mohr, 1967), 24.

[2] Cf. *Timaeus* 34ab and 36bc.

letter *Chi*, which is written in the form of a cross (like an X). The sign of the cross is inscribed upon the whole cosmos. Plato, again following more ancient traditions, connected this with the image of the deity: the Demiurge (the fashioner of the world) "stretched out" the world soul "throughout the whole universe". Saint Justin Martyr (d. ca. 165), the Palestinian-born first philosopher among the Fathers, came across this Platonic text and did not hesitate to link it with the doctrine of the triune God and his action in salvation history in the person of Jesus Christ. He sees the idea of the Demiurge and the world soul as premonitions of the mystery of the Father and the Son— premonitions that are in need of correction and yet also capable of correction. What Plato says about the world soul seems to him to refer to the coming of the Logos, the Son of God. And so he can now say that the shape of the cross is the greatest symbol of the lordship of the Logos, without which nothing in creation holds together.[3] The Cross of Golgotha is foreshadowed in the structure of the universe itself. The instrument of torment on which the Lord died is written into the structure of the universe. The cosmos speaks to us of the Cross, and the Cross solves for us the enigma of the cosmos. It is the real key to all reality. History and cosmos belong together. When we open our eyes, we can read the message of Christ in the language of the universe, and, conversely, Christ grants us understanding of the message of creation.

From Justin onward, this "prophecy of the Cross" in Plato, together with the connection of cosmos and history that it reveals, was one of the fundamental ideas in patristic theology. It must have been an overwhelming discovery for the Fathers to find that the philosopher who

[3] Cf. *I Apol.* 55.

summed up and interpreted the most ancient traditions had spoken of the cross as a seal imprinted on the universe. Saint Irenaeus of Lyons (d. ca. 200), the real founder of systematic theology in its Catholic form, says in his work of apologetics, the *Demonstration of the Apostolic Preaching*, that the Crucified One is "the very Word of Almighty God, who penetrates our universe by an invisible presence. And for this reason he embraces the whole world, its breadth and length, its height and depth, for through the Word of God all things are guided into order. And the Son of God is crucified in them, since, in the form of the Cross, he is imprinted upon all things" (1, 3). This text of the great Father of the Church conceals a biblical quotation that is of great importance for the biblical theology of the Cross. The epistle to the Ephesians exhorts us to be rooted and grounded in love, so that, together with all the saints, we "may have power to comprehend with all the saints what is the breadth and length and height and depth, and to know the love of Christ which surpasses knowledge" (3:18f.). There can be little doubt that this epistle emanating from the school of Saint Paul is referring to the cosmic Cross and thereby taking up traditions about the cross-shaped tree of the world that holds everything together—a religious idea that was also well known in India. Saint Augustine has a wonderful interpretation of this important passage from Saint Paul. He sees it as representing the dimensions of human life and as referring to the form of the crucified Christ, whose arms embrace the world and whose path reaches down into the abyss of the underworld and up to the very height of God himself.[4] Hugo Rahner has assembled the most beautiful patristic texts relevant to the cosmic mystery of the Cross. I should

---

[4] Cf. *De doctrina christiana* 2, 41, 62; *Corpus Christianorum* 32, 75f.

like to add only two more. In Lactantius (d. ca. 325) we read: "In his Passion God spread out his arms and thus embraced the globe as a sign that a future people, from the rising of the sun to its setting, would gather under his wings" (81). An unknown Greek author of the fourth century, contrasting the Cross with the cult of the sun, says that *Helios* (the sun) has now been conquered by the Cross. "Behold, man, whom the created sun in the heavens could not instruct, is now irradiated by the sunlight of the Cross and (in Baptism) enlightened." Then the anonymous author takes up some words of Saint Ignatius of Antioch (d. ca. 110), who described the Cross as the cosmic hoist (*mēchanē*) for going up to heaven, and says: "O what truly divine wisdom is this! O Cross, thou hoist to heaven! The Cross was driven into the ground—and behold, idol worship was destroyed. No ordinary wood is this, but the wood that God used for victory" (87f.).

In his eschatological discourse, Jesus had announced that at the end of time "the sign of the Son of man" would appear in heaven (Mt 24:30). The eye of faith was now able to recognize that this sign had been inscribed into the cosmos from the beginning and thus see faith in the crucified Redeemer confirmed by the cosmos. At the same time, Christians thus realized that the paths of religious history converged on Christ, that their expectations, expressed in many different images, led to him. Conversely, this meant that philosophy and religion gave faith the images and concepts in which alone it could fully understand itself.

"[Y]ou will be a blessing", God had said to Abraham at the beginning of salvation history (Gen 12:2). In Christ, the Son of Abraham, these words are completely fulfilled. He is a blessing, and he is a blessing for the whole of creation as well as for all men. Thus the Cross, which is his sign in heaven and on earth, was destined to become the characteristic gesture of blessing for Christians. We make the sign of the Cross on ourselves and thus enter the power of the blessing of Jesus Christ. We make the sign over people to whom we wish a blessing; and we also make it over things that are part of our life and that we want, as it were, to receive anew from the hand of Jesus Christ. Through the Cross, we can become sources of blessing for one another. I shall never forget the devotion and heartfelt care with which my father and mother made the sign of the Cross on the forehead, mouth, and breast of us children when we went away from home, especially when the parting was a long one. This blessing was like an escort that we knew would guide us on our way. It made visible the prayer of our parents, which went with us, and it gave us the assurance that this prayer was supported by the blessing of the Savior. The blessing was also a challenge to us not to go outside the sphere of this blessing. Blessing is a priestly gesture, and so in this sign of the Cross we felt the priesthood of parents, its special dignity and power. I believe that this blessing, which is a perfect expression of the common priesthood of the baptized, should come back in a much stronger way into our daily life and permeate it with the power of the love that comes from the Lord.

c. *Posture*

Kneeling (prostratio)

There are groups, of no small influence, who are trying to talk us out of kneeling. "It doesn't suit our culture", they say (which culture?). "It's not right for a grown

man to do this—he should face God on his feet." Or
again: "It's not appropriate for redeemed man—he has
been set free by Christ and doesn't need to kneel anymore." If we look at history, we can see that the Greeks
and Romans rejected kneeling. In view of the squabbling,
partisan deities described in mythology, this attitude was
thoroughly justified. It was only too obvious that these
gods were not God, even if you were dependent on their
capricious power and had to make sure that, whenever
possible, you enjoyed their favor. And so they said that
kneeling was unworthy of a free man, unsuitable for the
culture of Greece, something the barbarians went in for.
Plutarch and Theophrastus regarded kneeling as an expression of superstition. Aristotle called it a barbaric form of
behavior.[5] Saint Augustine agreed with him in a certain
respect: the false gods were only the masks of demons,
who subjected men to the worship of money and to self-
seeking, thus making them "servile" and superstitious.
He said that the humility of Christ and his love, which
went as far as the Cross, have freed us from these powers. We now kneel before that humility. The kneeling of
Christians is not a form of inculturation into existing customs. It is quite the opposite, an expression of Christian
culture, which transforms the existing culture through a
new and deeper knowledge and experience of God.

Kneeling does not come from any culture—it comes
from the Bible and its knowledge of God. The central
importance of kneeling in the Bible can be seen in a very
concrete way. The word *proskynein* alone occurs fifty-nine
times in the New Testament, twenty-four of which are in
the Apocalypse, the book of the heavenly liturgy, which

[5] Cf. *Rhetoric* 1361 a 36.

is presented to the Church as the standard for her own liturgy. On closer inspection, we can discern three closely related forms of posture. First, there is *prostratio*—lying with one's face to the ground before the overwhelming power of God; secondly, especially in the New Testament, there is falling to one's knees before another; and thirdly, there is kneeling. Linguistically, the three forms of posture are not always clearly distinguished. They can be combined or merged with one another.

For the sake of brevity, I should like to mention, in the case of *prostratio*, just one text from the Old Testament and another from the New. In the Old Testament, there is an appearance of God to Joshua before the taking of Jericho, an appearance that the sacred author quite deliberately presents as a parallel to God's revelation of himself to Moses in the burning bush. Joshua sees "the commander of the army of the LORD" and, having recognized who he is, throws himself to the ground. At that moment he hears the words once spoken to Moses: "Put off your shoes from your feet; for the place where you stand is holy" (Josh 5:15). In the mysterious form of the "commander of the army of the LORD", the hidden God himself speaks to Joshua, and Joshua throws himself down before him. Origen gives a beautiful interpretation of this text: "Is there any other commander of the powers of the Lord than our Lord Jesus Christ?" According to this view, Joshua is worshipping the One who is to come —the coming Christ. In the case of the New Testament, from the Fathers onward, Jesus' prayer on the Mount of Olives was especially important. According to Saint Matthew (26:39) and Saint Mark (14:35), Jesus throws himself to the ground; indeed, he falls to the earth (according to Matthew). However, Saint Luke, who in his whole work (both the Gospel and the Acts of the Apostles) is in a special way the theologian of kneeling prayer, tells us that Jesus prayed on his knees. This prayer, the prayer by which Jesus enters into his Passion, is an example for us, both as a gesture and in its content. The gesture: Jesus assumes, as it were, the fall of man, lets himself fall into man's fallenness, prays to the Father out of the lowest depths of human dereliction and anguish. He lays his will in the will of the Father's: "Not my will but yours be done." He lays the human will in the divine. He takes up all the hesitation of the human will and endures it. It is this very conforming of the human will to the divine that is the heart of redemption. For the fall of man depends on the contradiction of wills, on the opposition of the human will to the divine, which the tempter leads man to think is the condition of his freedom. Only one's own autonomous will, subject to no other will, is freedom. "Not my will, but yours . . ."—those are the words of truth, for God's will is not in opposition to our own, but the ground and condition of its possibility. Only when our will rests in the will of God does it become truly will and truly free. The suffering and struggle of Gethsemane is the struggle for this redemptive truth, for this uniting of what is divided, for the uniting that is communion with God. Now we understand why the Son's loving way of addressing the Father, "Abba", is found in this place (cf. Mk 14:36). Saint Paul sees in this cry the prayer that the Holy Spirit places on our lips (cf. Rom 8:15; Gal 4:6) and thus anchors our Spirit-filled prayer in the Lord's prayer in Gethsemane.

In the Church's liturgy today, prostration appears on two occasions: on Good Friday and at ordinations. On Good Friday, the day of the Lord's crucifixion, it is the fitting expression of our sense of shock at the fact that we by our sins share in the responsibility for the death of Christ. We throw ourselves down and participate in his shock, in his descent into the depths of anguish. We throw ourselves down and so acknowledge where we are and who we are: fallen creatures whom only he can set on their feet. We throw ourselves down, as Jesus did, before the mystery of God's power present to us, knowing that the Cross is the true burning bush, the place of the flame of God's love, which burns but does not destroy. At ordinations, prostration comes from the awareness of our absolute incapacity, by our own powers, to take on the priestly mission of Jesus Christ, to speak with his "I". While the ordinands are lying on the ground, the whole congregation sings the Litany of the Saints. I shall never forget lying on the ground at the time of my own priestly and episcopal ordination. When I was ordained bishop, my intense feeling of inadequacy, incapacity, in the face of the greatness of the task was even stronger than at my priestly ordination. The fact that the praying Church was calling upon all the saints, that the prayer of the Church really was enveloping and embracing me, was a wonderful consolation. In my incapacity, which had to be expressed in the bodily posture of prostration, this prayer, this presence of all the saints, of the living and the dead, was a wonderful strength—it was the only thing that could, as it were, lift me up. Only the presence of the saints with me made possible the path that lay before me.

Secondly, we must mention the gesture of falling to one's knees before another, which is described four times in the Gospels (cf. Mk 1:40; 10:17; Mt 17:14; 27:29) by means of the word *gonypetein*. Let us single out Mark 1:40. A leper comes to Jesus and begs him for help. He falls to his knees before him and says: "If you will, you can make me clean." It is hard to assess the significance of the gesture. What we have here is surely not a proper act of adoration but, rather, a supplication expressed fervently in bodily form, while showing a trust in a power beyond the merely human. The situation is different, though, with the classical word for adoration on one's knees—*proskynein*. I shall give two examples in order to clarify the question that faces the translator. First there is the account of how, after the multiplication of the loaves, Jesus stays with the Father on the mountain, while the disciples struggle in vain on the lake with the wind and the waves. Jesus comes to them across the water. Peter hurries toward him and is saved from sinking by the Lord. Then Jesus climbs into the boat, and the wind lets up. The text continues: "And the ship's crew came and said, falling at his feet, 'Thou art indeed the Son of God'" (Mt 14:33, Knox version). Other translations say: "[The disciples] in the boat worshiped [Jesus], saying . . ." (RSV). Both translations are correct. Each emphasizes one aspect of what is going on. The Knox version brings out the bodily expression, while the RSV shows what is happening interiorly. It is perfectly clear from the structure of the narrative that the gesture of acknowledging Jesus as the Son of God is an act of worship. We encounter a similar set of problems in Saint John's Gospel when we read the account of the healing of the man born blind. This narrative, which is structured in a truly "theo-dramatic" way, ends with a dialogue between Jesus and the man he has healed. It serves as a model for the dialogue of conversion, for the whole narrative must also be seen as a profound exposition of the existential and theological significance of Baptism. In the dialogue, Jesus asks the man whether he believes in the Son of Man. The man born blind replies: "Tell me who he is, Lord." When Jesus says, "It is he who is speaking to you", the man makes the confession of faith: "I do believe, Lord", and then he "[falls] down to worship him" (Jn 9:35–38, Knox version adapted). Earlier translations said: "He worshipped him." In fact, the whole scene is directed toward the act of faith and the worship of Jesus, which follows from it. Now the eyes of the heart, as well as of the body, are opened. The man has in truth begun to see. For the exegesis of the text it is important to note that the word *proskynein* occurs eleven times in Saint John's Gospel, of which nine occurrences are found in Jesus' conversation with the Samaritan woman by Jacob's well (Jn 4:19–24). This conversation is entirely devoted to the theme of worship, and it is indisputable that here, as elsewhere in Saint John's Gospel, the word always has the meaning of "worship". Incidentally, this conversation, too, ends—like that of the healing of the man born blind—with Jesus' revealing himself: "I who speak to you am he" (Jn 4:26).

I have lingered over these texts because they bring to light something important. In the two passages that we looked at most closely, the spiritual and bodily meanings of *proskynein* are really inseparable. The bodily gesture itself is the bearer of the spiritual meaning, which is precisely that of worship. Without the worship, the bodily gesture would be meaningless, while the spiritual act must of its very nature, because of the psychosomatic unity of man, express itself in the bodily gesture. The two aspects are united in the one word because in a very profound way they belong together. When kneeling becomes merely external, a merely physical act, it becomes meaningless. On the other hand, when someone tries to

take worship back into the purely spiritual realm and re-
fuses to give it embodied form, the act of worship evap-
orates, for what is purely spiritual is inappropriate to the
nature of man. Worship is one of those fundamental acts
that affect the whole man. That is why bending the knee
before the presence of the living God is something we
cannot abandon.

In saying this, we come to the typical gesture of kneeling on one or both knees. In the Hebrew of the Old Testament, the verb *barak*, "to kneel", is cognate with the
word *berek*, "knee". The Hebrews regarded the knees as
a symbol of strength; to bend the knee is, therefore, to
bend our strength before the living God, an acknowledg-
ment of the fact that all that we are we receive from him.
In important passages of the Old Testament, this gesture
appears as an expression of worship. At the dedication of
the Temple, Solomon kneels "in the presence of all the
assembly of Israel" (2 Chron 6:13). After the Exile, in
the afflictions of the returned Israel, which is still without a Temple, Ezra repeats this gesture at the time of the
evening sacrifice: "I . . . fell upon my knees and spread
out my hands to the LORD my God" (Ezra 9:5). The great
psalm of the Passion, Psalm 22 ("My God, my God, why
have you forsaken me?"), ends with the promise: "Yes,
to him shall all the proud of the earth fall down; before
him all who go down to the dust shall throw themselves
down" (v. 29, RSV adapted). The related passage Isaiah
45:23 we shall have to consider in the context of the New
Testament. The Acts of the Apostles tells us how Saint
Peter (9:40), Saint Paul (20:36), and the whole Christian
community (21:5) pray on their knees. Particularly important for our question is the account of the martyrdom
of Saint Stephen. The first man to witness to Christ with

his blood is described in his suffering as a perfect image of Christ, whose Passion is repeated in the martyrdom of the witness, even in small details. One of these is that Stephen, on his knees, takes up the petition of the crucified Christ: "Lord, do not hold this sin against them" (7:60). We should remember that Luke, unlike Matthew and Mark, speaks of the Lord kneeling in Gethsemane, which shows that Luke wants the kneeling of the first martyr to be seen as his entry into the prayer of Jesus. Kneeling is not only a Christian gesture but a christological one.

For me, the most important passage for the theology of kneeling will always be the great hymn of Christ in Philippians 2:6-11. In this pre-Pauline hymn, we hear and see the prayer of the apostolic Church and can discern within it her confession of faith in Christ. However, we also hear the voice of the apostle, who enters into this prayer and hands it on to us, and, ultimately, we perceive here both the profound inner unity of the Old and New Testaments and the cosmic breadth of Christian faith. The hymn presents Christ as the antitype of the First Adam. While the latter high-handedly grasped at likeness to God, Christ does not count equality with God, which is his by nature, "a thing to be grasped", but humbles himself unto death, even death on the Cross. It is precisely this humility, which comes from love, that is the truly divine reality and procures for him the "name which is above every name, that at the name of Jesus every knee should bow, in heaven and on earth and under the earth" (Phil 2:5-10). Here the hymn of the apostolic Church takes up the words of promise in Isaiah 45:23: "By myself I have sworn, from my mouth has gone forth in righteousness a word that shall not return: 'To me every knee shall bow, every tongue shall swear.'" In the interweaving of

Old and New Testaments, it becomes clear that, even as crucified, Jesus bears the "name above every name"—the name of the Most High—and is himself God by nature. Through him, through the Crucified, the bold promise of the Old Testament is now fulfilled: all bend the knee before Jesus, the One who descended, and bow to him precisely as the one true God above all gods. The Cross has become the world-embracing sign of God's presence, and all that we have previously heard about the historical and cosmic Christ should now, in this passage, come back into our minds. The Christian liturgy is a cosmic liturgy precisely because it bends the knee before the crucified and exalted Lord. Here is the center of authentic culture —the culture of truth. The humble gesture by which we fall at the feet of the Lord inserts us into the true path of life of the cosmos.

There is much more that we might add. For example, there is the touching story told by Eusebius in his history of the Church as a tradition going back to Hegesippus in the second century. Apparently, Saint James, the "brother of the Lord", the first bishop of Jerusalem and "head" of the Jewish Christian Church, had a kind of callous on his knees, because he was always on his knees worshipping God and begging for forgiveness for his people.[6] Again, there is a story that comes from the sayings of the Desert Fathers, according to which the devil was compelled by God to show himself to a certain Abba Apollo. He looked black and ugly, with frighteningly thin limbs, but, most strikingly, *he had no knees*. The inability to kneel is seen as the very essence of the diabolical.

But I do not want to go into more detail. I should like to make just one more remark. The expression used by

---

[6] Eusebius of Caesarea, *Church History*, 2, 23, 6.

Saint Luke to describe the kneeling of Christians (*theis ta gonata*) is unknown in classical Greek. We are dealing here with a specifically Christian word. With that remark, our reflections return full circle to where they began. It may well be that kneeling is alien to modern culture—insofar as it is a culture, for this culture has turned away from the faith and no longer knows the One before whom kneeling is the right, indeed, the intrinsically necessary gesture. The man who learns to believe learns also to kneel, and a faith or a liturgy no longer familiar with kneeling would be sick at the core. Where it has been lost, kneeling must be rediscovered, so that, in our prayer, we remain in fellowship with the apostles and martyrs, in fellowship with the whole cosmos, indeed, in union with Jesus Christ himself.

Standing and Sitting—Liturgy and Culture

We can be considerably more brief in what we say about these two postures, because they are not very controversial these days, and the importance that each has is not hard to see. In the Old Testament, standing is a classic posture for prayer. Let us content ourselves with just one example—the prayer of the childless Hannah, who becomes, in answer to her prayers, the mother of Samuel. In the New Testament, Saint Luke paints a portrait of Elizabeth, the mother of John the Baptist, with colors reminiscent of Hannah. After she has weaned the child Samuel, the happy mother comes to the Temple, in order to hand over the child of promise to the Lord: "I am the woman", she says, "who was standing here in your presence, praying to the LORD" (1 Sam 1:26). A whole series of New Testament texts show us that in Jesus' time standing was the ordinary posture for prayer among the Jews (cf. Mt 6:5; Mk 11:25; Lk 18:11–13.). Among Christians, standing was primarily the Easter form of prayer. The twentieth canon of Nicaea decrees that Christians should stand, not kneel, during Eastertide. It is the time of the victory of Jesus Christ, the time of joy, in which we show forth the Paschal victory of the Lord, even in the posture of our prayer. This may remind us once again of the passion of Saint Stephen. Faced with the fury of his persecutors, he looks up to heaven, where he sees Jesus standing at the right hand of the Father (cf. Acts 7:55). Standing is the posture of the victor. Jesus stands in God's presence —he stands, because he has trodden death and the power of the Evil One underfoot. At the end of this struggle, he is the one who stands upright, the one who remains standing. This standing is also an expression of readiness: Christ is standing up at the right hand of God in order to meet us. He has not withdrawn. It is for us that he stands, and, in the very hour of anguish, we can be sure that he will set off and come to us, just as once he set off from the Father and came to his own across the water, when wind and waves were overpowering their boat. When we stand, we know that we are united to the victory of Christ, and when we stand to listen to the Gospel, it is an expression of reverence. When this Word is heard, we cannot remain sitting; it pulls us up. It demands both reverence and courage, when he calls us to set off in some new direction, to do his will, and to carry it into our lives and into the world.

Just one further reminder may help us here. We are familiar, from the painting in the catacombs, with the figure of the *orans*, the female figure standing and praying with outstretched hands. According to recent research, the *orans* normally represents, not the praying Church, but the soul that has entered into heavenly glory and stands in adoration before the face of God. This has two important aspects. First, the soul is almost always represented as a woman because what is specific to human existence in relation to God is expressed in the form of a woman: the bridal element, in regard to the eternal nuptials and also the ready acceptance of the grace bestowed upon us. The second point is this: it is not the earthly liturgy, the liturgy of pilgrimage, that is represented here, but prayer in the state of glory. Thus, once again, this time in light of the *orans*, it becomes clear that standing prayer is an anticipation of the future, of the glory that is to come; it is meant to orient us toward it. Insofar as liturgical prayer is an anticipation of what has been promised, standing is its proper posture. However, insofar as liturgical prayer belongs to that "between" time in which we live, then kneeling remains indispensable to it as an expression of the "now" of our life.

Finally, the liturgy permits sitting during the readings, the homily, and the meditative assimilation of the Word (the responsorial psalm, and so on). Whether it is also appropriate during the Preparation of the Gifts may be regarded as an open question. In recent times, sitting has been introduced here because of a particular understanding of this part of the sacred liturgy. Certain people deny it has a sacred character and regard it as something purely practical. I shall not debate the issue here. New research —including the theological comparison of the different rites—is necessary. Sitting should be at the service of recollection. Our bodies should be relaxed, so that our hearing and understanding are unimpeded.

Today (as, doubtless, in different ways, also in the past)

it is noticeable that there is some curious mixing and matching going on with the different postures. Here and there, sitting has become very like the lotus position of Indian religiosity, which is regarded as the proper posture for meditation. Now I do not want absolutely to rule out the Christian use of the lotus position, which is again being practiced, in different ways, by some Christians. However, I do not believe it has any place in the liturgy. If we try to understand the inner language of bodily gestures, then we can begin to understand their origin and spiritual purpose. When a man kneels, he lowers himself, but his eyes still look forward and upward, as when he stands, toward the One who faces him. To kneel is to be oriented toward the One who looks upon us and toward whom we try to look, as the epistle to the Hebrews says, "looking to Jesus the pioneer and perfecter of our faith" (Heb 12:2; cf. 3:1). Keep your eyes fixed on Jesus—that is a maxim of the Fathers' doctrine of prayer, which takes up again the Old Testament motif of "seeking [God's] face". The man who prays looks beyond himself to the One who is above him and approaches him. He in turn, by his gazing and praying, tries to approach the Lord and thus seeks to enter into nuptial union with him. In the sitting position of oriental meditation, it is all quite different. Man looks into himself. He does not go away from himself to the Other but tends to sink inward, into the nothing that is at the same time everything. True, the Christian tradition is also familiar with the God who is more interior to us than we are to ourselves— the God whom we seek precisely by breaking away from aimless wandering in the external world and going inward. It is there, inside ourselves, that we find ourselves and the deepest ground of our being. In this sense, there are real bridges from the one attitude to the other. With all of today's empiricism and pragmatism, with its loss of soul, we have good reason to learn again from Asia. But however open Christian faith may be, must be, to the wisdom of Asia, the difference between the personal and the a-personal understandings of God remains. We must, therefore, conclude that kneeling and standing are, in a unique and irreplaceable way, the Christian posture of prayer—the Christian's orientation of himself toward the face of God, toward the face of Jesus Christ, in seeing whom we are able to see the Father (Jn 14:9).

Dancing is not a form of expression for the Christian liturgy. In about the third century, there was an attempt in certain Gnostic-Docetic circles to introduce it into the liturgy. For these people, the Crucifixion was only an appearance. Before the Passion, Christ had abandoned the body that in any case he had never really assumed. Dancing could take the place of the liturgy of the Cross, because, after all, the Cross was only an appearance. The cultic dances of the different religions have different purposes—incantation, imitative magic, mystical ecstasy—none of which is compatible with the essential purpose of the liturgy of the "reasonable sacrifice". It is totally absurd to try to make the liturgy "attractive" by introducing dancing pantomimes (wherever possible performed by professional dance troupes), which frequently (and rightly, from the professionals' point of view) end with applause. Wherever applause breaks out in the liturgy because of some human achievement, it is a sure sign that the essence of liturgy has totally disappeared and been replaced by a kind of religious entertainment. Such attractiveness fades quickly—it cannot compete in the market of leisure pursuits, incorporating as it increasingly does various forms of religious titillation. I myself have experienced the replacing of the penitential rite by a dance performance, which, needless to say, received a round of applause. Could there be anything farther removed from true penitence? Liturgy can only attract people when it looks, not at itself, but at God, when it allows him to enter and act. Then something truly unique happens, beyond competition, and people have a sense that more has taken place than a recreational activity. None of the Christian rites includes dancing. What people call dancing in the Ethiopian rite or the Zairean form of the Roman liturgy is in fact a rhythmically ordered procession, very much in keeping with the dignity of the occasion. It provides an inner discipline and order for the various stages of the liturgy, bestowing on them beauty and, above all, making them worthy of God. Once again we face the question: What do we have here, liturgy or popular piety? Very often these old forms of religious expression, which could not be inserted as such into the liturgy, have been integrated into the world of faith. Popular piety has a special importance as a bridge between the faith and each culture. Of its very nature, it is directly indebted to its culture. It enlarges the world of faith and gives it its vitality in the various circumstances of life. It is less universal than the liturgy, which connects vast regions with each other and embraces different cultures. Consequently, the various forms of popular piety are farther removed from each other than the liturgies are, and yet they embody the humanity of man, which, for all the differences of culture, remains similar in so many ways. The best-known example in Europe is the spring procession in

Echternach.[7] In a little sanctuary in the middle of the desert of northern Chile, I was once able to attend some Marian devotions that were followed in the open air by a dance, in honor of the Madonna, employing masks that looked rather frightening to me. Doubtless behind this lay very ancient, pre-Columbian traditions. What once might have been marked by a terrifying seriousness, in view of the power of the gods, had now been set free, transformed into an act of homage to the humble woman who can be called the Mother of God and the ground of our trust. Once again, it is something different if, after the liturgy, the joy that it contains turns into a "secular" feast, which is expressed in a common meal and dancing but does not lose sight of the reason for the joy, of what gives it its purpose and measure. This connection between the liturgy and cheerful earthiness ("Church and inn") has always been regarded as typically Catholic, and so it is still.

At this point, a brief remark about the theme of liturgy and inculturation suggests itself. Needless to say, we cannot go into it too widely and deeply, but, by the same token, it should not be overlooked. Everywhere these days the liturgy seems to be the proving ground for experiments in inculturation. Whenever people talk about inculturation, they almost always think only of the liturgy,

---

[7] Echternach, in the Grand Duchy of Luxembourg, holds an annual "Dancing Procession" (*Springprozession, procession dansante*) in honor of Saint Willibrord, the Apostle of the Netherlands, who died in 739 in the Abbey of Echternach, which he founded. It is a tradition that goes back to the Middle Ages and takes place on the Tuesday after Pentecost. As the thousands of pilgrims pass round the tomb of the saint and through the streets of the little town, they dance to an ancient melody, hopping twice on the right foot and twice on the left. At the same time they call upon the saint for his protection against epilepsy and St. Vitus' Dance.

which then has to undergo often quite dismal distortions. The worshippers usually groan at this, though it is happening for their sake. An inculturation that is more or less just an alteration of outward forms is not inculturation at all, but a misunderstanding of inculturation. Moreover, it frequently insults cultural and religious communities, from whom liturgical forms are borrowed in an all too superficial and external way. The first and most fundamental way in which inculturation takes place is the unfolding of a Christian culture in all its different dimensions: a culture of cooperation, of social concern, of respect for the poor, of the overcoming of class differences, of care for the suffering and dying; a culture that educates mind and heart in proper cooperation; a political culture and a culture of law; a culture of dialogue, of reverence for life, and so on. This kind of authentic inculturation of Christianity then creates culture in the stricter sense of the word, that is, it leads to artistic work that interprets the world anew in the light of God. As the Greeks so rightly saw, culture is, before all else, education, taking that word in its deepest sense as the inner opening up of a man to his possibilities, in which his external abilities are developed in harmony with his gifts. In the religious sphere, culture manifests itself above all in the growth of authentic popular piety. Despite all the inadequacies of the Christian mission in Latin America, and despite the fact that so much still needs to be done, Christian faith has put down deep roots in souls. This can be seen in the popular piety in which the mystery of Christ has come very close to people, in which Christ has become truly their own. Think, for example, of devotion to the Passion, in which these suffering peoples, after the cruelty of the gods of the past, gratefully look upon the God who suffers with them as the answer to their deepest longings. Think, too, of Marian devotion, in which the whole mystery of the Incarnation, the tenderness of God, the participation of man in God's own nature, and the nature of God's saving action are experienced at a profound level. Popular piety is the soil without which the liturgy cannot thrive. Unfortunately, in parts of the Liturgical Movement and on the occasion of the postconciliar reform, it has frequently been held in contempt or even abused. Instead, one must love it, purifying and guiding it where necessary, but always accepting it with great reverence, even when it seems alien or alienating, as the dedicated sanctuary of faith in the hearts of the people. It is faith's secure inner rooting; when it dries up, rationalism and sectarianism have an easy job. Tried and tested elements of popular piety may pass over, then, into liturgical celebration, without officious and hasty fabrication, by a patient process of lengthy growth. Incidentally, the liturgy, without any manipulation of the rite, has always quite spontaneously, through the way it is celebrated, borne the imprint of each culture in which it is celebrated. A liturgy in an Upper Bavarian village looks very different from High Mass in a French cathedral, which in turn seems quite unlike Mass in a southern Italian parish, and again that looks different from what you would find in a mountain village in the Andes, and so on. The decoration and arrangement of the altar and the interior of the church, the style of singing and praying—all of these give the liturgy its own special character, enabling people to feel completely at home. And yet, in every place, we can experience it as one and the same liturgy, and in this way we experience, too, the great communion of faith. The unity of the rite gives us a real experience of *communio*. When the rite is respected and animated from within, unity and diversity are not in opposition.

d. *Gestures*

The oldest gesture of prayer in Christendom is prayer with arms extended, the *orans* posture, which we have already briefly mentioned. This is one of the primal gestures of man in calling upon God and is found in virtually every part of the religious world. It is, first of all, an expression of nonviolence, a gesture of peace. A man opens his arms and thus opens himself to another person. It is also a gesture of seeking and hoping. Man reaches out to the hidden God, stretches out toward him. Arms extended have been compared to wings: man seeks the heights, he wants to be, as it were, carried upward by God on the wings of prayer. But for Christians, arms extended also have a christological meaning. They remind us of the extended arms of Christ on the Cross. The crucified Lord has given this primal human gesture of prayer a new depth. By extending our arms, we resolve to pray with the Crucified, to unite ourselves to his "mind" (Phil 2:5). In the arms of Christ, stretched on the Cross, Christians see a twofold meaning. In his case too, in his case above all, this gesture is the radical form of worship, the unity of his human will with the will of the Father, but at the same time these arms are opened toward us—they are the wide embrace by which Christ wants to draw us to himself (Jn 12:32). Worship of God and love of neighbor—the content of the chief commandment, which sums up the law and the prophets —coincide in this gesture. To open oneself to God, to

surrender oneself completely to him, is at the same time
—the two things cannot be separated—to devote oneself
to one's neighbor. This combining of the two directions
of love in the gesture of Christ on the Cross reveals, in a
bodily and visible way, the new depth of Christian prayer
and thus expresses the inner law of our own prayer.

A later development was the gesture of praying with
hands joined. This comes from the world of feudalism.
The recipient of a feudal estate, on taking tenure, placed
his joined hands in those of his lord—a wonderful symbolic act. I lay my hands in yours, allow yours to enclose
mine. This is an expression of trust as well as of fidelity.
The gesture has been retained in priestly ordination. The
newly ordained man receives his priestly task as a kind
of feudal estate held on tenure. He is not the source of
his priesthood. He is a priest, not through his own skills
and abilities, but by the gift of the Lord, a gift that always
remains a gift and never becomes simply his possession,
a power of his own. The new priest receives the gift and
task of priesthood as a gift from another, from Christ,
and recognizes that all he is ever able and allowed to be
is a "steward of the mysteries of God" (cf. 1 Cor 4:1), "a
good steward of God's varied grace" (cf. 1 Pet 4:10). If
this is what he is to become, he must commit his whole
existence to the task. And that can only take place in the
"house of God" (Heb 3:2–6), the Church, in which the
bishop, in the place of Christ, accepts the individual into
the priesthood, into a relationship of fidelity to Christ.
When the ordinand lays his joined hands in the hands of
the bishop and promises him reverence and obedience, he
is dedicating his service to the Church as the living Body
of Christ, laying his hands in the hands of Christ, entrusting himself to him and giving him his hands, so that they

may be his. What within feudalism may be questionable
—for all human lordship is questionable and can only be
justified if it represents and is faithful to the real Lord—
finds its true meaning in the relationship of the believer
to Christ the Lord. This, then, is what is meant when we
join our hands to pray: we are placing our hands in his,
and with our hands we place in his hands our personal
destiny. Trusting in his fidelity, we pledge our fidelity to
him.

We have already said something about kneeling as a
gesture of prayer. I should like at this point to mention
bowing. One of the petitions for acceptance in the Roman Canon (Eucharistic Prayer I) begins with the word
supplices: Bowing low, we implore thee. Here again, the
bodily gesture and the spiritual process are inseparable
and flow into one another. This is the gesture of the tax
collector, who knows that he cannot endure the gaze of
God and so bows low before it. And yet this prayer asks
that our sacrifice may come before the face of God, into
his sight, and be for us a blessing. Out of the depths of our
insufficiency, we call upon God, that he may set us upright, enable us to gaze upon him, and make us such that
he may gaze upon us. The *supplices*—our being "bowed
low"—is the bodily expression, so to speak, of what the
Bible calls humility (cf. "he humbled himself", Phil 2:8).
For the Greeks, humility was the attitude of a slave, and
so they rejected it. The transformation of values brought
about by Christianity sees in it something different. Humility is the ontologically appropriate attitude, the state
that corresponds to the truth about man, and as such it
becomes a fundamental attitude of Christian existence.
Saint Augustine constructed his whole Christology, indeed, I would say his entire apologetics for Christianity,

upon the concept of *humilitas*. He took up the teaching of the ancients, of the Greek and Roman world, that *hybris* —self-glorifying pride—is the real sin of all sins, as we see in exemplary form in the fall of Adam. Arrogance, the ontological lie by which man makes himself God, is overcome by the humility of God, who makes himself the slave, who bows down before us. The man who wants to come close to God must be able to look upon him—that is essential. But he must likewise learn to bend, for God has bent himself down. In the gesture of humble love, in the washing of feet, in which he kneels at our feet—that is where we find him. Thus the *supplices* is a gesture of great profundity. It is a physical reminder of the spiritual attitude essential to faith. Astonishingly, several modern translations of the Roman Canon have simply omitted the *supplices*. Perhaps they regarded the physical expression, which as a matter of fact has disappeared, as unimportant. Perhaps, too, they thought it was an unsuitable thing for a modern man to do. To bow low before a human being, to win his favor, is indeed unfitting. But to bow low before God can never be unmodern, because it corresponds to the truth of our being. And if modern man has forgotten this truth, then it is all the more incumbent on Christians in the modern world to rediscover it and teach it to our fellowmen.

Another gesture came into Christianity from the narrative already mentioned of the Pharisee and the Tax Collector (cf. Lk 18:9–14): striking the breast. Apparently, in the North Africa of Saint Augustine, it was very popular and practiced in a somewhat exaggerated and superficial manner, so much so, in fact, that the Bishop of Hippo had to remind his flock, with gentle irony, to moderate their "sin-bashing". However, this gesture, by which we point, not at someone else, but at ourselves as the guilty party, remains a meaningful gesture of prayer. This is exactly what we need, time and again, to do: to see and acknowledge our guilt and so also to beg for forgiveness. When we say *mea culpa* (through my fault), we turn, so to speak, to ourselves, to our own front door, and thus we are able rightly to ask forgiveness of God, the saints, and the people gathered around us, whom we have wronged. During the *Agnus Dei* (Lamb of God), we look upon him who is the Shepherd and for us became Lamb and, as Lamb, bore our iniquities. At this moment, it is only right and proper that we should strike our breasts and remind ourselves, even physically, that our iniquities lay on his shoulders, that "with his stripes we are healed" (Is 53:5).

e. *The Human Voice*

It is clear that in the liturgy of the Logos, of the Eternal Word, the word and thus the human voice have an essential role to play. In this little book, which is not intended to give instructions for liturgical practice but only insights into the spirit of the liturgy, we do not need to discuss the detailed forms in which the human voice is deployed in the liturgy. We have seen much of this already in early chapters, especially in connection with sacred music. First there is the *oratio*, the priestly mode of prayer, in which the priest, in the name of the whole community, speaks through Christ, in the Holy Spirit, to the Father. Then there are the various forms of proclamation: the readings ("Prophet and Apostle", as they used to say in the early Church, meaning by "prophecy" the whole of the Old Testament), the Gospel (solemnly sung at High Mass), and the homily, which in the strict sense is reserved to the bishop and then to the priest and deacon as well. Then there is the response to the Word [*Ant-Wort*], by which the assembled congregation takes up and accepts the Word. This structure of Word and response, which is essential to the liturgy, is modeled on the basic structure of the process of divine revelation, in which Word and response, the speech of God and the receptive hearing of the Bride, the Church, go together. In the liturgy, the response has different forms. For example, there is the acclamation ("shout"), which is of great importance in the world of ancient law. The responsive acclamation confirms the arrival of the Word and makes the process of revelation, of God's giving of himself in the Word, at last complete. The Amen, the Alleluia, and the *Et cum spiritu tuo*, and so on, are all part of this. One of the important results of the liturgical renewal is the fact that the people really do again respond in the acclamation and do not have to leave it to a representative, the altar server. This is the only way the true structure of the liturgy can be restored, a structure that, as we have just seen, makes concrete in divine worship the fundamental structure of divine action. God, the Revealer, did not want to stay as *solus Deus, solus Christus* (God alone, Christ alone). No, he wanted to create a Body for himself, to find a Bride —he sought a response. It was really for her that the Word went forth. Alongside the acclamation are the various forms of meditative appropriation of the Word, especially in the singing of psalms (but also in hymns), the different forms of which (responsorial and antiphonal) do not need to be discussed in detail here. Then there is the "new song", the great song the Church sings as she goes off toward the music of the New Heaven and New Earth.

This explains why, in addition to congregational singing, Christian liturgy of its very nature finds a suitable place for the choir and for musical instruments, too, which no purism about collective singing should be allowed to contest. The possibilities will, of course, always differ from place to place, but the Church as a whole must, for the sake of God, strive for the best, for from the very nature of the liturgy, by an inner necessity, comes a culture that becomes a standard for all secular culture.

We are realizing more and more clearly that silence is part of the liturgy. We respond, by singing and praying, to the God who addresses us, but the greater mystery, surpassing all words, summons us to silence. It must, of course, be a silence with content, not just the absence of speech and action. We should expect the liturgy to give us a positive stillness that will restore us. Such stillness will not be just a pause, in which a thousand thoughts and desires assault us, but a time of recollection, giving us an inward peace, allowing us to draw breath and rediscover the one thing necessary, which we have forgotten. That is why silence cannot be simply "made", organized as if it were one activity among many. It is no accident that on all sides people are seeking techniques of meditation, a spirituality for emptying the mind. One of man's deepest needs is making its presence felt, a need that is manifestly not being met in our present form of the liturgy.

For silence to be fruitful, as we have already said, it must not be just a pause in the action of the liturgy. No, it must be an integral part of the liturgical event. How is that to be done? In recent times, the attempt has been made to insert two short periods of silence into the liturgy as a way of addressing the problem: a pause for reflection after the homily and a period of silent prayer after the reception of Holy Communion. The pause for silence after the homily has not proved to be very satisfactory: it seems artificial, with the congregation just waiting for as long as the celebrant feels inclined to let it go on. What is more, the homily often leaves questions and contradictions in people's minds rather than an invitation to meet the Lord. As a general rule, the homily should conclude with an encouragement to prayer, which would give some content to the brief pause. But even then, it remains just a pause in the liturgy, not something from which a liturgy of silence can develop. More helpful and spiritually appropriate is the silence after Communion. This, in all truth, is the moment for an interior conversation with the Lord who has given himself to us, for that essential "communicating", that entry into the process of communication, without which the external reception of the Sacrament becomes mere ritual and therefore unfruitful. Unfortunately, there are often hindrances that spoil this precious moment. The distribution of Communion continues with the noise of people going back and forth. In relation to the rest of the liturgical action, the distribution often lasts too long, which means that the priest feels the need to move the liturgy on quickly so that there is no empty period of waiting and restlessness, with people already getting ready to leave. Nevertheless, whenever possible, this silence after Communion should be used, and the faithful should be given some guidance for interior prayer.

In some places, the Preparation of the Gifts is intended as a time for silence. This makes good sense and is fruitful, if we see the Preparation, not as just a pragmatic external action, but as an essentially interior process. We need to see that we ourselves are, or should be, the real gift in the "Word-centered sacrifice" through our sharing in Jesus Christ's act of self-offering to the Father (of which we spoke in the first part). Then this silence is not just a period of waiting, something external. Then something happens inwardly that corresponds to what is going on outwardly—we are disposing ourselves, preparing the way, placing ourselves before the Lord, asking him to make us ready for transformation. Shared silence becomes shared prayer, indeed shared action, a journey out of our everyday life toward the Lord, toward merging our time with his own. Liturgical education ought to regard it as its duty to facilitate this inner process, so that in the common experience of silence the inner process becomes a truly liturgical event and the silence is filled with content.

The structure of the liturgy itself provides for other moments of silence. First there is the silence of the Consecration at the elevation of the consecrated species. It is an invitation to direct our eyes toward Christ, to look at him from within, in a gaze that is at once gratitude, adoration, and petition for our own transformation. There are fashionable objections that would try to talk us out of this silence at the Consecration. The showing of the Gifts, it is said, is a medieval error, which disturbs the structure of the Eucharistic Prayer, the expression of a false and too grossly materialistic piety. The argument is that the elevation is out of keeping with the essential direction of the Eucharist. At this moment, so it is claimed, we should not be worshipping Christ—the whole Canon addresses the Father, to whom we pray through Christ. We do not need to go into these criticisms in detail. The essential answer to them is provided by what was said in chapter 2 about reverence for the Blessed Sacrament and the rightfulness of the medieval developments, which unfolded what had been there from the beginning in the faith of the Church. It is correct to say that the Canon has a trinitarian structure and consequently as a totality moves "through Christ, in the Holy Spirit, to the Father". But the liturgy in this respect knows nothing of rigidity and fixation. The reformed Missal of 1970 itself places on our lips a greeting directed toward the Lord: "We proclaim your death, O Lord, and we confess your Resurrection, until you come [in glory]!" The moment when the Lord comes down and transforms bread and wine to become his Body and Blood cannot fail to stun, to the very core of their being, those who participate in the Eucharist by faith and prayer. When this happens, we cannot do other than fall to our knees and greet him. The Consecration is the moment of God's great *actio* in the world for us. It draws our eyes and hearts on high. For a moment the world is silent, everything is silent, and in that silence we touch the eternal—for one beat of the heart we step out of time into God's being-with-us.

Another approach to the question of content-filled silence is provided by the liturgy itself. There is a silence that is part of the liturgical action, not an interruption. I am thinking of the silent prayers of the priest. Those who hold a sociological or activistic view of the priest's duties in the Mass frown upon these prayers, and, whenever possible, they leave them out. The priest is defined in a narrowly sociological and functionalistic way as the "presider" at the liturgical celebration, which is thought of as a kind of meeting. If that is what he is, then, of course, for the sake of the meeting, he has to be in action all the time. But the priest's duties in the Mass are much more than a matter of chairing a meeting. The priest presides over an encounter with the living God and as a person who is on his way to God. The silent prayers of the priest invite him to make his task truly personal, so that he may give his whole self to the Lord. They highlight the way in which all of us, each one personally yet together with everyone else, have to approach the Lord. The number of these priestly prayers has been greatly reduced in the liturgical reform, but, thank God, they do exist—they have to exist, now as before. First, there is the short prayer of preparation before the proclamation of the Gospel. The priest should pray it with real recollection and devotion, conscious of his responsibility to proclaim the Gospel aright, conscious, too, of the need that that entails for a purification of lips and heart. When the priest does this, he shows the congregation the dignity and grandeur of the Gospel and helps them understand how tremendous it is that God's Word should come into our midst. The priest's prayer creates reverence and a space for hearing the Word. Again, liturgical education is necessary if the priest's prayer is to be understood, and the people are not only to stand up physically but also to rise up spiritually and open the ears of their hearts to the Gospel. We have already spoken of the Preparation of the Gifts, the significance of which in the new rite is not entirely clear. The priest's reception of Holy Communion is preceded by two very beautiful and profound prayers, from which, to avoid the silence being too long, he is to choose one. Perhaps we shall again one day take the time to use both. But even if only one of them is prayed, the priest should with all the more reason really pray it in recollected silence as a personal preparation for receiving the Lord. This will help to bring everyone else into silence before the Sacred Presence, and then going to Communion will not degenerate into something merely external. This is particularly necessary, because in the present order of the Mass, the sign of peace frequently causes a lot of hustle and bustle in the congregation, into which the invitation to "Behold the Lamb of God" then comes as a rather abrupt intervention. If, in a moment of quiet, the eyes of the hearts of all are directed toward the Lamb, this can become a time of blessed silence. After the priest's reception of Communion, another (formerly, there were two) silent prayer of thanksgiving is provided for him, which again can and should be made their own by the faithful.

I should like to mention at this point that old prayer books contain, alongside a lot of kitsch, much that is a valuable resource for prayer, much that has grown out of deep interior experience and can again become today a school for prayer. What Saint Paul says in the epistle to the Romans—that we do not know how to pray as we ought (Rom 8:26)—applies even more to us today. So often we are without words in our encounter with God. The Holy Spirit does indeed teach us to pray; he does indeed give us the words, as Saint Paul says; but he also uses human mediation. The prayers that have risen up from the hearts of believers under the guidance of the Holy Spirit are a school, provided us by the Holy Spirit, that will slowly open our mute mouths and help us to learn how to pray and to fill the silence.

In 1978, to the annoyance of many liturgists, I said that in no sense does the whole Canon always *have* to be said out loud. After much consideration, I should like to repeat and underline the point here in the hope that, twenty years later, this thesis will be better understood. Meanwhile, in their efforts to reform the Missal, the German liturgists have explicitly stated that, of all things, the

Eucharistic Prayer, the high point of the Mass, is in crisis. Since the reform of the liturgy, an attempt has been made to meet the crisis by incessantly inventing new Eucharistic Prayers, and in the process we have sunk farther and farther into banality. Multiplying words is no help—that is all too evident. The liturgists have suggested all kinds of remedies, which certainly contain elements that are worthy of consideration. However, as far as I can see, they balk, now as in the past, at the possibility that silence, too, silence especially, might constitute communion before God. It is no accident that in Jerusalem, from a very early time, parts of the Canon were prayed in silence and that in the West the silent Canon—overlaid in part with meditative singing—became the norm. To dismiss all this as the result of misunderstandings is just too easy. It really is not true that reciting the whole Eucharistic Prayer out loud and without interruptions is a prerequisite for the participation of everyone in this central act of the Mass. My suggestion in 1978 was as follows. First, liturgical education ought to aim at making the faithful familiar with the essential meaning and fundamental orientation of the Canon. Secondly, the first words of the various prayers should be said out loud as a kind of cue for the congregation, so that each individual in his silent prayer can take up the intonation and bring the personal into the communal and the communal into the personal. Anyone who has experienced a church united in the silent praying of the Canon will know what a really *filled* silence is. It is at once a loud and penetrating cry to God and a Spirit-filled act of prayer. Here everyone does pray the Canon together, albeit in a bond with the special task of the priestly ministry. Here everyone is united, laid hold of by Christ, and led by the Holy Spirit into that common prayer to the Father which is the true sacrifice—the love that reconciles and unites God and the world.

f. *Vestments*

The liturgical attire worn by the priest during the celebration of Holy Mass should, first and foremost, make clear that he is not there as a private person, as this or that man, but stands in place of Another—Christ. What is merely private, merely individual, about him should disappear and make way for Christ. "[I]t is no longer I who live, but Christ who lives in me" (Gal 2:20). These words of Saint Paul, in which, from his own, very personal experience of Christ, he describes the newness of the baptized person, apply in a special way to the priest in celebrating Mass. It is not he himself who is important, but Christ. It is not he himself whom he is communicating to men, but Christ. He makes himself the instrument of Christ, acting, not from his own resources, but as the messenger, indeed, as the presence, of Another—*in persona Christi*, as the liturgical tradition says. Liturgical vestments are a direct reminder of those texts in which Saint Paul speaks of being clothed with Christ: "For as many of you as were baptized into Christ have put on Christ" (Gal 3:27). In the epistle to the Romans, the image is connected with the opposition between two ways of living. To those who waste their lives in immoderate eating and drinking, in debauchery and licentiousness, Saint Paul shows the Christian way: "But put on the Lord Jesus Christ, and make no provision for the flesh, to gratify its desires" (Rom 13:14). In the epistles to the Ephesians and Colossians, the same idea is interpreted in an even more fundamental way in relation to the anthropology of the new man: "[P]ut on the new man, created after the likeness of God in true righteousness and holiness" (Eph 4:24). "[You] have put on the new man, who is being renewed in knowledge after the image of his creator. Here there cannot be Greek and Jew, circumcised and uncircumcised, barbarian, Scythian, slave, free man, but Christ is all, and in all" (Col 3:10f.). The assumption is that the image of putting on Christ was developed by analogy with a man's putting on of the cultic mask of the deity when he was initiated into mystery cults. For Saint Paul, it is no longer a question of masks and rituals, but a question of a process of spiritual transformation. The goal is the inward renewal of man, his real assimilation to God, and thus his unity, the overcoming of all the barriers that have been, and continue to be, erected in the history of human sinfulness. The image of putting on Christ is, therefore, a dynamic image, bearing on the transformation of man and the world, the new humanity. Vestments are a reminder of all this, of this transformation in Christ, and of the new community that is supposed to arise from it. Vestments are a challenge to the priest to surrender himself to the dynamism of breaking out of the capsule of self and being fashioned anew by Christ and for Christ. They remind those who participate in the Mass of the new way that began with Baptism and continues with the Eucharist, the way that leads to the future world already delineated in our daily lives by the sacraments.

In his two epistles to the Corinthians, Saint Paul gives further elaboration to the eschatological orientation of the image of clothing. In the first epistle he says: "[T]his perishable nature must put on the imperishable, and this mortal nature must put on immortality" (15:53). The apostle gives us an even deeper insight into his own hopes and struggles in the fifth chapter of the second epistle. Paul describes the body of this earthly time as an "earthly tent", which will be taken down, and looks ahead to the house not made with human hands, "eternal in the heavens". He is anxious about the taking down of the tent, anxious about the "nakedness" in which he will then find himself. His hope is to be, not "unclothed", but "further clothed", to receive the "heavenly house"—the definitive body—as a new garment. The apostle does not want to discard his body, he does not want to be bodiless. He is not interested in any flight of the soul from the "prison of the body", as envisaged by the Pythagorean tradition taken up by Plato. He does not want flight but transformation. He hopes for resurrection. Thus the theology of clothing becomes a theology of the body. The body is more than an external dressing up of man—it is part of his very being, of his essential constitution. And yet this body is subject to decay. It is only a tent. It is provisional. But, at the same time, it is an anticipation of the definitive body, the definitive and complete form of human existence. The liturgical vestment carries this message in itself. It is a "further clothing", not an "unclothing", and the liturgy guides us on the way to this "further clothing", on the way to the body's salvation in the risen body of Jesus Christ, which is the new "house not made with hands, eternal in the heavens" (2 Cor 5:1). The Body of Christ, which we receive in the Eucharist, to which we are united in the Eucharist ("one Body with him", cf. 1 Cor 6:12–20), saves us from "nakedness", from the bareness in which we cannot stand before God. In the context of this teaching of Saint Paul, I am very fond of the old formula for the distribution of Holy Communion:

"The Body of our Lord Jesus Christ preserve thy soul unto everlasting life." These words turn the teaching of 2 Corinthians 5:1–10 into prayer. The soul on its own would be a sad fragment. But even before the general resurrection, it enters into the Body of Christ, which in a sense becomes our body, just as we are supposed to become his Body. The Body (of Christ) saves our soul for eternal life—for Greek thought, a nonsensical paradox, but because of the risen Christ, living hope. The liturgical vestment has a meaning that goes beyond that of external garments. It is an anticipation of the new clothing, the risen Body of Jesus Christ, that new reality which awaits us when the earthly "tent" is taken down and which gives us a "place to stay" (cf. Jn 14:2: "In my Father's house are many rooms": the word translated "room" here really means "place to stay", highlighting the definitiveness, the privilege of having somewhere we can remain).

When the Fathers were thinking about the theology of clothing, two other biblical texts came to their minds, which I should like to include in my reflections here to give us a better understanding of liturgical vestments. First, there is the story of the Prodigal Son, in which the father, having embraced his son on his return, gives this instruction: "Bring quickly the best robe . . ." (Lk 15:22). In the Greek text, it says "the *first* robe", and that is how the Fathers read and understood it. For them, the first robe is the robe in which Adam was created and which he lost after he had grasped at likeness to God. All the clothes subsequently worn by man are only a poor substitute for the light of God coming from within, which was Adam's true "robe". Thus, in reading the account of the Prodigal Son and his return, the Fathers heard the account of Adam's fall, the fall of man (cf. Gen 2:7), and interpreted Jesus' parable as a message about the return home and reconciliation of mankind as a whole. The man who in faith returns home receives back the first "robe", is clothed again in the mercy and love of God, which are his true beauty. The white garment presented at Baptism is meant to suggest these great connections in salvation history, and at the same time it points toward the white garment of eternity, of which the Apocalypse speaks (cf. 19:8)—an expression of the purity and beauty of the risen body. The great arch that connects Adam's creation and fall with the white garment of eternity is contained in the symbolism of liturgical vestments, and the cornerstone supporting the whole arch is Christ: "Put on Christ"— even now be one with him, even now be members of his Body.

g. *Matter*

The Catholic liturgy is the liturgy of the Word made flesh —made flesh for the sake of the resurrection. And, as we have seen, it is a cosmic liturgy. Thus it is clear that not only do the human body and signs from the cosmos play an essential role in the liturgy but that the matter of this world is part of the liturgy. Matter comes into the liturgy in two ways: first, in the form of many kinds of symbols —the holy fire of Easter night, the candle and the flame that burns on it, the various kinds of liturgical objects such as the bell, the altar cloth, and so on. In the last century, Romano Guardini opened up our understanding of this symbolic world in a new way by his little book *Sacred Signs*. Recently, Bishop Kapellari of Klagenfurt gave us a new book, with many pictures, in which Guardini's insights are developed, deepened, and applied to our present situation. There is no need, therefore, to discuss the matter here.

The second, even more important way in which matter comes into the liturgy is in the sacraments, the sacred actions that go back to Christ himself, which in the strict sense constitute the liturgy—precisely because they were not invented by men but were given to us in their substance by the Lord himself. Three of the seven sacraments relate directly to man as a person at very particular points in his life and consequently do not need any other "matter" than man himself in the situation to which the sacrament is ordered. First, there is Penance, in which as sinners we beg for the word of forgiveness and renewal. Then, there is Holy Orders, in which the Lord, by the bishop's laying on of hands, gives a man mission and authority in succession to the ministry of the apostles. Finally, there is Matrimony, in which two human beings give themselves to each other for a lifelong union and thereby become a real, living, and tangible image of the covenant between Christ and his Church (cf. Eph 5:27–32).

But then there are four sacraments—Baptism, Confirmation, the Eucharist, and the Anointing of the Sick—in which material things become the vessels of God's action upon us. It is not for this little book to develop a theology of the sacraments. I should just like to highlight the elements that come into the liturgy here as a mediation of the divine action. For these elements, which the Lord himself chose, are full of meaning. We need to meditate on them as such if we are to understand the spirit of the liturgy better. They are: water, (olive) oil, (wheaten) bread, and wine. Let us remember in parenthesis here that of the four elements in antiquity—water, air, fire, earth

—the first three are all symbols of the Holy Spirit, while the earth represents man, who comes from the earth and to the earth returns. Fire and air in the form of breath are present in many ways in the symbolism of the liturgy, but only water, which comes from above and yet belongs to the earth, has become, as the primordial element of life, sacramental matter in the strict sense. The Church's tradition discerns a twofold symbolism in water. The salt water of the sea is a symbol of death, a threat and a danger; it reminds us of the Red Sea, which was deadly to the Egyptians, though the Israelites were rescued from it. Baptism is a kind of passing through the Red Sea. A death occurs within it. It is more than a bath or washing —it touches the very depths of existence, as far as death itself. It is a crucifying communion with Christ. This is precisely what is signified by the Red Sea, which is an image of death and resurrection (cf. Rom 6:1–11). On the other hand, water flowing from a spring is a symbol of the source of all life, *the* symbol of life. That is why the early Church laid down that Baptism had to be administered by means of "living water", spring water, so that Baptism could be experienced as the beginning of new life. In this connection, the Fathers always had at the back of their minds the conclusion of the Passion narrative according to Saint John: blood and water flow from the opened side of Jesus; Baptism and Eucharist spring from the pierced heart of Jesus. He has become the living spring that makes us alive (cf. Jn 19:34f.; 1 Jn 5:6). At the Feast of Tabernacles, Jesus had prophesied that streams of living water would flow from the man who came to him and drank: "Now this he said about the Spirit, which those who believed in him were to receive" (Jn 7:39). The baptized man himself becomes a spring. When we think of the great saints of history, from whom streams of faith, hope, and love really came forth, we can understand these words and thus understand something of the dynamism of Baptism, of the promise and vocation it contains.

When we look at the three other elements in the sacraments of the Church—olive oil, wheaten bread, and wine, we are struck by the characteristic that distinguishes them from the gift of water. Whereas water is the common element of life for the whole earth and is therefore suitable in all places as a door of entry to communion with Christ, in the case of the other three elements, we are dealing with the typical gifts of Mediterranean culture. We encounter this triad in explicit association in the glorious psalm of creation, Psalm 104, where the Psalmist thanks God for giving man the food of the earth and "wine to gladden the heart of man, oil to make his face shine, and bread to strengthen man's heart" (v. 15). These three elements of Mediterranean life express the goodness of creation, in which we receive the goodness of the Creator himself. And now they become the gift of an even higher goodness, a goodness that makes our face shine anew in likeness to the "Anointed" God, to his beloved Son, Jesus Christ, a goodness that changes the bread and wine of the earth into the Body and Blood of the Redeemer, so that, through the Son made man, we may have communion with the triune God himself.

At this point comes the objection that these gifts have a symbolic force only in the Mediterranean area and that in other growing regions they ought to be replaced by elements appropriate to those regions. This is the same issue that we encountered when we were discussing the inversion of the cosmic symbolism of the seasons in the

Southern Hemisphere. The answer we gave there applies again here: in the interplay of culture and history, history has priority. God has acted in history and, through history, given the gifts of the earth their significance. The elements become sacraments through connection with the unique history of God in relation to man in Jesus Christ. As we have said before, Incarnation does not mean doing as we please. On the contrary, it binds us to the history of a particular time. Outwardly, that history may seem fortuitous, but it is the form of history willed by God, and for us it is the trustworthy trace he has imprinted on the earth, the guarantee that we are not thinking up things for ourselves but are truly touched by God and come into touch with him. Precisely through what is particular and once-for-all, the here and now, we emerge from the "ever and never" vagueness of mythology. It is with this particular face, with this particular human form, that Christ comes to us, and precisely thus does he make us brethren beyond all boundaries. Precisely thus do we recognize him: "It is the Lord!" (Jn 21:7).

Bibliography

General Works on the Liturgy

The presentation of the theology of the liturgy in the *Catechism of the Catholic Church* (*CCC*) is fundamental (cf. nos. 1077–1112).

Adam, A., and R. Berger. *Pastoralliturgisches Handlexikon.* Freiburg: Herder, 1980.

Corbon, J. *Liturgie de source.* Paris: Cerf, 1980. Translated by Matthew J. O'Connell as *The Wellspring of Worship.* New York: Paulist Press, 1988.

Kunzler, M. *Die Liturgie der Kirche.* AMATECA: Lehr-bücher zur katholischen Theologie. Vol. 10. Paderborn: Bonifatius, 1995.

———. *Porta orientalis: Fünf Ost-West-Versuche über Theologie und Ästhetik der Liturgie.* Paderborn: Bonifatius, 1993.

Lang, B. *Heiliges Spiel: Eine Geschichte des christlichen Gottesdienstes.* Munich: Beck, 1998.

Martimort, G., ed. *L'Église en prière: Introduction à la liturgie.* New ed., 4 vols. Paris: Desclée, 1983–1984. Translated by Matthew O'Connell as *The Church at Prayer: An Introduction to the Liturgy.* New ed. 4 vols. Collegeville, Minn.: Liturgical Press, 1986–1988.

Meyer, H. B., H. Auf der Maur, B. Fischer, A. A. Häussling, B. Kleinheyer, eds. *Gottesdienst der Kirche: Handbuch der Liturgiewissenschaft*. Regensburg: Pustet, 1984ff.
The parts to appear so far are: 3 (*Gestalt des Gottesdienstes*), 4 (*Eucharistie*), 5 and 6/1 (*Feiern im Rhythmus der
Zeit*), 7/1 (*Sakramentliche Feiern* I), 7/2 (*Sakramentliche
Feiern* I/2), 8 (*Sakramentliche Feiern*).

Nichols, O.P., A. *Looking at the Liturgy: A Critical View
of Its Contemporary Form*. San Francisco: Ignatius Press,
1996.

Ratzinger, J. *Das Fest des Glaubens*. Einsiedeln: Johannes
Verlag, 1981. Translated by Graham Harrison as *The
Feast of Faith: Approaches to a Theology of the Liturgy*. San
Francisco: Ignatius Press, 1986.

————. *Ein neues Lied für den Herrn: Christusglaube und
Liturgie in der Gegenwart*. Freiburg: Herder, 1995. Trans-
lated by Martha M. Matesich as *A New Song for the Lord:
Faith in Christ and Liturgy Today*. New York: Crossroad
Pub., 1996.

Sartore, D., and A. Triacca, eds. *Nuovo dizionario di liturgia*. Rome: Edizioni Paoline, 1983.

PART ONE

Chapter 1

Particularly important for the theme of play is J. Huiz-
inga, *Homo ludens* (Amsterdam, 1939 [English translation:
New York: J. and J. Harper, 1970]) as well as the precious
little book of Hugo Rahner's, drawn entirely from the Fathers: *Der spielende Mensch* (Einsiedeln: Johannes Verlag,

1952); translated by Brian Battershaw and Edward Quinn as *Man at Play* (New York: Herder and Herder, 1967).

In *The Spirit of the Liturgy*, Romano Guardini to a large extent unfolded the special nature of the liturgy with the help of the concept of play. However, in the fourth and fifth printing (1920), he inserted a chapter "On the Seriousness of the Liturgy", which clearly limits the concept of play.

Chapter 2

On the *exitus-reditus* theme:

Ratzinger, J. *Die Geschichtstheologie des heiligen Bonaventura.* Munich & Zurich, 1959. 2d ed., St. Ottilien, 1992. Translated by Zachary Hayes as *The Theology of History in St. Bonaventure.* Chicago, Ill.: Franciscan Herald Press, 1971.

Seckler, M. *Das Heil in der Geschichte: Geschichtstheologisches Denken bei Thomas von Aquin.* Munich: Kösel, 1954.

Torrell, J. P. *Initiation à St. Thomas d'Aquin.* Fribourg: Éditions universitaires, 1993. Translated by Robert Royal as *Saint Thomas Aquinas.* Vol. 1. Washington, D.C.: Catholic Univ. of America Press, 1996.

Chapter 3

The view set out here, of the path from the Old Testament to the New and of the nature of the liturgy in general, is one I have developed over the course of many years through my acquaintance with the Scriptures and the liturgy. Preliminary sketches for it, together with references to the literature, can be found in the two works of mine mentioned above, *The Feast of Faith* and *A New Song for the Lord* as well as in the article "Eucharistie und Mission" (*Forum katholische Theologie* 14 [1998]: 81–98), which has been published in several different languages.

PART TWO

Chapter 1

On the "Church between the Testaments", see:

Ratzinger, J. *Volk und Haus Gottes in Augustins Lehre von der Kirche*. 2d ed. Pp. 304–8. St. Ottilien, 1992.

On *semel quia semper*, see:

St. Bernard of Clairvaux, *Sermo 5 de diversis* 1. In *Bernhard von Clairvaux. Sämtliche Werke*. Latin/German. Edited by G. Winkler. Vol. 9, p. 218. Innsbruck, 1998.

Chapter 2

My presentation here takes its bearings from L. Bouyer, *Architecture et liturgie* (Paris: Cerf, 1991). The page numbers given refer to the English edition: *Liturgy and Architecture* (Notre Dame, Ind.: Univ. of Notre Dame Press, 1967).

From the abundant literature on this matter, I should like to mention only the following:

Norman, E. *The House of God*. New York: Thames and Hudson, 1990.

White, L. M. *Building God's House in the Roman World*. Baltimore and London: Johns Hopkins Univ. Press, 1990.

Chapter 3

Here once again I refer to Bouyer and my own *Feast of Faith*. More of the literature can be found in the latter.

Chapter 4

On faith in the Real Presence and its unfolding in theology, see:

Betz, J. *Eucharistie in der Schrift und Patristik:* Handbuch der Dogmengeschichte. Edited by Schmaus, Grillmeier, Scheffczyk, and Seybold. Vol. 4/4a. Freiburg: Herder, 1979.

―――. *Die Eucharistie in der Zeit der griechischen Väter*. Vol. 2/1. Freiburg: Herder, 1961.

Gerken, A. *Theologie der Eucharistie*. Munich: Kösel, 1973.

Lubac, H. de. *Corpus mysticum: L'Eucharistie et L'Église au Moyen âge*. 2d ed. Paris: Aubier, 1949. Translated by Gemma Simmonds with Richard Price and Christopher Stephens as *Corpus mysticum: The Eucharist and the Church in the Middle Ages: Historical Survey*. Notre Dame, Ind.: Univ. of Notre Dame Press, 2007.

Sayes, J. A. *La presencia real de Cristo en la Eucaristia*. BAC. Madrid: EDICA, 1976.

Chapter 5

As ever, the handbooks of liturgiology mentioned above should be consulted. On the question of Sunday, see also my own book, *A New Song for the Lord*.

In addition, see:

Fedalto, G. *Quando festeggiare il 2000? Problemi di cronologia cristiana*. Edizioni San Paolo, 1998.

Rahner, H. *Griechische Mythen in christlicher Deutung*. Darmstadt, 1957. Translated by Brian Battershaw as *Greek Myths and Christian Mystery*. New York: Harper and Row, 1963. My references to the Fathers are taken from this book.

Schade, H. *Lamm Gottes und Zeichen des Widders: Zur kosmologisch-psychologischen Hermeneutik der Ikonographie des "Lammes Gottes"*. Edited by V. H. Elbern. Freiburg: Herder, 1998.

Voss, G. "Christen auf der Suche nach einem gemeinsamen Osterdatum", parts 1 and 2, especially 2. In KNA. *Ökumenische Information* 24 (June 9, 1998): 5–10.

Weigl, E. "Die Oration *Gratiam tuam, quaesumus, Domine*: Zur Geschichte des 25 März in der Liturgie". *Liturgisches Jahrbuch*, 3 (1923): 57–73.

PART THREE

Chapter 1

Evdokimov, P. *L'Art de l'icône: Théologie de la beauté*. Paris: Desclée, 1970. Translated by Steven Bigham as *The Art of the Icon: A Theology of Beauty*. Redondo Beach, Calif.: Oakwood Pub., 1990. The page numbers given refer to the English edition of this book.

Onasch, K. *Kunst und Liturgie der Ostkirche in Stichworten unter Berücksichtigung der Alten Kirche*. Vienna: H. Böhlau, 1981.

Van der Meer, F. *Die Ursprünge christlicher Kunst*. Freiburg: Herder, 1982.

Various authors. *Arte e liturgia: L'arte sacra a trent'anni dal Concilio*. Milan: Edizioni San Paolo, 1983.

Chapter 2

Fellerer, K. G., ed. *Geschichte der katholischen Kirchenmusik*. 2 vols. Bärenreiter, 1972–1976. Translated by Francis A. Brunner as *The History of Catholic Church Music*. Westport, Conn.: Greenwood Press, 1979.

Forte, B. *La porta della bellezza: Per un'estetica teologica*. Especially pp. 85–108. Morcelliana, 1999.

Jaschinski, E. *Musica sacra oder Musik im Gottesdienst?* Regensburg: Pustet, 1990.

Ravasi, G. *Il canto della rana: Musica et teologia nella Bibbia*. Regensburg: Piemme, 1990.

I should also like to refer especially to the relevant chapters in *Feast of Faith* and *A New Song for the Lord*.

PART FOUR

Chapter 1

A good survey of the Eastern rites can be found in:

Bux, N. *Il quinto sigillo*. Libreria editrice Vaticana, 1997.

Vazheeparampil, Prasanna. *The Making and Unmaking of Tradition*. Especially the diagram of the rites on p. 57. Rome, 1998.

For information about the large world of the non-Byzantine Eastern Churches, the great work by M. Zibawi is very important: *Orienti cristiani*. Milan: Jaca Book, 1995.

I should also like to refer to the article "Liturgien" in *Lexikon für Theologie und Kirche*. 3d ed. Vol. 6, pp. 972–87.

Chapter 2

Cordes, P. J. *Actuosa participatio—tätige Teilnahme*. Paderborn: Bonifatius, 1995.

Dinkler, E. *Signum crucis: Aufsätze zum Neuen Testament und zur christlichen Archäologie*. Especially pp. 1–76. Tübingen: Mohr, 1967.

Rahner, H. *Griechische Mythen in christlicher Deutung*. Darmstadt, 1957. Translated by Brian Battershaw as *Greek Myths and Christian Mystery*. New York: Harper and Row, 1963.

A helpful synthesis of the patristic testimonies is provided by V. Pfnür, "Das Kreuz: Lebensbaum in der Mitte des Paradiesgartens". In *Garten des Lebens: Festschrift für Winfrid Cramer*, edited by M.-B. von Stritzky and Christian Uhrig, pp. 203–22. Altenberge: Oros, 1999.

The section on kneeling is to a large extent dependent on:

Sinoir, P. *La Prière à genoux dans l'Écriture Sainte*. Paris: Téqui, 1997.

Many references relevant to the various sections of this chapter can be found in the book mentioned above (part 3, chapter 1), *Arte e liturgia*, especially pp. 139–209.

Kapellari, E. *Heilige Zeichen in Liturgie und Alltag*. Graz: Styria, 1997.

General Index

Aaron (high priest), 29, 36, 77
Abba, 201
Abel, 73, 112
Abodah (prayer), 81
Abraham (patriarch), 30, 51–52, 73, 131, 197
abstraction, 140
acclamation, 222
acheiropoietos (image), 133–35
actio, 71, 185–86, 188–89, 226
action, liturgical, 74, 186, 189, 224, 226
action of God, 187
active participation, 91, 94, 185–91, 229
Adam, 135, 206, 220, 233
Addai, St., 176
adoration, 12–13, 50–51, 61–63, 129, 134, 174, 203, 210, 225; Eucharistic, 63, 99, 104; of the Magi, 124. *See also* worship
"aesthetic", the, 143
Africa, 121, 176, 220
agnosticism, 143
Agnus Dei (hymn), 221
aiōnios, 70
air (element), 235–36
aisles (architecture), 81
Alexandria (city), 54, 59, 113, 121, 174–76, 178

"all in all", 42, 44, 47, 64, 73, 111
All Saints (feast), 146
allegory, 132
altar (church), 36, 61, 84–99, 216, 234; altarpiece, 141, 144; position, 84–87, 90–92, 95, 216
Amos (prophet), 54
anarchy, 32, 169
angels, 121, 131, 139, 167–69; of death, 116. *See also* cherubim and seraphim
Annunciation (feast), 114, 121–22
Anointing of the Sick (sacrament), 235
Antioch (city), 100, 120, 174–76, 178, 197
Antiochus IV Epiphanes, 59
antiquity, 43–44, 60, 92, 95–96, 99, 143, 166–67, 199, 220, 235
Antonians (order), 141
Apollo (Greek god), 164–65
apophatic theology, 138
apostasy, 36–37, 54
apostles, 87, 109, 125, 176–78, 208, 235
apostolic tradition, 82, 84, 178, 180, 183

247

Scripture Index

FATHER ROMANO GUARDINI

The Spirit
of the Liturgy

Translated by Ada Lane

The Prayer of the Liturgy

A N OLD theological proverb says, "Nothing done by
nature and grace is done in vain." Nature and grace
obey their own laws, which are based upon certain established hypotheses. Both the natural and the supernatural
life of the soul, when lived in accordance with these principles, remain healthy, develop, and are enriched. In isolated cases, the rules may be waived without any danger,
when such a course is required or excused by reason of a
spiritual disturbance, imperative necessity, extraordinary
occasion, important end in view, or the like. In the end,
however, this cannot be done with impunity. Just as the
life of the body droops and is stunted when the conditions of its growth are not observed, so it is with spiritual
and religious life—it sickens, losing its vigor, strength,
and unity.

This is even more true where the regular spiritual life
of a corporate body is concerned. Exceptions play a far
greater part, after all, in the life of the individual than
in that of the group. As soon as a group is in question,
concern is immediately aroused with regard to the regulation of those practices and prayers that will constitute
the permanent form of its devotion in common; and then
the crucial question arises whether the fundamental laws
that govern normal interior life—in the natural as in the
supernatural order—are in this case to have currency or
not. For it is a question no longer of the correct attitude to

be adopted, from the spiritual point of view, toward the adjustment of some temporary requirement or need, but of the form to be taken by the permanent legislation that will henceforth exercise an enduring influence upon the soul. This is not intended to regulate entirely independent cases, each on its own merits, but to take into account the average requirements and demands of everyday life. It is to serve as a model, not for the spiritual life of the individual, but for that of a corporate body, composed of the most distinct and varied elements. From this it follows that any defect in its organization will inevitably become both apparent and obtrusive. It is true that at first every mistake will be completely overshadowed by the particular circumstances—the emergency or disturbance—that justified the adoption of that particular line of conduct. But in proportion as the extraordinary symptoms subside and the normal existence of the soul is resumed, the more forcibly every interior mistake is bound to come to light, sowing destruction on all sides in its course.

The fundamental conditions essential to the full expansion of spiritual life as it is lived in common are most clearly discernible in the devotional life of any great community that has spread its development over a long period of time. Its scheme of life has by then matured and developed its full value. In a corporate body—composed of people of highly varied circumstances, drawn from distinct social strata, perhaps even from different races, in the course of different historical and cultural periods— the ephemeral, adventitious, and locally characteristic elements are, to a certain extent, eliminated, and that which is universally accepted as binding and essential comes to the fore. In other words, the canon of spiritual administration becomes, in the course of time, objective and impartial.

The Catholic liturgy is the supreme example of an objectively established rule of spiritual life. It has been able to develop κατὰ τὸν ὅλον, that is to say, in every direction and in accordance with all places, times, and types of human culture. Therefore, it will be the best teacher of the *via ordinaria*—the regulation of religious life in common, with, at the same time, a view to actual needs and requirements.[1]

The significance of the liturgy must, however, be more exactly defined. Our first task will be to establish the quality of its relation to the non-liturgical forms of spiritual life.

The primary and exclusive aim of the liturgy is not the expression of the individual's reverence and worship for God. It is not even concerned with the awakening, formation, and sanctification of the individual soul as such. Nor does the onus of liturgical action and prayer rest with the individual. It does not even rest with the collective groups, composed of numerous individuals, who periodically achieve a limited and intermittent unity in their capacity as the congregation of a church. The liturgical entity consists rather of the united body of the faithful as such—the Church—a body that infinitely outnumbers

---

[1] It is not by chance that "the religious pope" so resolutely took in hand the revision of the liturgy. The internal revival of the Catholic community will not make progress until the liturgy again occupies its rightful position in Catholic life. And the Eucharistic movement can only effectually distribute its blessings when it is in close touch with the liturgy. It was the pope who issued the Communion decrees who also said, "You must not *pray* at Mass, you must *say* Mass!" Only when the Blessed Sacrament is understood from the point of view of the liturgy can it take that active share in the religious regeneration of the world which Pius X expected of it. (In the same way, the full active and moral power of the Blessed Sacrament is only free to operate unchecked when its connection with the problems and tasks of public and family life, and with those of Christian charity and of vocational occupations, is fully comprehended.)

the mere congregation. The liturgy is the Church's public and lawful act of worship, and it is performed and conducted by the officials whom the Church herself has designated for the post—her priests. In the liturgy, God is to be honored by the body of the faithful, and the latter is in its turn to derive sanctification from this act of worship. It is important that this objective nature of the liturgy should be fully understood. Here the Catholic conception of worship in common sharply differs from the Protestant, which is predominatingly individualistic. The fact that the individual Catholic, by his absorption into the higher unity, finds liberty and discipline originates in the twofold nature of man, who is both social and solitary.

Now, side by side with the strictly ritual and entirely objective forms of devotion, others exist, in which the personal element is more strongly marked. To this type belong those that are known as "popular devotions," such as afternoon prayers accompanied by hymns, devotions suited to varying periods, localities, or requirements, and so on. They bear the stamp of their time and surroundings and are the direct expression of the characteristic quality or temper of an individual congregation.

Although in comparison with the prayer of the individual, which is expressive of purely personal needs and aspirations, popular devotions are both communal and objective, they are to a far greater degree characteristic of their origin than is the liturgy, the entirely objective and impersonal method of prayer practiced by the Church as a whole. This is the reason for the greater stress laid by popular devotion upon the individual need of edification. Hence the rules and forms of liturgical practice cannot be taken, without more ado, as the authoritative and decisive standard for non-liturgical prayer. The claim that the liturgy should be taken as the exclusive pattern of devotional practice in common can never be upheld. To do so would be to confess complete ignorance of the spiritual requirements of the greater part of the faithful. The forms of popular piety should rather continue to exist side by side with those of the liturgy and should constitute themselves according to the varying requirements of historical, social, and local conditions. There could be no greater mistake than that of discarding the valuable elements in the spiritual life of the people for the sake of the liturgy or than the desire of assimilating them to it. But in spite of the fact that the liturgy and popular devotion have each their own special premises and aims, still it is to liturgical worship that preeminence of right belongs. The liturgy is and will be the *lex orandi*. Non-liturgical prayer must take the liturgy for its model and must renew itself in the liturgy if it is to retain its vitality. It cannot precisely be said that as dogma is to private religious opinion, so is the liturgy to popular devotion; but the connection between the latter does to a certain degree correspond with that special relation, characteristic of the former, which exists between the government and the governed. All other forms of devotional practice can always measure their shortcomings by the standard of the liturgy and with its help find the surest way back to the *via ordinaria* when they have strayed from it. The changing demands of time, place, and special circumstance can express themselves in popular devotion; facing the latter stands the liturgy, from which clearly issue the fundamental laws—eternally and universally unchanging—that govern all genuine and healthy piety.

In the following pages, an attempt will be made to

select from the liturgy and to analyze several of these laws. But it is an attempt pure and simple, which professes to be neither exhaustive nor conclusive.

The first and most important lesson that the liturgy has to teach is that the prayer of a corporate body must be sustained by thought. The prayers of the liturgy are entirely governed by and interwoven with dogma. Those who are unfamiliar with liturgical prayer often regard them as theological formulae, artistic and didactic, until on closer acquaintance they suddenly perceive and admit that the clear-cut, lucidly constructed phrases are full of interior enlightenment. To give an outstanding example, the wonderful Collects of the Masses of Sunday may be quoted. Wherever the stream of prayer wells abundantly upward, it is always guided into safe channels by means of plain and lucid thought. Interspersed among the pages of the Missal and the Breviary are readings from Holy Scripture and from the works of the Fathers, which continually stimulate thought. Often these readings are introduced and concluded by short prayers of a characteristically contemplative and reflective nature—the antiphons —during which that which has been heard or read has time to cease echoing and to sink into the mind. The liturgy, the *lex orandi*, is, according to the old proverb, the law of faith—the *lex credendi*—as well. It is the treasure-house of the thought of revelation.

This is not, of course, an attempt to deny that the heart and the emotions play an important part in the life of prayer. Prayer is, without a doubt, "a raising of the heart to God". But the heart must be guided, supported, and purified by the mind. In individual cases or on definite and explicit occasions, it may be possible to persist in, and to derive benefit from, emotion pure and simple, either spontaneous or occasioned by a fortunate chance. But a regular and recurrent form of devotion lights upon the most varied moods, because no one day resembles another. If the content of these devotional forms is of a predominatingly emotional character, it will bear the stamp of its fortuitous origin, since the feeling engendered by solitary spiritual occurrences flows for the most part into special and particular channels. Such a prayer therefore will always be unsuitable if it does not harmonize, to a certain degree at least, with the disposition of the person who is to offer it. Unless this condition is complied with, either it is useless or it may even mar the sentiment experienced. The same thing occurs when a form of prayer intended for a particular purpose is considered to be adapted to the most varied occasions.

Only thought is universally current and consistent and, as long as it is really thought, remains suited, to a certain degree, to every intelligence. If prayer in common, therefore, is to prove beneficial to the majority, it must be primarily directed by thought, and not by feeling. It is only when prayer is sustained by and steeped in clear and fruitful religious thought that it can be of service to a corporate body, composed of distinct elements, all actuated by varying emotions.

We have seen that thought alone can keep spiritual life sound and healthy. In the same way, prayer is beneficial only when it rests on the bedrock of truth. This is not meant in the purely negative sense that it must be free from error; in addition to this, it must spring from the fullness of truth. It is only truth—or dogma, to give it its other name—that can make prayer efficacious and impregnate it with that austere, protective strength without which it degenerates into weakness. If this is true of private prayer, it is doubly so of popular devotion, which in many directions verges on sentimentality.[2] Dogmatic thought brings release from the thraldom of individual caprice and from the uncertainty and sluggishness that follow in the wake of emotion. It makes prayer intelligible and causes it to rank as a potent factor in life.

If, however, religious thought is to do justice to its mission, it must introduce into prayer truth in all its fullness.

Various individual truths of revelation hold a special attraction for the temperaments and conditions to which they correspond. It is easy to see that certain people have a pronounced predilection for certain mysteries of faith. This is shown in the case of converts, for instance, by the religious ideas that first arrested their attention at their entry into the Church or that decided them on the step they were taking and, in other cases, by the truths that at the approach of doubt form the mainstay and buttress of the whole house of faith. In the same way, doubt does not charge at random but attacks for the most part those mysteries of faith that appeal least to the temperament of the people concerned.[3]

If a prayer, therefore, stresses any one mystery of faith

[2] A proof of this is to be found in the often sugary productions of sacred art—holy pictures, statues, etc.—which appeal to the people. The people are susceptible to powerful art when it is national; the Middle Ages are a witness to this as are certain aspects of modern art. But the danger of lapsing into mere insipidity is very great. The same thing applies to popular songs and holds good in other directions as well.

[3] This does not mean that these truths are merely a mental indication of the existing spiritual condition of the person concerned. It is rather a proof of the saying, "grace takes nature for granted." Revelation finds in a man's natural turn of mind the necessary spiritual premises by which the truths, which are of themselves mysteries, can be more easily grasped and adhered to.

in an exclusive or an excessive manner, in the end, it will adequately satisfy none but those who are of a corresponding temperament, and even the latter will eventually become conscious of their need of truth in its entirety. For instance, if a prayer deals exclusively with God's mercy, it will not ultimately satisfy even a delicate and tender piety, because this truth calls for its complement—the fact of God's justice and majesty. In any form of prayer, therefore, that is intended for the ultimate use of a corporate body, the whole fullness of religious truth must be included.

Here, too, the liturgy is our teacher. It condenses into prayer the entire body of religious truth. Indeed, it is nothing else but truth expressed in terms of prayer. For it is the great fundamental truths[4] that above all fill the liturgy —God in his mighty reality, perfection, and greatness, One, and Three in One: his creation, providence, and omnipresence; sin, justification, and the desire of salvation; the Redeemer and his Kingdom; the four last things. It is only such an overwhelming abundance of truth that can never pall but continue to be, day after day, all things to all men, ever fresh and inexhaustible.

In the end, therefore, prayer in common will be fruitful only insofar as it does not concentrate markedly, or at any rate exclusively, on particular portions of revealed truth, but embraces, as far as possible, the whole of divine teaching. This is especially important where the people are concerned, because they easily tend to develop a

---

[4] It is a further proof of Pius X's perspicacity that he made universally accessible precisely those portions of the liturgy—Sundays, the weekly office, and especially the daily Masses of Lent—that stress the great fundamental mysteries of faith.

partiality for particular mysteries of faith that for some reason have become dear to them.[5] On the other hand, it is obvious that prayer must not be overladen and, as a result, form a mere hotchpotch of ill-assorted thoughts and ideas—a thing that sometimes does occur. Yet without the element of spaciousness, spiritual life droops and becomes narrow and petty. "The truth shall make you free"—free not only from the thralldom of error, but free as a preparation for the vastness of God's Kingdom.

While the necessity of thought is emphasized, it must not be allowed to degenerate into the mere frigid domination of reason. Devotional forms, on the contrary, should be permeated by warmth of feeling.

On this point as well, the liturgy has many recommendations to make. The ideas that fill it are vital: that is to say, they spring from the impulses of the heart that has been molded by grace and must again, in their turn, affect other eager and ardent hearts. The Church's worship is full of deep feeling, of emotion that is intense and sometimes even vehement. Take the Psalms, for instance —how deeply moving they often are! Listen to the expression of longing in the *Quemadmodum*, of remorse in the *Miserere*, of exultation in the Psalms of praise, and of indignant righteousness in those denouncing the wicked. Or consider the remarkable spiritual tension that lies between the mourning of Good Friday and the joy of Easter morning.

Liturgical emotion is, however, exceedingly instructive.

---

[5] By this we do not mean that specific times (e.g., the stress of war) and conditions (e.g., the special needs of an agricultural or seafaring population) do not bring home certain truths more vividly than others. We are dealing here with the universal principle, which is, however, adaptable and must make allowances for special cases.

It has its moments of supreme climax, in which all bounds are broken, as, for instance, in the limitless rejoicing of the *Exsultet* on Holy Saturday. But, as a rule, it is controlled and subdued. The heart speaks powerfully, but thought at once takes the lead; the forms of prayer are elaborately constructed, the constituent parts carefully counterbalanced; and, as a rule, they deliberately keep emotion under strict control. In this way, in spite of the deep feeling to be found in, say, the Psalms (to instance them once more), a sense of restraint pervades liturgical form.

The liturgy as a whole is not favorable to exuberance of feeling. Emotion glows in its depths, but it smolders merely, like the fiery heart of the volcano, whose summit stands out clear and serene against the quiet sky. The liturgy *is* emotion, but it is emotion under the strictest control. We are made particularly aware of this at Holy Mass, and it applies equally to the prayers of the Ordinary and of the Canon and to those of the Proper of the Time. Among them are to be found masterpieces of spiritual restraint.

The restraint characteristic of the liturgy is at times very pronounced—so much so as to make this form of prayer appear at first as a frigid intellectual production, until we gradually grow familiar with it and realize what vitality pulsates in the clear, measured forms.

And how necessary this discipline is! At certain moments and on certain occasions, it is permissible for emotion to have a vent. But a prayer that is intended for the everyday use of a large body of people must be restrained. If, therefore, it has uncontrolled and unbalanced emotion for a foundation, it is doubly dangerous. It will operate in one of two ways. Either the people who use it will take it seriously and probably will then feel obliged to force themselves into acquiescence with an emotion that they have never, generally speaking, experienced, or which, at any rate, they are not experiencing at that particular moment, thus perverting and degrading their religious feeling. Or else indifference, if they are of a phlegmatic temperament, will come to their aid; they then take the phrases at less than their face value, and consequently the word is depreciated.

Written prayer is certainly intended as a means of instruction and of promoting an increased sensibility. But its remoteness from the average emotional attitude must not be allowed to become too great. If prayer is ultimately to be fruitful and beneficial to a corporate body, it must be intense and profound, but at the same time normally tranquil in tone. The wonderful verses of the hymn— hardly translatable, so full are they of penetrating insight —may be quoted in this connection:

> *Laeti bibamus sobriam*
> *Ebrietatem Spiritus*[6]

Certainly we must not try to measure off the lawful share of emotion with a foot-rule; but where a plain and straightforward expression suffices, we must not aggrandize or embellish it; and a simple method of speech is always to be preferred to an overloaded one.

Again, the liturgy has many suggestions to make on the quality of the emotion required for the particular form of prayer under discussion, which is ultimately to prove universally beneficial. It must not be too choice in expression or spring from special sections of dogma, but it must clearly express the great fundamental feelings, both

[6] From the Benedictine Breviary, Lauds (i.e., the prayer at daybreak) of Tuesday. [Literally, "Let us joyfully taste of the sober drunkenness of the Spirit."]

natural and spiritual, as do the Psalms, for instance, where we find the utterance of adoration, longing for God, gratitude, supplication, awe, remorse, love, readiness for sacrifice, courage in suffering, faith, confidence, and so on. The emotion must not be too acutely penetrating, too tender, or too delicate, but strong, clear, simple, and natural.

Then the liturgy is wonderfully reserved. It scarcely expresses, even, certain aspects of spiritual surrender and submission, or else it veils them in such rich imagery that the soul still feels that it is hidden and secure. The prayer of the Church does not probe and lay bare the heart's secrets; it is as restrained in thought as in imagery; it does, it is true, awaken very profound and very tender emotions and impulses, but it leaves them hidden. There are certain feelings of surrender, certain aspects of interior candor that cannot be publicly proclaimed, at any rate in their entirety, without danger to spiritual modesty. The liturgy has perfected a masterly instrument that has made it possible for us to express our inner life in all its fullness and depth, without divulging our secrets—*secretum meum mihi*. We can pour out our hearts and still feel that nothing has been dragged to light that should remain hidden.[7]

This is equally true of the system of moral conduct that is to be found in prayer.

Liturgical action and liturgical prayer are the logical

[7] The liturgy here accomplishes on the spiritual plane what has been done on the temporal by the dignified forms of social intercourse, the outcome of the tradition created and handed down by sensitive people. This makes communal life possible for the individual and yet insures him against unauthorized interference with his inner self; he can be cordial without sacrificing his spiritual independence; he is in communication with his neighbor without on that account being swallowed up and lost among the crowd. In the same way, the liturgy preserves freedom of spiritual movement for the soul by means of a wonderful union of spontaneity and the finest erudition. It extols *urbanitas* as the best antidote to barbarism, which triumphs when spontaneity and culture alike are no more.

consequences of certain moral premises—the desire for justification, contrition, readiness for sacrifice, and so on —and often issue afresh into moral actions. But here again, it is possible to observe a fine distinction. The liturgy does not lightly exact moral actions of a very far-reaching nature, especially those that denote an interior decision. It requires them where the matter is of real importance, for example, the abjuration at Baptism or the vows at the final reception into an Order. When, however, it is a question of making regular daily prayer fruitful in everyday intentions and decisions, the liturgy is very cautious. For instance, it does not rashly utter such things as vows or full and permanent repudiations of sin, entire and lasting surrender, all-embracing consecration of one's entire being, utter contempt for and renouncement of the world, promises of exclusive love, and the like. Such ideas are present at times, fairly frequently even, but generally under the form of a humble entreaty that the suppliant may be vouchsafed similar sentiments or that he is encouraged to ponder upon their goodness and nobility or is exhorted on the same subject. But the liturgy avoids the frequent use of those prayers in which these moral actions are specifically expressed.

How right this is! In moments of exaltation and in the hour of decision, such a manner of speech may be justified and even necessary. But when it is a question of the daily spiritual life of a corporate body, such formulas, when frequently repeated, offer those who are using them an unfortunate selection from which to make their choice. Perhaps they take the formulas literally and endeavor to kindle the moral sentiments expressed in them, discovering later that it is often difficult, and sometimes impossible, to do so truthfully and effectually. They are consequently in danger of developing artificial sentiments, of forcing intentions that still remain beyond their compass, and of daily performing moral actions that of their very nature cannot be frequently accomplished. Or else they take the words merely as a passing recommendation of a line of conduct that it would be well to adopt and, in this way, depreciate the intrinsic moral value of the formula, although it may be used frequently and in all good faith. In this connection are applicable the words of Christ, "Let what you say be simply 'Yes' or 'No'" (Mt 5:37).

The liturgy has solved the problem of providing a constant incentive to the highest moral aims and, at the same time, of remaining true and lofty, while satisfying everyday needs.

Another question that arises is that concerning the form to be taken by prayer in common. We may put it like this: What method of prayer is capable of transforming the souls of a great multitude of people and of making this transformation permanent?

The model of all devotional practice in common is to be found in the Divine Office, which day after day gathers together great bodies of people at stated times for a particular purpose. If anywhere, then it is in the Office that those conditions will be found that are favorable to the framing of rules for the forms of prayer in common.[8]

It is of paramount importance that the whole gathering should take an active share in the proceedings. If those

---

[8] We do not overlook the fact that the Office, in its turn, presupposes its special relations and conditions, from which useful hints may be gained for private devotion, such as the necessity for a great deal of leisure, which enables the soul to meditate more deeply; and a special erudition, which opens the mind to the world of ideas and to artistry of form, and so on.

composing the gathering merely listen, while one of the number acts as spokesman, the interior movement soon stagnates. All present, therefore, are obliged to take part. It is not even sufficient for the gathering to do so by repeating the words of their leader. This type of prayer does, of course, find a place in the liturgy, for example, in the litany. It is perfectly legitimate, and people desirous of abandoning it totally fail to recognize the requirements of the human soul. In the litany, the congregation answers the varying invocations of the leader with an identical act, for example, with a request. In this way, the act each time acquires a fresh content and fresh fervor, and an intensification of ardor is the result. It is a method better suited than any other to express a strong, urgent desire or a surrender to God's will, presenting as it does the petition of all sides effectively and simultaneously.

But the liturgy does not employ this method of prayer frequently; we may even say, when we consider divine worship as a whole, that it employs it but seldom. And rightly so, for it is a method that runs the risk of numbing and paralyzing spiritual movement.[9] The liturgy adapts the dramatic form by choice to the fundamental require-

---

[9] The foregoing remarks on the liturgy have already made it abundantly clear that the justification of methods of prayer such as, e.g., the Rosary, must not be gainsaid. They have a necessary and peculiar effect in the spiritual life. They clearly express the difference that exists between liturgical and popular prayer. The liturgy has for its fundamental principle *Ne bis idem* [there must be no repetition]. It aims at a continuous progress of ideas, mood, and intention. Popular devotion, on the contrary, has a strongly contemplative character and loves to linger around a few simple images, ideas, and moods without any swift changes of thought. For the people, the forms of devotion are often merely a means of being with God. On this account, they love repetition. The ever-renewed requests of the Our Father, Hail Mary, etc., are for them at the same time receptacles into which they can pour their hearts.

ments of prayer in common. It divides those present into two choirs and causes prayer to progress by means of dialogue. In this way, all present join the proceedings and are obliged to follow with a certain amount of attention at least, knowing as they do that the continuation of their combined action depends upon each one personally.

Here the liturgy lays down one of the fundamental principles of prayer that cannot be neglected with impunity.[10] However justified the purely responsive forms of prayer may be, the primary form of prayer in common is the actively progressive—that much we learn from the *lex orandi*. And the question, intensely important today, as to the right method to employ in again winning people to the life of the Church is most closely connected with the question under discussion. For it is modern people precisely who insist upon vital and progressive movement and an active share in things. The fluid mass of this overwhelming spiritual material, however, needs cutting down and fashioning. It requires a leader to regulate the beginning, omissions, and end and, in addition, to organize the external procedure. The leader also has to model it interiorly; thus, for instance, he has to introduce the recurrent thought-theme, himself undertaking the harder portions, in order that they may be adequately and conscientiously dealt with; he must express the emotion of

[10] In earlier ages, the Church practiced by preference the so-called "responsive" form of chanting the Psalms. The Precentor chanted one verse after the other, and the people answered with the identical verse or the partially repeated verse. But at the same time, another method was in use, according to which the people divided into two choirs, and each alternately chanted a verse of the psalm. It says much for the sureness of liturgical instinct that the second method entirely supplanted the first. Cf. Valentin Thalhofer and Ludwig Eisenhofer, *Handbuch der katholischen Liturgik*, (Freiburg: Herder, 1902), 1:261ff.

all present by means of climaxes and introduce certain restful pauses by the inclusion of didactic or meditative portions. Such is the task of the choir-leader, which has undergone a carefully graduated course of development in the liturgy.

Attention has already been called to the deep and fruitful emotion that is contained in the liturgy. It also embraces the two fundamental forces of human existence: nature and civilization.

In the liturgy, the voice of nature makes itself heard clearly and decisively. We only need to read the Psalms to see man as he really is. There the soul is shown as courageous and despondent, happy and sorrowful, full of noble intentions, but of sin and struggles as well, zealous for everything that is good and then again apathetic and dejected. Or let us take the readings from the Old Testament. How frankly human nature is revealed in them! There is no attempt at extenuation or excuse. The same thing applies to the Church's words of ordination and to the prayers used in administering the sacraments. A truly refreshing spontaneity characterizes them; they call things by their names. Man is full of weakness and error, and the liturgy acknowledges this. Human nature is inexplicable, a tangled web of splendor and misery, of greatness and baseness, and as such it appears in the prayer of the Church. Here we find no carefully adapted portrait from which the harsh and unpleasing traits have been excluded, but man as he is.

Not less rich is the liturgy's cultural heritage. We become conscious of the fact that many centuries have cooperated in its formation and have bequeathed to it of their best. They have fashioned its language; expanded its ideas and conceptions in every direction; developed

its beauty of construction down to the smallest detail—
the short verses and the finely forged links of the prayers,
the artistic form of the Divine Office and of the Mass,
and the wonderful whole that is the ecclesiastical year.
Action, narrative, and choral forms combine to produce
the cumulative effect. The style of the individual forms
continually varies—simple and clear in the Hours, rich
in mystery on the festivals of Mary, resplendent on the
more modern feasts, delightful and full of charm in the
offices of the early virgin-martyrs. To this we should add
the entire group of ritual gestures and action, the liturgical vessels and vestments, and the works of sculptors and
artists and musicians.

In all this is to be learned a really important lesson on
liturgical practice. Religion needs civilization. By civilization we mean the essence of the most valuable products
of man's creative, constructive, and organizing powers—
works of art, science, social orders, and the like. In the
liturgy, it is civilization's task to give durable form and
expression to the treasure of truths, aims, and supernatural activity that God has delivered to man by revelation,
to distill its quintessence, and to relate this to life in all
its multiplicity. Civilization is incapable of creating a religion, but it can supply the latter with a *modus operandi*,
so that it can freely engage in its beneficent activity. That
is the real meaning of the old proverb, *Philosophia ancilla
theologiae*—philosophy is the handmaid of theology. It applies to all the products of civilization, and the Church
has always acted in accordance with it. Thus she knew
very well what she was doing, for instance, when she absolutely obliged the Order of Saint Francis—brimming
over with high aspirations and spiritual energy and initiative—to adopt a certain standard of living, property,

learning, and so on. Only a prejudiced mind, with no conception of the fundamental conditions essential to normal spiritual life, would see in this any deterioration of the first high aims. By her action in the matter, the Church, on the contrary, prepared the ground for the Order, so that in the end it could remain healthy and productive. Individuals, or short waves of enthusiasm, can to a wide degree dispense with learning and culture. This is proved by the beginnings of the desert Orders in Egypt and of the mendicant friars and by holy people in all ages. But, generally speaking, a fairly high degree of genuine learning and culture is necessary in the long run in order to keep spiritual life healthy. By means of these two things, spiritual life retains its energy, clearness, and catholicity. Culture preserves spiritual life from the unhealthy, eccentric, and one-sided elements with which it tends to get involved only too easily. Culture enables religion to express itself and helps it to distinguish what is essential from what is non-essential, the means from the end, and the path from the goal. The Church has always condemned every attempt at attacking science, art, property, and so on. The same Church that so resolutely stresses the "one thing necessary" and that upholds with the greatest impressiveness the teaching of the Evangelical Counsels —that we must be ready to sacrifice everything for the sake of eternal salvation—nevertheless desires, as a rule, that spiritual life should be impregnated with the wholesome salt of genuine and lofty culture.

But spiritual life is in precisely as great a need of the subsoil of healthy nature—"grace takes nature for granted." The Church has clearly shown her views on the subject by the gigantic struggles waged against Gnosticism and Manicheeism, against the Catharists and the Albigenses, against Jansenism and every kind of fanaticism. This was done by the same Church that, in the face of Pelagius and Celestius, of Jovinian and Helvidius, and of the immoderate exaltation of nature, powerfully affirmed the existence of grace and of the supernatural order and asserted that the Christian must overcome nature. The lack of fruitful and lofty culture causes spiritual life to grow numbed and narrow; the lack of the subsoil of healthy nature makes it develop on mawkish, perverted, and unfruitful lines. If the cultural element of prayer declines, the ideas become impoverished, the language coarse, the imagery clumsy and monotonous; in the same way, when the life-blood of nature no longer flows vigorously in its veins, the ideas become empty and tedious, the emotion paltry and artificial, and the imagery lifeless and insipid. Both—the lack of natural vigor and the lack of lofty culture—together constitute what we call barbarism, that is, the exact contradiction of that *scientia vocis* which is revealed in liturgical prayer and is reverenced by the liturgy itself as the sublime prerogative of the holy Creative Principle.[11]

Prayer must be simple, wholesome, and powerful. It must be closely related to actuality and not afraid to call things by their names. In prayer, we must find our entire life over again. On the other hand, it must be rich in ideas

[11] The above remarks must not be misunderstood. Certainly the grace of God is self-sufficient; neither nature nor the work of man is necessary in order that a soul may be sanctified. God "can awaken of these stones children to Abraham". But as a rule, he wishes that everything that belongs to man in the way of good, lofty, natural, and cultural possessions shall be placed at the disposal of religion and so serve the Kingdom of God. He has interconnected the natural and the supernatural order and has given natural things a place in the scheme of his supernatural designs. It is the duty of his representative on earth, ecclesiastical authority, to decide how and to what extent these natural means of attaining the supernatural goal are to be utilized.

and powerful images and speak a developed but restrained language; its construction must be clear and obvious to the simple man, stimulating and refreshing to the man of culture. It must be intimately blended with an erudition that is in nowise obtrusive but that is rooted in breadth of spiritual outlook and in inward restraint of thought, volition, and emotion.

And that is precisely the way in which the prayer of the liturgy has been formed.

The Fellowship of the Liturgy

T HE LITURGY does not say "I", but "We", unless the
particular action that is being performed specifically
requires the singular number (for example, a personal
declaration, certain prayers offered by the bishop or the
priest in his official capacity, and so on). The liturgy is
celebrated, not by the individual, but by the body of the
faithful. This is not composed merely of the persons who
may be present in church; it is not the assembled congregation. On the contrary, it reaches out beyond the bounds
of space to embrace all the faithful on earth. Simultaneously it reaches beyond the bounds of time, to this extent, that the body that is praying upon earth knows itself
to be at one with those for whom time no longer exists,
who, being perfected, exist in eternity.

Yet this definition does not exhaust the conception of
the universality and the all-embracingness that characterize the fellowship of the liturgy. The entity that performs
the liturgical actions is not merely the sum total of all
individual Catholics. It *does* consist of all these united in
one body, but only insofar as this unity is of itself something, apart from the millions who compose it. And that
something is the Church.

Here we find an analogy with what happens in the body
politic. The State is more than the sum total of citizens,
authorities, laws, organizations, and so on. In this connection, discussion of the time-honored question—whether

this higher unity is real or imagined—is beside the point. In any case, as far as personal perception is concerned, it does exist. The members of a State are conscious not only of being parts of a greater whole, but also of being, as it were, members of an overlapping, fundamental, living unity.

On an essentially different plane—the supernatural—a more or less corresponding phenomenon may be witnessed in the Church. The Church is self-contained, a structure-system of intricate and invisible vital principles, of means and ends, of activity and production, of people, organizations, and laws. It does consist of the faithful, then; but it is more than the mere body of these, passively held together by a system of similar convictions and regulations. The faithful are actively united by a vital and fundamental principle common to them all. That principle is Christ himself; his life is ours; we are incorporated in him; we are his Body, *Corpus Christi mysticum*.[1] The active force that governs this living unity, grafting the individual onto it, granting him a share in its fellowship and preserving this right for him, is the Holy Spirit.[2] Every individual Catholic is a cell of this living organism or a member of this Body.

The individual is made aware of the unity that comprehends him on many and various occasions, but chiefly in the liturgy. In it he sees himself face to face with God, not as an entity, but as a member of this unity. It is the unity that addresses God; the individual merely speaks in it, and it requires of him that he should know and acknowledge that he is a member of it.

[1] Cf. Rom 12:4–5; 1 Cor 12:4–6; Eph, chaps. 1–4; Col 1:15–20, and elsewhere.
[2] Cf. 1 Cor 12:4–11; M.J. Scheeben, *Die Mysterien des Christentums* (Freiburg: Herder, 1912), 314–508.

It is on the plane of liturgical relations that the individual experiences the meaning of religious fellowship. The individual—provided that he actually desires to take part in the celebration of the liturgy—must realize that it is as a member of the Church that he, and the Church within him, acts and prays; he must know that in this higher unity, he is at one with the rest of the faithful, and he must desire to be so.

From this, however, arises a very perceptible difficulty. It is chiefly to be traced to a more common one, concerning the relation between the individual and the community. The religious community, like every other, exacts two things from the individual. The first is a sacrifice, which consists in the renouncement by the individual of everything in him that exists merely for itself and excludes others, while and insofar as he is an active member of the community: he must lay self aside and live with, and for, others, sacrificing to the community a proportion of his self-sufficiency and independence. In the second place, he must produce something; and that something is the widened outlook resulting from his acceptance and assimilation of a more comprehensive scheme of life than his own—that of the community.

This demand will be differently met, according to the disposition of each individual. Perhaps it will be the more impersonal element of spiritual life—the ideas, the ordering of instruments and designs, the objectives, laws, and rules, the tasks to be accomplished, the duties and rights, and so on—that first arrests the attention. Both the sacrifice and production indicated above will in such cases assume a more concrete character. The individual has to renounce his own ideas and his own way. He is obliged to subscribe to the ideas and to follow the lead of the liturgy. To it he must surrender his independence; pray

with others, and not alone; obey, instead of freely disposing of himself; and stand in the ranks, instead of moving
about at his own will and pleasure. It is, furthermore,
the task of the individual to apprehend clearly the ideal
world of the liturgy. He must shake off the narrow tram-
mels of his own thought and make his own a far more
comprehensive world of ideas; he must go beyond his
little personal aims and adopt the educative purpose of
the great fellowship of the liturgy. It goes without saying, therefore, that he is obliged to take part in exercises
that do not respond to the particular needs of which he is
conscious; that he must ask for things that do not directly
concern him; espouse and plead before God causes that
do not affect him personally and that merely arise out of
the needs of the community at large; he must at times
—and this is inevitable in so richly developed a system
of symbols, prayer, and action—take part in proceedings
of which he does not entirely, if at all, understand the
significance.

All this is particularly difficult for modern people, who
find it so hard to renounce their independence. And yet
people who are perfectly ready to play a subordinate part
in State and commercial affairs are all the more susceptible
and the more passionately reluctant to regulate their spiritual lives by dictates other than those of their private and
personal requirements. The requirements of the liturgy
can be summed up in one word, humility. Humility by
renunciation; that is to say, by the abdication of self-rule
and self-sufficiency. And humility by positive action; that
is to say, by the acceptance of the spiritual principles that
the liturgy offers and that far transcend the little world
of individual spiritual existence.

The demands of the liturgy's communal life wear a different aspect for the people who are less affected by its concrete and impersonal side. For the latter, the problem of fellowship does not so much consist in the question of how they are to assimilate the universal and, as it were, concrete element, at the same time subordinating themselves to and dovetailing into it. The difficulty rather lies in their being required to divide their existence with other people, to share the intimacy of their inner life, their feeling and willing, with others; and to know that they are united with these others in a higher unity. And by others we mean, not one or two neighbors or a small circle of people, congenial by reason of similar aims or special relations, but with all, even with those who are indifferent, adverse, or even hostilely minded.

The demand here resolves itself into the breaking down of the barriers that the more sensitive soul sets around its spiritual life. The soul must issue forth from these if it is to go among others and share their existence. Just as in the first case the community was perceived as a great concrete order, in the second it is perceived as a broad tissue of personal affinities, an endless interweaving of living reciprocal relations. The sacrifice required in the first place is that of renouncing the right of self-determination in spiritual activity; in the second, that of renouncing spiritual isolation. There it is a question of subordinating self to a fixed and objective order, here of sharing life in common with other people. There, humility is required; here, charity and vigorous expansion of self. There, the given spiritual content of the liturgy must be assimilated; here, life must be lived in common with the other members of Christ's Body, their petitions included with one's own, their needs voiced as one's own. There, "We" is the expression of selfless objectivity; here, it signifies that he who employs it is expanding his inner life in order to include that of others and to assimilate theirs to his. In the first case, the pride that insists upon independence and the aggressive intolerance often bred by individual existence must be overcome, while the entire system of communal aims and ideas must be assimilated; in the second, the repulsion occasioned by the strangeness of corporate life must be mastered, and the shrinking from self-expansion and that exclusiveness triumphed over which leads us to desire only the company of such as we have ourselves chosen and to whom we have voluntarily opened out. Here, too, is required continual spiritual abnegation, a continuous projection of self at the desire of others, and a great and wonderful love that is ready to participate in their life and to make that life its own.

Yet the subordination of self is actually facilitated by a peculiarity inherent in liturgical life itself. It forms at once the complement of and contrast to what has already been discussed. Let us call the disposition manifesting itself in the two forms indicated above the individualistic. Facing it stands the social disposition, which eagerly and consistently craves for fellowship and lives in terms of "we" just as involuntarily as the former bases itself on the exclusive "I". The social disposition will, when it is spiritually active, automatically seek out congenial associates; and their joint striving toward union will be characterized by a firmness and decision alien to the liturgy. It is sufficient to recall in this connection the systems of spiritual association and fellowship peculiar to certain sects. Here at times the bounds of personality diminish to such an extent that all spiritual reserve is lost and, frequently, all external reserve as well. Naturally this description only applies to extreme cases, but it still shows the tendency of the social urge in such dispositions. For this reason, people like this will not find all their expectations immediately fulfilled in the liturgy. The fellowship of the liturgy will to them appear frigid and restricted. From which it follows that this fellowship, however complete and genuine it may be, still acts as a check upon unconditional self-surrender. The social urge is opposed by an equally powerful tendency that sees to it that a certain fixed boundary is maintained. The individual is, it is true, a member of the whole—but he is only a member. He is not utterly merged in it; he is added to it, but in such a way that he throughout remains an entity, existing of himself. This is notably borne out by the fact that the union of the members is not directly accomplished from man to man. It is accomplished by and in their joint aim, goal, and spiritual resting place—God—by their identical creed, sacrifice, and sacraments. In the liturgy, it is of very rare occurrence that speech and response and action or gesture are immediately directed from one member of the fellowship to the other.[3] When this does occur, it is generally worthwhile to observe the great restraint that characterizes such communication. It is governed by strict regulations. The individual is never drawn into contacts that are too extensively direct. He is always free to decide how far he is to get into touch, from the spiritual point of view, with others in that which is common to them all, in God. Take the kiss of peace, for instance; when it is performed according to the rubric, it is a masterly manifestation of restrained and elevated social solidarity.

This is of great importance. It is hardly necessary to point out what would be the infallible consequences of

[3] This does not apply, of course, to the communication between the hierarchical persons and the faithful. This relation is continual and direct.

attempting to transmit the consciousness of their fellow-ship in the liturgy directly from one individual to another. The history of the sects teems with examples bearing on this point. For this reason, the liturgy sets strict bounds between individuals. Their union is moderated by a continually watchful sentiment of disparity and by reciprocal reverence. Their fellowship notwithstanding, the one individual can never force his way into the intimacy of the other, never influence the latter's prayers and actions or force upon the latter his own characteristics, feelings, and perceptions. Their fellowship consists in community of intention, thought, and language, in the direction of eyes and heart to the one aim; it consists in their identical belief, the identical sacrifice that they offer, the Divine Food that nourishes them all alike; in the one God and Lord who unites them mystically in himself. But individuals in their quality of distinct corporeal entities do not among themselves intrude upon each other's inner life.

It is this reserve alone that in the end makes fellow-ship in the liturgy possible; but for it the latter would be unendurable. By this reserve, again, the liturgy keeps all vulgarizing elements at a distance. It never allows the soul to feel that it is imprisoned with others or that its independence and intimacy are threatened with invasion.

From the man of individualistic disposition, then, a sacrifice for the good of the community is required; from the man of social disposition, submission to the austere restraint that characterizes liturgical fellowship. While the former must accustom himself to frequenting the company of his fellows and must acknowledge that he is only a man among men, the latter must learn to subscribe to the noble, restrained forms that etiquette requires in the House and at the Court of the Divine Majesty.

The Style of the Liturgy

S TYLE IS chiefly spoken of in a universal sense. By style we understand those particular characteristics that distinguish every valid and genuine production or organism as such, whether it is a work of art, a personality, a form of society, or anything whatever; it denotes that any given vital principle has found its true and final expression. But this self-expression must be of such a nature that it simultaneously imparts to the individual element a universal significance, reaching far beyond its own particular sphere. For the essence of individuality embraces within itself a second element; it is true that it is particular and unreproducible, but it is at the same time universal, standing in relationship to the other individuals of its kind and manifesting in its permanent existence traits that are also borne by others. The greater the originality and forcefulness of an individual thing, the greater its capacity of comprehensively revealing the universal essence of its kind,[1] the greater is its significance. Now if a personality, a work of art, or a form of society has, by virtue of its existence and activity, expressed in a convincing manner that which it really is, and if at the same time by its quality of specialness it does not merely represent an arbitrary mood, but its relation to a corporate life, then and to that extent it may be said to have style.

---

[1] The essence of genius, of the man of genius (e.g., of the saint), and of the really great work or deed consists in this, that it is immeasurably original and yet is still universally applicable to human life.

In this sense, the liturgy undoubtedly has created a style. It is unnecessary to waste further words on the subject.

The conception can, however, be given a narrower sense. Why is it that in front of a Greek temple we are more intensely conscious of style than we are in front of a Gothic cathedral? The inner effect of both these structures is identically powerful and convincing. Each is the perfect expression of a particular type or form of space-perception. Each reveals the individuality of a people but, at the same time, affords a profound insight into the human soul and the significance of the world in general. Yet before the temple of Praetum we are more strongly conscious of style than we are before the cathedrals of Cologne and of Rheims. What is the reason? Why is it that for the uncultured observer Giotto has the more style in comparison with Grünewald, who is without any doubt equally powerful; and the figure of an Egyptian king more than Donatello's wonderful statue of Saint John?

In this connection, the word *style* has a specialized meaning. It conveys that in the works of art to which reference has been made the individual yields place to the universal. The fortuitous element—determined by place and time, with its significance restricted to certain specific people—is superseded by that which is essentially, or at least more essentially, intended for many times, places, and people. The particular is to a great degree absorbed by the universal and ideal. In such works, an involved mental or spiritual condition, for instance, that could only have expressed itself in an abstruse utterance or in an unreproducible action, is simplified and reduced to its elements.[2] By this process, it is made universally comprehensible.

[2] Cf. the inner life in Ibsen's plays, for instance, with that of Sophoclean tragedy, *Ghosts*, perhaps, with *Oedipus*.

The incalculable ebullition is given a permanent basis. It then becomes easily penetrable and capable of demonstrating in itself the interweaving of cause and effect.[3] The solitary historical event serves to throw into relief the vital significance, universal and unaffected by time, that reposes within it. The figure that appears but once is made to personify characteristics common to the whole of society. The hasty, impetuous movement is restrained and measured. Whereas it was formerly confined to specific relationships or circumstances, it can now to a certain degree be accepted by everyone.[4] Things, materials, and instruments are divested of their fortuitous character, their elements revealed, their purpose defined, and their power of expressing certain moods or ideas is heightened.[5] In a word, while one type of art and of life is endeavoring to express that which is special and particular, this other, on the contrary, is striving to hold up to our view that which is universally significant. The latter type of art fashions simple reality, which is always specialized, in such a manner that the ideal and universal comes to the fore; that is to say, its style is developed and its form is fixed. And so whenever life, with its entanglements and its multiplicity, has been simplified in this way, whenever its inner lawfulness is emphasized and it is raised from the particular to the universal, we are always conscious of style in the narrower sense of the word. Admittedly, it is difficult to say where style ends and arrangement begins. If the arrangement is too accentuated, if the modeling is carried out according to rules and ideas, and not according to its vital connection with reality, if the production is the result, not of exact observation, but of deliberate

---

[3] Cf. the line of action adopted by, e.g., Hedda Gabler and Antigone.

[4] Such is the origin of social deportment and of court usage.

[5] Such is the origin of symbols—social, state, religious, and otherwise.

planning, then it will be universal only and, therefore, lifeless and void.[6] True style, even in its strictest form, still retains the developed faculty of convincing expression. Only that which is living has style; pure thought, and the productions of pure thought, have none.

Now the liturgy—at any rate, as far as the greater part of its range is concerned—has style in the stricter sense of the word. It is not the direct expression of any particular type of spiritual disposition, either in its language and ideas or in its movements, actions, and the materials that it employs. If we compare, for instance, the Sunday Collects with the prayers of an Anselm of Canterbury or of a Newman; the gestures of the officiating priest with the involuntary movements of the man who fancies himself unobserved while at prayer; the Church's directions on the adornment of the sanctuary, on vestments and altar-vessels, with popular methods of decoration and of dress on religious occasions; and Gregorian chant with the popular hymn—we shall always find, within the sphere of the liturgy, that the medium of spiritual expression, whether it consists of words, gestures, colors, or materials, is to a certain degree divested of its singleness of purpose, intensified, tranquilized, and given universal currency.

Many causes have contributed to this result. For one thing, the passing centuries have continually polished, elaborated, and adapted the form of liturgical expression. Then the strongly generalizing effect of religious thought must be taken into account. Finally, there is the influence of the Greco-Latin spirit, with its highly significant tendency toward style in the strict sense of the word.

Now if we consider the fact that these quietly construc-

[6] It is this that differentiates various classical periods from the classical age.

tive forces were at work on the vital form of expression, not of an individual, but of an organic unity, composed of the greatness, exclusiveness, and strength of the collective consciousness that is the Catholic Church; if we consider further that the vital formula thus fashioned steadily concentrates its whole attention upon the hereafter, that it aspires from this world to the next and, as a natural result, is characterized by eternal, sublime, and superhuman traits, then we shall find assembled here all the preliminary conditions essential to the development of a style of great vigor and intensity. If it were capable of doing so anywhere, here above all should develop a living style, spiritual, lofty, and exalted. And that is precisely what has happened. If we reflect upon the liturgy as a whole and upon its important points, not upon the abbreviated form in which it is usually presented, but as it should be, we shall have the good fortune to experience the miracle of a truly mighty style. We shall see and feel that an inner world of immeasurable breadth and depth has created for itself so rich and so ample an expression, and one at the same time so lucid and so universal in form, that its like has never been seen, either before or since.

And it is style in the stricter sense of the word as well —clear in language, measured in movement, severe in its modeling of space, materials, colors, and sounds; its ideas, languages, ceremonies, and imagery fashioned out of the simple elements of spiritual life; rich, varied, and lucid; its force further intensified by the fact that the liturgy employs a classic language, remote from everyday life.

When all these considerations are borne in mind, it is easy to understand that the liturgy possesses a tremendously compelling form of expression, which is a school of religious training and development to the Catholic who rightly understands it and which is bound to appear to the impartial observer as a cultural formation of the most lofty and elevated kind.

It cannot, however, be denied that great difficulties lie in the question of the adaptability of the liturgy to every individual and, more especially, to the modern man. The latter wants to find in prayer—particularly if he is of an independent turn of mind—the direct expression of his spiritual condition. Yet in the liturgy, he is expected to accept, as the mouthpiece of his inner life, a system of ideas, prayer, and action that is too highly generalized and, as it were, unsuited to him. It strikes him as being formal and almost meaningless. He is especially sensible of this when he compares the liturgy with the natural outpourings of spontaneous prayer. Liturgical formulas, unlike the language of a person who is spiritually congenial, are not to be grasped straightway without any further mental exertion on the listener's part; liturgical actions have not the same direct appeal as, say, the involuntary movement of understanding on the part of someone who is sympathetic by reason of circumstances and disposition; the emotional impulses of the liturgy do not so readily find an echo as does the spontaneous utterance of the soul. These clear-cut formulas are liable to grate more particularly upon the modern man, so intensely sensitive in everything that affects his scheme of life, who looks for a touch of nature everywhere and listens so attentively for the personal note. He easily tends to consider the idiom of the liturgy as artificial and its ritual as purely formal. Consequently, he will often take refuge in forms of prayer and devotional practices whose spiritual value is far inferior to that of the liturgy but that seem to have one advantage over the latter—that of contemporary or, at any rate, of congenial origin.

Those who honestly want to come to grips with this problem in all its bearings should for their own guidance note the way in which the figure of Christ is represented, first in the liturgy and then in the Gospels. In the latter, everything is alive; the reader breathes the air of earth; he sees Jesus of Nazareth walking about the streets and among the people, hears his incomparable and persuasive words, and is aware of the heart-to-heart intercourse between Jesus and his followers. The charm of vivid actuality pervades the historical portrait of Christ. He is so entirely one of us, a real person—Jesus, "the carpenter's son"—who lived in Nazareth in a certain street, wore certain clothes, and spoke in a certain manner. That is just what the modern man longs for; and he is made happy by the fact that in this actual historical figure is incarnate the living and eternal Godhead, One with the body, so that he is in the fullest sense of the word "true God and true Man".

But how differently does the figure of Jesus appear in the liturgy! There he is the Sovereign Mediator between God and man, the eternal High Priest, the divine Teacher, the Judge of the living and of the dead; in his Body, hidden in the Eucharist, he mystically unites all the faithful in the great society that is the Church; he is the God-Man, the Word that was made Flesh. The human element, or—involuntarily the theological expression rises to the lips—the Human Nature certainly remains intact, for the battle against Eutyches was not fought in vain; he is truly and wholly human, with a body and soul that have actually lived. But they are now utterly transformed by the Godhead, rapt into the light of eternity, and remote from time and space. He is the Lord, "sitting at the right hand of the Father", the mystic Christ living on in his Church.

It will be objected that in the Gospels of the Mass, we can still follow the historical life of Jesus in its entirety. That is absolutely true. But if we endeavor to listen more attentively, we shall still find that a particular light is thrown on these narratives by their context. They are a part of the Mass, of the *mysterium magnum*, pervaded by the mystery of sacrifice, an integral part of the structure of the particular Sunday office, current season, or ecclesiastical year, swept along by that powerful straining upward to the Hereafter that runs through the entire liturgy. In this way, the contents of the Gospels, which we hear chanted and in a foreign language, are in their turn woven into the pattern. Of ourselves, we come to consider, not the particular traits that they contain, but their eternal, super-historical meaning.

Yet by this the liturgy has not—as Protestantism has sometimes accused it of doing—disfigured the Christ of the Gospels. It has not set forth a frigid intellectual conception instead of the living Jesus.

The Gospels themselves, according to the aims and purpose of the respective Evangelists, stress first one, then another aspect of the personality and activity of Christ. Facing the portrait contained in the first three Gospels, in the epistles of Saint Paul, Christ appears as God, mystically living on in his Church and in the souls of those who believe in him. The Gospel of Saint John shows the Word made Flesh and, finally, in the Apocalypse, God is made manifest in his eternal splendor. But this does not mean that the historical facts of Christ's human existence are in any way kept back; on the contrary, they are always taken for granted and often purposely emphasized.[7] The

---

[7] As, for instance, in the beginning of the Gospel of Saint John.

liturgy therefore has done nothing that Holy Scripture itself does not do. Without discarding one stroke or trait of the historical figure of Christ, it has, for its own appointed purpose, more strongly stressed the eternal and super-temporal elements of that figure, and for this reason —the liturgy is no mere commemoration of what once existed, but is living and real; it is the enduring life of Jesus Christ in us and that of the believer in Christ, eternally God and Man.

It is precisely because of this, however, that the difficulty still persists. It is good to make it absolutely clear, since the modern man experiences it more especially. More than one—according to his instinctive impulse— would be content to forego the most profound knowledge of theology if as against that it were permitted to him to watch Jesus walking about the streets or to hear the tone in which he addresses a disciple. More than one would be willing to sacrifice the most beautiful liturgical prayer if, in exchange, he might meet Christ face to face and speak to him from the bottom of his heart.

Where is the angle to be found from which this difficulty is to be tackled and overcome? It is in the view that it is hardly permissible to play off the spiritual life of the individual, with its purely personal bearing, against the spiritual life of the liturgy, with its generalizing bias. They are not mutually contradictory; they should both combine in active cooperation.

When we pray on our own behalf, only we approach God from an entirely personal standpoint, precisely as we feel inclined or impelled to do according to our feelings and circumstances. That is our right, and the Church would be the last to wish to deprive us of it. Here we live our own life and are, as it were, face to face with

God.[8] His Face is turned toward us, as to no one else; he belongs to each one of us. It is this power of being a personal God, ever fresh to each of us, equally patient and attentive to each one's wants, that constitutes the inexhaustible wealth of God. The language that we speak on these occasions suits us entirely, and much of it apparently is suited to us alone. We can use it with confidence because God understands it, and there is no one else who needs to do so.

We are, however, not only individuals but members of a community as well; we are not merely transitory, but something of us belongs to eternity, and the liturgy takes these elements in us into account. In the liturgy, we pray as members of the Church; by it, we rise to the sphere that transcends the individual order and is therefore accessible to people of every condition, time, and place. For this order of things, the style of the liturgy—vital, clear, and universally comprehensible—is the only possible one. The reason for this is that any other type of prayer, based upon one particular set of hypotheses or requirements, would undoubtedly prove a totally unsuitable form for a content of different origin. Only a system of life and thought that is truly Catholic—that is to say, actual and universal—is capable of being universally adopted without violence to the individual. Yet there is still an element of sacrifice involved in such adoption. Each one is bound to strive within himself and to rise superior to self. Yet in so doing, he is not swallowed up by, and lost in, the majority; on the contrary, he becomes more independent, rich, and versatile.

[8] Even if here, as in the whole range of spiritual things, the Church is our guide. But she is so in a different manner than where the liturgy is concerned.

Both methods of prayer must cooperate. They stand together in a vital and reciprocal relationship. The one derives its light and fruitfulness from the other. In the liturgy, the soul learns to move about the wider and more spacious spiritual world. It assimilates—if the comparison is permissible—that freedom and dignified restraint which in human intercourse is acquired by the man who frequents good society and who limits his self-indulgence by the discipline of time-honored social usage; the soul expands and develops in that width of feeling and clearness of form which together constitute the liturgy, just as it does through familiarity and communion with great works of art. In a word, the soul acquires, in the liturgy, the "grand manner" of the spiritual life—and that is a thing that cannot be too highly prized. On the other hand, as the Church herself reminds us—and the example of the Orders who live by the liturgy is a proof of this—side by side with the liturgy there must continue to exist that private devotion which provides for the personal requirements of the individual and to which the soul surrenders itself according to its particular circumstances. From the latter, liturgical prayer in its turn derives warmth and local color.

If private devotion were nonexistent, and if the liturgy were the final and exclusive form of spiritual exercise, that exercise might easily degenerate into a frigid formula; but if the liturgy were nonexistent—well, our daily observations amply show what would be the consequences and how fatally they would take effect.

The Symbolism of the Liturgy

I N THE LITURGY, the faithful are confronted by a new world, rich in types and symbols that are expressed in terms of ritual, actions, vestments, implements, places, and hours, all of which are highly significant. Out of this the question arises—what is the precise significance of all this as regards the soul's intercourse with God? God is above space; what has he to do with directions as to specific localities? God is above time; what does time, beginning with the liturgical hours and ending with the ecclesiastical year, matter to him? God is Simplicity; then how is he concerned with specific ritual, actions, and instruments? Let us desist from the attempt to enter more fully into the question and content ourselves with asking: God is a Spirit—can matter therefore have any significance in the soul's intercourse with him? Is not the intervention of material things bound to pervert and to degrade this intercourse? And even if we admit that man consists of soul and body, that he is not pure spirit and, therefore, as a logical conclusion, that a material element will always play a certain part in his spiritual life—must we not regard this as a defect against which we must strive? Should it not be the task of all true religion to come to be the "worship of God in spirit and in truth" and at least to aim at, if not to succeed in, eliminating the bodily and material element as far as possible?

This question penetrates deeply into the essence and nature of the liturgy.

What meaning has matter—regarded as the medium of spiritual receptivity and utterance, of spiritual impression and expression—for us?

The question depends upon the manner in which the ego, within its bodily-spiritual personality, experiences the relationship between body and soul.[1] There exists a peculiar form of this self-experience, in which the boundary between the "spiritual" and the "bodily" or "physical" is sharply defined. In such cases, the spiritual plane appears as entirely self-contained, lying within—or perhaps it would be better to say beyond—the physical plane and having little or nothing to do with the latter. The two planes—spiritual and physical—are felt to be two distinct orders, lying closely adjacent, between which communication certainly takes place; but communication of such a nature that it rather appears as a transposition from the one into the other than as the direct cooperation of both. Such is the frame of mind that has probably drawn its conception of the external world from Leibniz' theory of monads and its conception of the soul from the teaching of psycho-physical parallelism.

It is obvious that people who favor such a system of thought will only attach a more or less fortuitous significance to the relationship between the physical and the spiritual. The latter, they consider, is intimately bound up with the former and is also in need of it, but as far as the life of the soul proper is concerned, the physical has no importance; it merely appears to encumber and to degrade spiritual activity. The soul strives to attain its goal—that is to say, truth, the moral impulse, God, and the divine—by purely spiritual means. Even when such people know that this endeavor cannot possibly succeed,

[1] The more precise discussion of the question belongs to the domain, as yet but little explored, of typological psychology.

they still exert themselves to approach to the purely spiritual at least as nearly as they can. To them the physical is an alloy, an innate imperfection, of which they endeavor to rid themselves. They may perhaps credit it with a limited external significance and look upon it as an aid to the elucidation of the spiritual, as an illustration or as an allegory; but they are all the time conscious that they are making what is actually an inadmissible concession. Moreover, the physical does not appeal to them as a medium of vividly expressing their inner life. They scarcely even feel the need of expressing that life in a tangible manner; for them the spiritual is self-sufficing, or else it can express itself in a straightforward moral action and in a simply uttered word.

People of such a turn of mind will inevitably have great difficulties to face in the liturgy.[2] Somewhat naturally, they gravitate toward a strictly spiritual form of devotion, which aims at suppressing the physical or material element and at shaping its external manifestations in as plain and homely a manner as possible; it prizes the simple word as the most spiritual medium of communication.

Facing these, and in contrast with them, are people of a different mental constitution. For them, the spiritual and the physical are inextricably jumbled together;[3] they incline to amalgamate the two. While the former type of disposition labors to separate the physical and the spiri-

---

[2] This disposition does not, of course, actually exist in the extreme form portrayed here any more than does that which is described later. We are concerned, however, with giving an account of such conditions in the abstract and not in detail.

[3] It need hardly be said that no intention exists of discussing in this connection the real relationship of soul and body. We are concerned with describing the manner in which this relationship is felt and interiorly experienced. It is a question, not of metaphysics, but merely of descriptive psychology.

tual spheres, the latter endeavors to unite them. People like this are prone to look upon the soul merely as the lining of the body and upon the body as the outside, in some sort the condensation or materialization, of the spirit within. They interpret spiritual elements in terms of physical conditions or movements and directly perceive every material action as a spiritual experience. They extend their conviction of the essential oneness of the soul and the body beyond the province of the individual personality and include external things within its sphere of operation. As they frequently tend to regard externals as the manifestation of spiritual elements, they are also capable of utilizing them as a means of expressing their own innerness. They see this expressed in various substances, in clothing, in social formations, and in nature, while their inner struggles are reflected even in conditions, desires, and conflicts that are universal.[4]

Of the two types of spiritual character, the second at the first glance would seem to correspond the more closely to the nature of the liturgy. It is far more susceptible to the power of expression proper to liturgical action and materials and can the more readily apply these external phenomena to the expression of its own inner life. Yet in the liturgy, it has to face problems and difficulties all its own.

People who perceive the physical or material and the spiritual as inextricably mingled find it hard to confine the manifestations of the individual soul to set forms of expression and to adhere strictly to the clearly defined significance of the formulas, actions, and instruments employed in such expression. They conceive the inner life as being in a perpetual state of flux. They cannot create

[4] Cf., for instance, the feeling of the Romantics for nature.

definite and clearly outlined forms of expression because they are incapable of separating spiritual from physical or material objects. They find it equally difficult to distinguish clearly the specific substance behind the given forms of expression; they will always give it a fresh interpretation according to varying circumstances.[5]

In other words, in spite of the close relationship that in this case exists between the physical and the spiritual, such people lack the power of welding certain spiritual contents to certain external forms, which together will constitute either the expression of their inner selves or a receptacle for an extraneous content. That is to say, they lack one of the ingredients essential to the creation of symbols. The other type of people do not succeed any better, because they fail to realize how vital the relationship is between the spiritual and the physical. They are perfectly capable of differentiating and of delimiting the boundaries between the two, but they do this to such an extent that they lose all sense of cohesion. The second type possess a sense of cohesion, and with them the inner content issues directly into the external form. But they lack discrimination and objectiveness. Both—the sense of cohesion and the power of discrimination—are essential to the creation of a symbol.

A symbol may be said to originate when that which is interior and spiritual finds expression in that which is exterior and material. But it does not originate when[6] a spiritual element is by general consent coupled with a

---

[5] Hence the tendency of people like this to forsake the Church, with her clear and unequivocal formulas, and to turn to nature, there to seek an outlet for their vague and fluctuating emotions and to win from her the stimulus that suits them.

[6] As in allegory.

material substance, as, for instance, the image of the scales with the idea of justice. Rather must the spiritual element transpose itself into material terms because it is vital and essential that it should do so. Thus the body is the natural emblem of the soul, and a spontaneous physical movement will typify a spiritual event. The symbol proper is circumscribed; and it may be further distinguished by the total inability of the form selected as a medium of expression to represent anything else whatever. It must be expressed in clear and precise terms and therefore, when it has fulfilled the usual conditions, must be universally comprehensible. A genuine symbol is occasioned by the spontaneous expression of an actual and particular spiritual condition. But at the same time, like works of art, it must rise above the purely individual plane. It must not merely express isolated spiritual elements but must deal with life and the soul in the abstract.

Consequently, when a symbol has been created, it often enjoys widespread currency and becomes universally comprehensible and significant. The auspicious collaboration of both the types of temperament outlined above is essential to the creation of a symbol, in which the spiritual and the physical elements must be united in perfect harmony. At the same time, it is the task of the spiritual element to watch over and determine every stroke of the modeling, to sort and sift with a sure hand, to measure off and weigh together delicately and discreetly, in order that the given matter may be given its corresponding and appropriate form. The more clearly and completely a spiritual content is cast in its material mold, the more valuable is the symbol thus produced and the more worthy it is of its name, because it then loses its connection with the solitary incident that occasioned it and becomes a universal possession. The greater the depth of life from which it has sprung, and the greater the degree of clarity and of conviction that has contributed to its formation, the more true this is in proportion.

The power of symbol-building was at work, for instance, when the fundamental rules governing social intercourse were laid down. From it are derived those forms by which one person signifies to another interest or reverence, in which are externally expressed the inward happenings of civil and political life, and the like. Further—and in this connection it is specially significant—it is the origin of those gestures that convey a spiritual meaning; the man who is moved by emotion will kneel, bow, clasp his hands or impose them, stretch forth his arms, strike his breast, make an offering of something, and so on. These elementary gestures are capable of richer development and expansion or else of amalgamation. They are the source of the manifold ritual actions, such as the kiss of peace or the blessing. Or it may be that certain ideas are expressed in corresponding movements, thus belief in the mystery of absolution is shown by the sign of the Cross. Finally, a whole series of such movements may be coordinated. This gives rise to religious action by which a richly developed spiritual element—for example, a sacrifice—succeeds in attaining external and symbolic expression. It is when that form of self-experience which has been described above is extended to objects that lie without the personal province that the material concrete factor enters into the symbol. Material objects are used to reinforce the expressiveness of the body and its movements and, at the same time, form an extension of the permanent bodily powers. Thus, for instance, in a sacrifice, the victim is offered, not only by the hands, but in a vessel or dish. The smooth surface of the dish emphasizes the expressive motion of the hand; it forms a wide and open plane, displayed before the Godhead, and throws into powerful relief the upward straining line of the arm. Or again, as it rises, the smoke of the incense enhances the aspiration expressed by the upturned hands and gaze of those who are at prayer. The candle, with its slender, soaring, tapering column tipped with flame, and consuming itself as it burns, typifies the idea of sacrifice that is voluntarily offered in lofty spiritual serenity.

Both the before-mentioned types of temperament co-operate in the creation of symbols. The one, with its apprehension of the affinity between the spiritual and the physical, provides the material for the primary hypothesis essential to the creation of the symbol. The other, by its power of distinction and its objectiveness, brings to the symbol lucidity and form. They both, however, find in the liturgy the problems peculiar to their temperament. But because they have shared together in the creation of the liturgical symbol, both are capable of overcoming these difficulties as soon, that is, as they are at least in some way convinced of the binding value of the liturgy.

The former type, then, must abandon their exaggerated spirituality, admit the existence of the relationship between the spiritual and the physical, and freely avail themselves of the wealth of liturgical symbolism. They must give up their reserve and the Puritanism that prompts them to oppose the expression of the spiritual in material terms and must, instead, take the latter as a medium of lively expression. This will add a new warmth and depth to their emotional and spiritual experience.

The latter type must endeavor to stem their extravagance of sensation and to bind the vague and ephemeral

elements into clear-cut forms. It is of the highest importance that they should realize that the liturgy is entirely
free from any subjection to matter[7] and that all the natural
clements in the liturgy (cf. what has been previously said
concerning its style) are entirely recast as ritual forms.
So for people of this type, the symbolizing power of the
liturgy becomes a school of measure and of spiritual restraint.

The people who really live by the liturgy will come
to learn that the bodily movements, the actions, and the
material objects that it employs are all of the highest significance. It offers great opportunities of expression, of
knowledge, and of spiritual experience; it is emancipating
in its action and capable of presenting a truth far more
strongly and convincingly than can the mere word of
mouth.

[7] Such as is found in nature-religions, for instance, which are directly
derived from nature herself, from the forest, the sea, etc. The liturgy, on
the contrary, is entirely designed by human hands. It would be extremely
interesting to investigate in a detailed manner the transformation of natural
things, shapes, and sounds into ritual objects through the agency of the
liturgy.

The Playfulness of the Liturgy

G RAVE AND EARNEST PEOPLE, who make the knowledge of truth their whole aim, see moral problems in everything, and seek for a definite purpose everywhere, tend to experience a peculiar difficulty where the liturgy is concerned.[1] They incline to regard it as being to a certain extent aimless, as superfluous pageantry of a needlessly complicated and artificial character. They are affronted by the scrupulously exact instructions that the liturgy gives on correct procedure, on the right direction in which to turn, on the pitch of the voice, and so on. What is the use of it all? The essential part of Holy Mass—the action of Sacrifice and the divine Banquet—could be so easily consummated. Why, then, the need for the solemn institution of the priestly office? The necessary consecration could be so simply accomplished in so few words and the sacraments so straightforwardly administered—what is the reason of all the prayers and ceremonies? The liturgy tends to strike people of this turn of mind as—to use the words that are really most appropriate—trifling and theatrical.

The question is a serious one. It does not occur to everyone, but in the people whom it does affect it is a sign

[1] In what follows, the writer must beg the reader not to weigh isolated words and phrases. The matter under consideration is vague and intangible and not easy to put into words. The writer can only be sure of not being misunderstood if the reader considers the chapter and the general train of thought as a whole.

of the mental attitude that concentrates on and pursues that which is essential. It appears to be principally connected with the question of purpose.

That which we call purpose is, in the true sense of the word, the distributive, organizing principle that subordinates actions or objects to other actions or objects, so that the one is directed toward the other and one exists for the sake of the other. That which is subordinate, the means, is only significant insofar as it is capable of serving that which is superior, the end. The purpose does not infuse a spiritual value into its medium; it uses it as a passage to something else, a thoroughfare merely; aim and fulcrum alike reside in the former. From this point of view, every instrument has to prove in the first place whether, and in the second to what extent, it is fitted to accomplish the purpose for which it is employed. This proof will primarily be headed by the endeavor to eliminate from the instrument all the non-essential, unimportant, and superfluous elements. It is a scientific principle that an end should be attained with the minimum expenditure of energy, time, and material. A certain restless energy, an indifference to the cost involved, and accuracy in going to the point characterize the corresponding turn of mind.

A disposition like this is, on the whole, both appropriate and necessary to life, giving it earnestness and fixity of purpose. It also takes reality into consideration, to the extent of viewing everything from the standpoint of purpose. Many pursuits and professions can be shown to have their origin almost entirely in the idea of purpose. Yet no phenomenon can be entirely, and many can be to a minor degree only, comprehended in this category. Or, to put it more plainly, that which gives objects and events their right to existence and justifies their individuality is in many cases not the sole, and in others not even the primary, reason for their usefulness. Are flowers and leaves useful? Of course; they are the vital organs of plants. Yet because of this, they are not tied down to any particular form, color, or smell. Then what, upon the whole, is the use of the extravagance of shapes, colors, and scents in nature? To what purpose the multiplicity of species? Things could be so much more simple. Nature could be entirely filled with animate beings, and they could thrive and progress in a far quicker and more suitable manner. The indiscriminate application to nature of the idea of purpose is, however, open to objection. To go to the root of the matter, what is the object of this or that plant, and of this or that animal, existing at all? Is it in order to afford nourishment to some other plant or animal? Of course not. Measured merely by the standard of apparent and external utility, there is a great deal in nature that is only partially, and nothing that is wholly and entirely, intended for a purpose, or, better still, purpose*ful*. Indeed, considered in this light, a great deal is purposeless. In a mechanical structure—a machine, say, or a bridge— everything has a purpose; and the same thing applies to business enterprises or to the government of a State; yet even where these phenomena are concerned, the idea of purpose is not far-reaching enough to give an adequate reply to the query: Whence springs their right to existence?

If we want to do justice to the whole question, we must shift our angle of vision. The conception of purpose regards an object's center of gravity as existing outside that object, seeing it lie instead in the transition to further movement, that is, the movement toward the goal that the object provides. But every object is to a certain extent, and many are entirely, self-sufficient and an end in itself—if, that is, the conception can be applied at all in this extensive sense. The conception of meaning is more adaptable. Objects that have no purpose in the strict sense of the term have a meaning. This meaning is not realized by their extraneous effect or by the contribution that they make to the stability or the modification of another object, but their significance consists in being what they are. Measured by the strict sense of the word, they are purposeless, but still full of meaning.

Purpose and meaning are the two aspects of the fact that an existent principle possesses the motive for, and the right to, its own essence and existence. An object regarded from the point of view of purpose is seen to dovetail into an order of things that comprehends both it and more beyond it; from the standpoint of meaning, it is seen to be based upon itself.

Now what is the meaning of that which exists? That it should exist and should be the image of God the Everlasting. And what is the meaning of that which is alive? That it should live, bring forth its essence, and bloom as a natural manifestation of the living God.

This is true of nature. It is also true of the life of the soul. Has science an aim or an object in the real sense of the word? No. Pragmatism is trying to foist one upon it. It insists that the aim of science is to better humanity and to improve it from the moral point of view. Yet this constitutes a failure to appreciate the independent value of knowledge. Knowledge has no aim, but it has a meaning, and one that is rooted in itself—truth. The legislative activity of Parliament, for instance, has an end in view; it is intended to bring about a certain agreed result in the life of the State. Jurisprudence, on the contrary, has no object; it merely indicates where truth lies in questions of law. The same thing applies to all real science. According to its nature, it is either the knowledge of truth or the service of truth, but nothing else. Has art any aim or purpose? No, it has not. If it had, we should be obliged to conclude that art exists in order to provide a living for artists, or else, as the eighteenth-century German thinkers of the *Aufklärung*—the "age of enlightenment"—considered, it is intended to offer concrete examples of intelligent views and to inculcate virtue. This is absolutely untrue. The work of art has no purpose, but it has a meaning—*ut sit*—that it should exist and that it should clothe in clear and genuine form the essence of things and the inner life of the human artist. It is merely to be *splendor veritatis*, the glory of truth.

When life lacks the austere guidance of the sense of purpose, it degenerates into pseudo-aestheticism. But when it is forced into the rigid framework that is the purely purposeful conception of the world, it droops and perishes. The two conceptions are interdependent. Purpose is the goal of all effort, labor, and organization; meaning is the essence of existence, of flourishing, ripening life. Purpose and meaning, effort and growth, activity and production, organization and creation—these are the two poles of existence.

The life of the Universal Church is also organized on these lines. In the first place, there is the whole tremendous system of purposes incorporated in the Canon Law and in the constitution and government of the Church. Here we find every means directed to the one end, that of keeping in motion the great machinery of ecclesiastical government. The first-mentioned point of view will decide whether adjustment or modification best serves the collective purpose and whether the latter is attained with the least possible expenditure of time and energy.[2] The scheme of labor must be arranged and controlled by a strictly practical spirit.

The Church, however, has another side. She embraces a sphere that is in a special sense free from purpose. And that is the liturgy. The latter certainly comprehends a whole system of aims and purposes as well as the instruments to accomplish them. It is the business of the sacraments to act as the channels of certain graces. This mediation, however, is easily and quickly accomplished when the necessary conditions are present. The administration of the sacraments is an example of a liturgical action that is strictly confined to the one object. Of course, it can be said of the liturgy, as of every action and every prayer that it contains, that it is directed toward the providing of spiritual instruction. This is perfectly true. But the liturgy has no thought-out, deliberate, detailed plan of instruction. In order to sense the difference, it is sufficient to compare a week of the ecclesiastical year with the Spiritual Exercises of Saint Ignatius. In the latter, every element is determined by deliberate choice, everything is directed toward the production of a certain spiritual and didactic result; each exercise, each prayer, even the way in which the hours of repose are passed, all aim at the one thing, the conversion of the will. It is not so with the liturgy. The fact that the latter has no place in the Spiritual Exercises is a proof of this.[3] The liturgy wishes to teach, but not by means of an artificial system of aim-conscious

[2] Even when the Church is considered from her other aspect, that of a divine work of art. Yet the former conception is bound to recur in this connection.

[3] The Benedictines give it one, but do so in an obviously different system of spiritual exercises from that conceived by Saint Ignatius.

educational influences; it simply creates an entire spiritual world in which the soul can live according to the requirements of its nature. The difference resembles that which exists between a gymnasium, in which every detail of the apparatus and every exercise aims at a calculated effect, and the open woods and fields. In the first, everything is consciously directed toward discipline and development; in the second, life is lived with nature, and internal growth takes place in her. The liturgy creates a universe brimming with fruitful spiritual life and allows the soul to wander about in it at will and to develop itself there. The abundance of prayers, ideas, and actions, and the whole arrangement of the calendar are incomprehensible when they are measured by the objective standard of strict suitability for a purpose. The liturgy has no purpose, or, at least, it cannot be considered from the standpoint of purpose. It is not a means that is adapted to attain a certain end—it is an end in itself. This fact is important, because if we overlook it, we labor to find all kinds of didactic purposes in the liturgy that may certainly be stowed away somewhere but are not actually evident.

When the liturgy is rightly regarded, it cannot be said to have a purpose, because it exists, not for the sake of humanity, but for the sake of God. In the liturgy, man is no longer concerned with himself; his gaze is directed toward God. In it, man is not so much intended to edify himself as to contemplate God's majesty. The liturgy means that the soul exists in God's presence, originates in him, lives in a world of divine realities, truths, mysteries, and symbols, and really lives its true, characteristic, and fruitful life.[4]

---

[4] The fact that the liturgy moralizes so little is consistent with this conception. In the liturgy, the soul forms itself, not by means of deliberate

There are two very profound passages in Holy Scripture that are quite decisive on the point. One is found in the description of Ezekiel's vision.[5] Let us consider the flaming Cherubim, "each [one of whom] went straight forward; wherever the Spirit would go. When they went, they went . . . without turning. . . . Wherever the spirit would go, they went. . . . There was the likeness of a firmament, shining like crystal, spread out over their heads. And when they went, I heard the sound of their wings like the sound of many waters . . . [and] when they stood still, they let down their wings." How "aimless" they are! How discouraging for the zealous partisans of reasonable suitability for a purpose! They are only pure motion, powerful and splendid, acting according to the direction of the Spirit, desiring nothing save to express its inner drift and its interior glow and force. They are the living image of the liturgy.

In the second passage, it is Eternal Wisdom that speaks: "I was beside him, like a master workman, and I was daily his delight, rejoicing before him always, rejoicing in his inhabited world."[6]

This is conclusive. It is the delight of the Eternal Father that Wisdom (the Son, the perfect Fullness of Truth) should pour out its eternal essence before him in all its ineffable splendor, without any "purpose"—for what purpose should it have?—but full of decisive meaning, in pure and vocal happiness; the Son "rejoices" before the Father.

Such is the life of the highest beings, the angels, who,

---

teaching and the exercise of virtue, but by the fact that it exists in the light of eternal Truth and is naturally and supernaturally robust.

[5] Ezek 1:4–24, especially vv. 12, 17, 20, 22, 24, and 10:9–17.

[6] Prov 8:30–31.

without a purpose and as the Spirit stirs them, move before God and are a mystic diversion and a living song
before him.

In the earthly sphere, there are two phenomena that
tend in the same direction: the play of the child and the
creation of the artist.

The child, when he plays, does not aim at anything.
He has no purpose. He does not want to do anything but
to exercise his youthful powers, pour forth his life in an
aimless series of movements, words, and actions, and by
this to develop and to realize himself more fully; all of
which is purposeless, but full of meaning, nevertheless,
the significance lying in the unchecked revelation of this
youthful life in thoughts and words and movements and
actions, in the capture and expression of his nature, and
in the fact of his existence. And because it does not aim
at anything in particular, because it streams unbroken and
spontaneously forth, its utterance will be harmonious, its
form clear and fine; its expression will of itself become
picture and dance, rhyme, melody, and song. That is what
play means; it is life, pouring itself forth without an aim,
seizing upon riches from its own abundant store, significant through the fact of its existence. It will be beautiful,
too, if it is left to itself and if no futile advice and ped-
agogic attempts at enlightenment foist upon it a host of
aims and purposes, thus denaturizing it.

Yet, as life progresses, conflicts ensue, and it appears to
grow ugly and discordant. Man sets before himself what
he wants to do and what he should do and tries to realize
this in his life. But in the course of these endeavors, he
learns that many obstacles stand in his way, and he perceives that it is very seldom that he can attain his ideal.

It is in a different order, in the imaginary sphere of representation, that man tries to reconcile the contradiction

between that which he wishes to be and that which he is. In art he tries to harmonize the ideal and actuality, that which he ought to be and that which he is, the soul within and nature without, the body and the soul. Such are the visions of art. It has no didactic aims, then; it is not intended to inculcate certain truths and virtues. A true artist has never had such an end in view. In art, he desires to do nothing but to overcome the discord to which we have referred and to express in the sphere of representation the higher life of which he stands in need and to which in actuality he has only approximately attained. The artist merely wants to give life to his being and its longings, to give external form to the inner truth. And people who contemplate a work of art should not expect anything of it but that they should be able to linger before it, moving freely, becoming conscious of their own better nature, and sensing the fulfillment of their most intimate longings. But they should not reason and chop logic or look for instruction and good advice from it.

The liturgy offers something higher. In it man, with the aid of grace, is given the opportunity of realizing his fundamental essence, of really becoming that which according to his divine destiny he should be and longs to be, a child of God. In the liturgy he is to go "to God, who restores the joy of [his] youth."[7] All this is, of course, on the supernatural plane, but at the same time it corresponds to the same degree to the inner needs of man's nature. Because the life of the liturgy is higher than that to which customary reality gives both the opportunity and form of expression, it adopts suitable forms and methods from that sphere in which alone they are to be found, that is

---

[7] Entrance antiphon of the Mass.

to say, from art. It speaks measuredly and melodiously; it employs formal, rhythmic gestures; it is clothed in colors and garments foreign to everyday life; it is carried out in places and at hours that have been coordinated and systematized according to more sublime laws than ours. It is in the highest sense the life of a child, in which everything is picture, melody, and song.

Such is the wonderful fact that the liturgy demonstrates: it unites art and reality in a supernatural childhood before God. That which formerly existed in the world of unreality only, and was rendered in art as the expression of mature human life, has here become reality. These forms are the vital expression of real and frankly supernatural life. But this has one thing in common with the play of the child and the life of art—it has no purpose, but it is full of profound meaning. It is not work, but play. To be at play or to fashion a work of art in God's sight—not to create, but to exist—such is the essence of the liturgy. From this is derived its sublime mingling of profound earnestness and divine joyfulness. The fact that the liturgy gives a thousand strict and careful directions on the quality of the language, gestures, colors, garments, and instruments that it employs can only be understood by those who are able to take art and play seriously. Have you ever noticed how gravely children draw up the rules of their games, on the form of the melody, the position of the hands, the meaning of this stick and that tree? It is for the sake of the silly people who may not grasp their meaning and who will persist in seeing the justification of an action or object only in its obvious purpose. Have you ever read of or even experienced the deadly earnestness with which the artist-vassal labors for art, his lord? Of his sufferings on the score of language? Or of what an overweening mistress form is? And all this for something that has no aim or purpose! No, art does not bother about aims. Does anyone honestly believe that the artist would take upon himself the thousand anxieties and feverish perplexities incident to creation if he intended to do nothing with his work but to teach the spectator a lesson, which he could just as well express in a couple of facile phrases, one or two historical examples, or a few well-taken photographs? The only answer to this can be an emphatic negative. Being an artist means wrestling with the expression of the hidden life of man, avowedly in order that it may be given existence; nothing more. It is the image of the divine creation, of which it is said that it has made things *ut sint.*

The liturgy does the same thing. It too, with endless care, with all the seriousness of the child and the strict conscientiousness of the great artist, has toiled to express in a thousand forms the sacred, God-given life of the soul to no other purpose than that the soul may therein have its existence and live its life. The liturgy has laid down the serious rules of the sacred game that the soul plays before God. And, if we are desirous of touching bottom in this mystery, it is the Spirit of fire and of holy discipline "Who has knowledge of the word"[8]—the Holy Spirit— who has ordained the game that Eternal Wisdom plays before the Heavenly Father in the Church, its kingdom on earth. And "its delight" is in this way "to be with the children of men."

Only those who are not scandalized by this understand what the liturgy means. From the very first, every type of rationalism has turned against it. The practice of the

[8] Responsory at Terce, Pentecost.

liturgy means that by the help of grace, under the guidance of the Church, we grow into living works of art before God, with no other aim or purpose than that of living and existing in his sight; it means fulfilling God's word and "becoming as little children"; it means foregoing maturity with all its purposefulness and confining oneself to play, as David did when he danced before the Ark. It may, of course, happen that those extremely clever people, who merely from being grown-up have lost all spiritual youth and spontaneity, will misunderstand this and jibe at it. David probably had to face the derision of Michal.

It is in this very aspect of the liturgy that its didactic aim is to be found, that of teaching the soul not to see purposes everywhere, not to be too conscious of the end it wishes to attain, not to be desirous of being overly clever and grown-up, but to understand simplicity in life. The soul must learn to abandon, at least in prayer, the restlessness of purposeful activity; it must learn to waste time for the sake of God and to be prepared for the sacred game with sayings and thoughts and gestures, without always immediately asking "why?" and "wherefore?" It must learn not to be continually yearning to *do* something, to attack something, to accomplish something useful, but to play the divinely ordained game of the liturgy in liberty and beauty and holy joy before God.

In the end, eternal life will be its fulfillment. Will the people who do not understand the liturgy be pleased to find that the heavenly consummation is an eternal song of praise? Will they not rather associate themselves with those other industrious people who consider that such an eternity will be both boring and unprofitable?

The Seriousness of the Liturgy

THE LITURGY is art, translated into terms of life. Sensitive people clearly recognize its wealth of expression, its symmetry of form, and its delicate sense of proportion. As a result, such people are in danger of appreciating the Church's worship merely for the sake of its aesthetic value. It is on the whole understandable that poetic literature should apprehend the liturgy from its artistic side. It is a more serious matter when this is so emphatically stressed in writings that are particularly dedicated to liturgical worship. It is sufficient for our purpose to recall valuable works such as Staudenmaier's *Geist des Christentums*, or many of J. K. Huysman's books, *L'Oblat*, for instance. The present writer is anxious that this little work should not gravitate, however unconsciously, in the same direction. For this reason, in the chapter that has been begun, the question will be more closely examined.

It is an incontrovertible proposition that people who consider a work of art merely from the artistic point of view do it an injustice. Its significance as a composition can be fully estimated only when it is viewed in connection with the whole of life. A work of art is in less danger from the logician or the moral philosopher pure and simple, because they stand in no particular relation to it. Deadly destructive to the work of art, however, is the purely artistic perception of the aesthete—both word and matter being taken in the worst and most extreme sense that they have possessed since, for instance, Oscar Wilde.

Still more does this hold good when it is a question of the representation, not of a work of art, but of actual people, and even of that tremendous unity—the *Opus Dei* that is the liturgy—in which the Creator-Artist, the Holy Spirit, has garnered and expressed the whole fullness of reality and of creative art. Aesthetes are everywhere looked upon as unwelcome guests, as drones and as parasites sponging on life, but nowhere are they more deserving of anger and contempt than in the sphere of sacred things. The careworn man who seeks nothing at Mass but the fulfillment of the service that he owes to his God; the busy woman who comes to be a little lightened of her burden; the many people who, barren of feeling and perceiving nothing of the beauty and splendor of word and sound that surround them, but merely seek strength for their daily toil—all these penetrate far more deeply into the essence of the liturgy than does the connoisseur who is busy savoring the contrast between the austere beauty of a Preface and the melodiousness of a Gradual.

All of which impels us to the fundamental question: What is the importance of beauty in relation to the entire liturgical scheme?

First, however, a slight but necessary digression. We have already seen that the Church's life functions in two directions. On the one side, there exists an active communal life, a tremendous driving force of systematically directed activities, which, however, coalesce in the many-membered but strongly centralized organization. Such a unity alike presupposes and manifests power. But what is the purpose of power in the spiritual sphere?

This query deeply concerns every one of us, each according to his disposition. For the one, it is a question of satisfying himself as to the truth of the axiom that every type of society, including the spiritual, needs power if it is to subsist. The truth of this does not degrade the ideal, even if it ranks power next in order to doctrine, exhortation, and organization. This external power must not, of course, be allowed to usurp the place of truth and of justice or permitted to influence convictions. Where, however, a religion is concerned that does not confine itself to presenting ideals and opinions but undertakes the molding and adapting of human entities on behalf of the Kingdom of God, there power is necessary. It is this that adapts a truth, or a spiritual or ethical system, to the needs of actual existence.

But if there are people who find it hard to bear that things like justice and power should be named in the same breath with such intimate matters as religious convictions and spiritual life, there are others who are entirely differently constituted. Upon such people a tremendous force like the Catholic Church produces so direct an effect that they easily forget the real significance of such power. It is merely a means to an end. It is a tool, used to carve the Kingdom of God from the raw material of the world; it is the servant of divine truth and grace. If an attempt were to be made to constitute a form of spiritual society without a powerful discipline, it would inevitably dissolve into fleeting shadows. But if power, the servant, were to be promoted to the position of master, the means to that of the end, the tool to that of the guiding hand, religion would then be stifled by despotism and its consequence, slavery.

Somewhat analogous to the position of power in the Church's active life is that of beauty in relation to her contemplative side. The Church not only exists for a purpose, but she is of herself significant, viewed from her other aspect of art transformed into life—or, better still, in the process of transformation. For that is what the Church is in the liturgy.

The preceding chapter endeavored to demonstrate that artistic self-sufficiency is actually compatible with the liturgy. Only a sophist could argue that the justification of a form of life resides exclusively in its manifest purposes. On the other hand, one must not forget as well that artistic worth—beauty—is as dangerous to the susceptible person as is power in the corresponding sphere of active communal life. The danger inherent in the idea of power is only to be overcome by those who are clear about its nature and the method of employing it. Similarly, only those who force their way into perception of its import can break free from the illusive spell of beauty.

Apart from this stands the question of whence a spiritual value derives its currency, whether from itself or from an extraneous superior value. Associated with it, but entirely distinct, is the second question, as to the quality of the relation that exists between one value that is admittedly based upon itself and other independent values. The first question endeavors to trace one value back to another, for example, the validity of the administration of justice to justice in the abstract. The second investigates the existence, between two values of equal validity, of a determinate order that may not be inverted.

Truth is of itself a value, because it is truth, justice because it is justice, and beauty because and insofar as it is beauty. No one of these qualities can derive its validity from another; it can only do so from itself.[1] The most profound and true thought does not make a work beautiful, and the best intentions of the artist avail as little, if his creation, in addition to a concrete, vivid and robust form, has not—in a word—beauty. Beauty as such is valid of itself, entirely independent of truth and other values. An object or a work of art is beautiful when its inner essence and significance find perfect expression in its existence. This perfection of expression embraces the fact of beauty and is its accepted form of currency. Beauty means that the essence of an object or action has, from the first moment of its existence and from the innermost depths of its being, formulated its relation to the universe and to the spiritual world; that this interior formation, from which has developed a phenomenon susceptible of expression, has resolved upon symbolic unity; that everything is said that should be said, and no more; that the essential form is attained, and no other; that in it there is nothing that is lifeless and empty but everything that is vivid and animated; that every sound, every word, every surface, shade, and movement, emanates from within, contributes to the expression of the whole, and is associated with the rest in a seamless, organic unity. Beauty is the full, clear, and inevitable expression of the inner truth in the external manifestation. "Pulchritudo est splendor veritatis"—"est species boni", says ancient philosophy, "beauty is the splendid perfection that dwells in the revelation of essential truth and goodness."

[1] We are not concerned here with the question of if and how all forms of validity ultimately go back to an ultimately valid Absolute, i.e., to God.

Beauty, therefore, is an independent value; it is not truth and not goodness, nor can it be derived from them. And yet it stands in the closest relation to these other values. As we have already remarked, in order that beauty may be made manifest, something must exist that will reveal itself externally; there must be an essential truth that compels utterance or an event that will out. Pride of place, therefore, though not of rank or worth, belongs, not to beauty, but to truth. Although this applies incontestably to life as a whole and to the fundamentals of art as well, it will perhaps be difficult for the artist to accept without demur.

"Beauty is the splendor of truth", says scholastic philosophy. To us moderns, this sounds somewhat frigid and superficially dogmatic. But if we remember that this axiom was held and taught by men who were incomparable constructive thinkers, who conceived ideas, framed syllogisms, and established systems that still tower over others like vast cathedrals, we shall feel it incumbent upon us to penetrate more deeply into the meaning of these few words. Truth does not mean mere lifeless accuracy of comprehension; it means the right and appropriate regulation of life, a vital spiritual essence; it means the intrinsic value of existence in all its force and fullness. And beauty is the triumphant splendor that breaks forth when the hidden truth is revealed, when the external phenomenon is at all points the perfect expression of the inner essence. Perfection of expression, then, not merely superficial and external, but interior and contemporaneous with every step in the creation—can the essence of beauty be more profoundly and at the same time more briefly defined?

Beauty cannot be appreciated unless this fact is borne

in mind, and it is apprehended as the splendor of perfectly expressed intrinsic truth.

But there is a grave risk, which many people do not escape, of this order being reversed and of beauty being placed before truth or treated as entirely separate from the latter, the perfection of form from the content, and the expression from its substance and meaning. Such is the danger incurred by the aesthetic conception of the world, which ultimately degenerates into nerveless aestheticism.

No investigation of the aesthetic mind and ideas can be undertaken here. But we may premise that its primary characteristic is a more or less swift withdrawal from discussion of the reason for a thing's existence to the manner of it, from the content to the method of presentation, from the intrinsic value of the object to its value as a form, from the austerity of truth and the inflexible demands of morality to the relaxing harmony of beauty. This will happen more or less consistently and more or less consciously until everything terminates finally in a frame of mind that no longer recognizes intrinsic truth, with its severe "thus and not otherwise", or the moral idea with its unconditional "either—or", but that seeks for significance in form and expression alone. That which is objective, whether it is a natural object, a historical event, a man, a sorrow, a preference, a work, a legal transaction, knowledge, an idea, is merely viewed as a fact without significance. It serves as a pretext for expression, that is all.[2] Thus originates the shadowy image of absolute form, a manner without a matter, a radiance without heat, a fact without force.[3]

[2] Oscar Wilde's *Intentions* are quite clear on this point.

[3] The writer has been reproached for treating the subject too simply in this exposition. He has deliberately shortened it for the sake of the funda-

People who think like this have lost the ability to grasp the profundity of a work of art and the standard by which to measure its greatness. They no longer comprehend it as being what it is, as a victory and as an avowal. They do not even do justice to the form that is the exclusive object of their preoccupation; for form means the expression of a substance or the mode of life of an existent being.

Truth is the soul of beauty. People who do not understand what the one and the other are really worth turn their joyful play into mere empty trifling. There is something heroic in every great and genuine creation, in which the interior essence has won through opposition to its true expression. A good fight has been fought in which some essential substance, conscious of the best elements within itself, has set aside that which is extraneous to itself, submitted all disorder and confusion to a strict discipline, and obeyed the laws of its own nature. A tremendous ebullition takes place, and an inner substance gives external testimony to its essence and to the essential message that it holds. But the aesthete looks upon all this as pointless trifling.

Nay, more. Aestheticism is profoundly shameless. All true beauty is modest. This word is not used in a superficial sense. It has no relation to the suitability of this or that for utterance, portrayal, or existence. What it means is that all expression has been impelled by an interior urge, justified by immutable standards, and permitted, even offered, existence by the latter. This permission and

---

mental idea and has neglected many of its ramifications that should actually have been discussed. Yet after careful testing, he finds no reason for altering his method of procedure. In a more profound sense, that which he here says is nevertheless justified.

obligation, however, only reside in the intrinsic truth of an entity or a genuine spiritual experience. Expression, on the other hand, for the sake of expression, self-elected as both matter and form, has no longer any value.

We are led yet farther afield by these considerations. In spite of the most genuine impulse, and even when truth not only emphatically justifies the proceeding but also imperatively demands it, all true inwardness still shrinks from self-revelation just because it is full of all goodness. The desire for revelation, however, and the realization that it is only in articulation that it can obtain release from the tyranny of silence compel the expression of an inwardness; yet it still shrinks from disclosure because it fears that by this it will lose its noblest elements. The fulfillment of all inwardness lies in the instant when it discloses itself in a form appropriate to its nature. But it is immediately conscious of a painful reaction, of a sensation as of having irrevocably lost something inexpressibly precious.

This applies—or is it too sweeping a statement?—to all genuine creative art. It is like a blush after the word, readily enough spoken, but followed by a secret reproach, an often incomprehensible pain, arising from depths till now unexplored; it is like the quick compression of the lips that would give much to recall the hasty avowal. People who understand this are aware that further depths and modestly concealed riches still lie beyond that which, surrendering itself, has taken shape. This generosity, while at the same time the store remains undiminished, this advance, followed by withdrawal into resplendent fastnesses, this grappling with expression, triumphant expansion, and timid, dolorous contraction, together constitute the most tender charm of beauty.

But all this—the restrained yet youthful fullness of candor—vanishes before the glance, at once disrespectful and obtuse, of those who seek after articulation for the sake of articulation and after beauty for the sake of beauty.

Those who aspire to a life of beauty must, in the first place, strive to be truthful and good. If a life is true, it will automatically become beautiful, just as light shines forth when a flame is kindled. But if they seek after beauty in the first place, it will fare with them as it fared with Hedda Gabler, and in the end everything will become nauseating and loathsome.

In the same way—however strange it may sound—the creative artist must not seek after beauty in the abstract, not, that is, if he understands that beauty is something more than a certain grace of external form and a pleasing and elegant effect. He must, on the contrary, with all his strength endeavor to become true and just in himself, to apprehend truth and to live in and by it and, in this way, fully realize both the internal and external world. And then the artist, as the enemy of all vanity and showiness, must express truth as it should be expressed, without the alteration of a single stroke or trait. It follows that his work, if he is an artist at all, will, and not only will but *must*, be beautiful. If, however, he tries to avoid the toilsome path of truth and to distill form from form, that which he represents is merely empty illusion.

People who have not enjoyed—repulsive word, which puts beauty on a par with a titbit and originates from the worthless conception that we have just now censured—human perfection or the beauty of a work of art but desire closer familiarity with it must take the inner essence for their starting point. They will be well advised to ignore expression and harmony of form at first but to endeavor to penetrate instead to the inner truth of the vital essence. Viewed from this standpoint, the whole process by which the matter transposes itself into its form becomes apparent, and the spectators witness a miraculous flowering. This means that they are familiar with beauty, although perhaps they may not consciously recognize it for what it is but are merely aware of a sentiment of perfect satisfaction at the visible and adequate fulfillment of an object or of an existence.

Beauty eludes those who pursue it for its own sake, and their life and work are ruined because they have sinned against the fundamental order of values. If a man, however, desires to live for truth alone, to be truthful in himself and to speak the truth, and if he keeps his soul open, beauty, in the shape of richness, purity, and vitality of form—will come to meet him, unsought and unexpected.

What profound penetration and insight were shown by Plato, the master of aesthetics, in his warnings against the dangers of excessive worship of beauty! We need a new artist-seer to convince the young people of our day, who bend the knee in idolatrous homage before art and beauty, what must be the fruit of such perversion of the highest spiritual laws.

We must now refer what has already been propounded to the liturgy. There is a danger that in the liturgical sphere as well aestheticism may spread; that the liturgy will first be the subject of general eulogy, then gradually its various treasures will be estimated at their aesthetic value, until finally the sacred beauty of the House of God comes to provide a delicate morsel for the connoisseur. Until, that is, the "house of prayer" becomes once more, in a different way, a "den of thieves". But for the sake of him who dwells there and for that of our own souls, this must not be tolerated.

The Church has not built up the *Opus Dei* for the pleasure of forming beautiful symbols, choice language, and graceful, stately gestures, but she has done it—insofar as it is not completely devoted to the worship of God —for the sake of our desperate spiritual need. It is to give expression to the events of the Christian's inner life: the assimilation, through the Holy Spirit, of the life of the creature to the life of God in Christ; the actual and genuine rebirth of the creature into a new existence; the development and nourishment of this life, its stretching forth from God in the Blessed Sacrament and the means of grace toward God in prayer and sacrifice; and all this in the continual mystic renewal of Christ's life in the course of the ecclesiastical year. The fulfillment of all these processes by the set forms of language, gesture, and instruments, their revelation, teaching, accomplishment, and acceptance by the faithful, together constitute the liturgy. We see, then, that it is primarily concerned with reality, with the approach of a real creature to a real God, and with the profoundly real and serious matter of redemption. There is here no question of creating beauty, but only that of finding salvation for sin-stricken humanity. Here truth is at stake, and the fate of the soul, and real—yes, ultimately the only real—life. All this it is that must be revealed, expressed, sought after, found, and imparted by every possible means and method; and when this is accomplished, lo! it is turned into beauty.[4]

---

[4] The Abbot of Marialaach rightly remarks in this connection, "I stress the point that the liturgy has *developed* into a work of art; it was not deliber-

This is not a matter for amazement, since the principle here at work is the principle of truth and of mastery over form. The interior element has been expressed clearly and truthfully, the whole superabundance of life has found its utterance, and the fathomless profundities have been plainly mapped out. It is only to be expected that a gleam of the utmost splendor should shine forth at such a manifestation of truth.

For us, however, the liturgy must chiefly be regarded from the standpoint of salvation. We should steadfastly endeavor to convince ourselves of its truth and its importance in our lives. When we recite the prayers and psalms of the liturgy, we are to praise God, nothing more. When we assist at Holy Mass, we must know that we are close to the fount of all grace. When we are present at an ordination, the significance of the proceedings must lie for us in the fact that the grace of God has taken possession of a fragment of human life. We are not concerned here with the question of powerfully symbolic gestures, as if we were in a spiritual theater, but we have to see that our real souls should approach a little nearer to the real God, for the sake of all our most personal, profoundly serious affairs.

For it is only thus that perception of liturgical beauty will be vouchsafed to us. It is only when we participate in liturgical action with the earnestness begotten of deep personal interest that we become aware why, and in what perfection, this vital essence is revealed. It is only when we

---

ately formed as such by the Church. The liturgy bore within itself so much of the seed of beauty that it was of itself bound to flower ultimately. But the internal principle that controlled the form of that flowering was the essence of Christianity." Ildefons Herwegen, *Das Kunstprinzip der Liturgie*, (Paderborn: Junfermann, 1916), 18.

premise the truth of the liturgy that our eyes are opened to its beauty.

The degree of perception varies, according to our aesthetic sensitiveness. Perhaps it will merely be a pleasant feeling of which we are not even particularly conscious, of the profound appropriateness of both language and actions for the expression of spiritual realities, a sensation of quiet spontaneity, a consciousness that everything is right and exactly as it should be. Then perhaps an offertory suddenly flashes in upon us, so that it gleams before us like a jewel. Or bit by bit the whole sweep of the Mass is revealed, just as from out of the vanishing mist the peaks and summits and slopes of a mountain chain stand out in relief, shining and clear, so that we imagine we are looking at them for the first time. Or it may be that, in the midst of prayer, the soul will be pervaded by that gentle, blithe gladness which rises into sheer rapture. Or else the book will sink from our hands, while, penetrated with awe, we taste the meaning of utter and blissful tranquillity, conscious that the final and eternal verities that satisfy all longing have here found their perfect expression.

But these moments are fleeting, and we must be content to accept them as they come or are sent.

On the whole, however, and as far as everyday life is concerned, this precept holds good, "Seek first the Kingdom of God, and his justice, and all else shall be added to you"—all else, even the glorious experience of beauty.

The Primacy of the Logos
Over the Ethos

T HE LITURGY exhibits one peculiarity that strikes as very odd those natures in particular that are generously endowed with moral energy and earnestness—and that is its singular attitude toward the moral order.

People of the type instanced above chiefly regret one thing in the liturgy, that its moral system has few direct relations with everyday life. It does not offer any easily transposable motives, or ideas realizable at first hand, for the benefit of our daily conflicts and struggles. A certain isolation, a certain remoteness from actual life characterizes it; it is celebrated in the somewhat sequestered sphere of spiritual things. A contrast exists between the study, the factory, and the laboratory of today, between the arena of public and social life and the Holy Places of solemn, divine worship, between the intensely practical tendency of our time, which is opposed to life by its wholly material force and acrid harshness, and the lofty, measured domain of liturgical conceptions and determination, with its clearness and elevation of form.

From this it follows that we cannot directly translate into action that which the liturgy offers us. There will always be a constant need, then, for methods of devotion that have their origin in a close connection with modern life and for the popular devotions by which the Church meets the special demands and requirements of actual existence and that, since they directly affect the soul, are immediately productive of practical results.[1] The liturgy, on the contrary, is primarily occupied in forming the fundamental Christian temper. By it man is to be induced to determine correctly his essential relation to God and to put himself right in regard to reverence for God, love and faith, atonement and the desire for sacrifice. As a result of this spiritual disposition, it follows that when action is required of him, he will do what is right.

The question, however, goes yet deeper. What is the position of the liturgy generally to the moral order? What is the quality of the relation in it of the will to knowledge, as of the value of truth to the value of goodness? Or, to put it in two words, what is the relation in it of the Logos to the Ethos? It will be necessary to go back somewhat in order to find the answer.

It is safe to affirm that the Middle Ages, in philosophy at least, answered the question as to the relation between these two fundamental principles by decisively ranking knowledge before will and the activity attendant upon the functioning of the latter. They gave the Logos precedence over the Ethos. That is proved by the way in which certain frequently discussed questions are answered[2] and

---

[1] Both in this connection and in countless others, we find demonstrated the absolute necessity of the extraliturgical forms of spiritual exercise, the Rosary, the Stations of the Cross, popular devotions, meditation, etc. There could be no greater mistake than the attempt to build up liturgical life on an exclusively liturgical model. And it is equally mistaken merely to tolerate the other forms because the "lower classes" need them, while setting the liturgy as the only possible pattern and guide before struggling humanity. Both are necessary. The one complements the other. Pride of place, however, belongs of course to the liturgy, because it is the official prayer of the Church. Cf. my book, *Der Kreuzweg unseres Herrn und Heilandes*, (Mainz: Matthias Grünewald, 1921), introduction.

[2] Cf. the discussions on the significance of theology as to whether it is

by the absolute priority that was assigned to the contemplative life over the active;[3] this stands out as the fundamental attitude of the Middle Ages, which took the Hereafter as the constant and exclusive goal of all earthly striving.

Modern times brought about a great change. The great objective institutions of the Middle Ages—class solidarity, the municipalities, the empire—broke up. The power of the Church was no longer, as formerly, absolute and temporal. In every direction, individualism became more strongly pronounced and independent. This development was chiefly responsible for the growth of scientific criticism and, in a special manner, the criticism of knowledge itself. The inquiry into the essence of knowledge, which formally followed a constructive method, now assumes, as a result of the profound spiritual changes that have taken place, its characteristic critical form. Knowledge itself becomes questionable, and, as a result, the center of gravity and the fulcrum of the spiritual life gradually shift from knowledge to the will. The actions of the independent individual become increasingly important. In this way, active life forces its way before the contemplative, the will before knowledge.

Even in science, which, after all, is essentially dependent upon knowledge, a peculiar significance is assigned to the will. In place of the former penetration of guaran-

---

a "pure" science or one with an aim, that of bettering humanity; on the essence of eternal happiness, whether it ultimately consists in the contemplation of God or in the love of him; on the dependence of the will upon knowledge, and so on.

[3] It is significant that it was not until the seventeenth century, and then in the face of universal opposition, that active Orders for women were founded. The history of the Order of the Visitation is especially instructive in this connection.

teed truth, of tranquil assimilation and discussion, there now develops a restless investigation of obscure, questionable truth. Instead of explanation and assimilation, education tends increasingly toward independent investigation. The entire scientific sphere exhibits an enterprising and aggressive tendency. It develops into a powerful, restlessly productive, laboring community.

This importance of the will has been scientifically formulated in the most conclusive manner by Kant. He recognized, side by side with the order of perception, of the world of things, in which the understanding alone is competent, the order of practicality, of freedom, in which the will functions. Arising out of the postulations of the will, he admits the growth of a third order, the order of faith, as opposed to knowledge, the world of God and the soul. While the understanding is of itself incapable of asserting anything on these latter matters, because it is unable to verify them by the senses, it receives belief in their reality, and, thus, the final shaping of its conception of the world, from the postulations of the will that cannot exist and function without these highest data from which to proceed. This established the "primacy of the will". The will, together with the scale of moral values peculiar to it, has taken precedence over knowledge with its corresponding scale of values; the Ethos has obtained the primacy over the Logos.

The ice having been broken, there now follows the entire course of philosophic development that sets, in the place of the pure will logically conceived by Kant, the psychological will, constituting the latter the unique rule of life—a development due to Fichte, Schopenhauer, and von Hartmann—until it finds its clearest expression in Nietzsche. He proclaims the "will to power". For him, truth is that which makes life sound and noble, leading humanity farther toward the goal of the "Superman".

Such is the origin of pragmatism, by which truth is viewed no longer as an independent value in the case of a conception of the universe or in spiritual matters, but as the expression of the fact that a principle or a system benefits life and actual affairs and elevates the character and stability of the will.[4] Truth is fundamentally, if not entirely—though here we overstep the field marked out for our consideration—a moral, though hardly a vital, fact.

This predominance of the will and of the idea of its value gives the present day its peculiar character. It is the reason for its restless pressing forward, the stringent limiting of its hours of labor, the precipitancy of its enjoyment; hence, too, the worship of success, of strength, of action; hence the striving after power and, generally, the exaggerated opinion of the value of time and the compulsion to exhaust oneself by activity till the end. This is the reason, too, why spiritual organizations such as the old contemplative orders, which formerly were automatically accepted by spiritual life everywhere and which were the darlings of the orthodox world, are not infrequently misunderstood even by Catholics and have to be defended by their friends against the reproach of idle trifling. And if it is true that this attitude of mind has already become firmly established in Europe, whose culture is rooted in the distant past, it is doubly true where the New World is concerned. There it comes to light unconcealed and

---

[4] This tendency has also influenced Catholic thought. A great deal of modernistic thought endeavors to make theological truth—dogma—dependent upon Christian life and to estimate its importance, not as a standard of truth, but as a value in life.

unalloyed. The practical will is everywhere the decisive factor, and the Ethos has complete precedence over the Logos, the active side of life over the contemplative.

What is the position of Catholicism in relation to this development? It must be premised that the best elements of every period and of every type of mind can and will find their fulfillment in this religion, which is truly capable of being all things to all men. So it has been possible to adapt the tremendous development of power during the last five centuries in Catholic life and to summon ever fresh aspects from its inexhaustible store. A long investigation would be needed if we were to point out how many highly valuable personalities, tendencies, activities, and views have been called forth from Catholic life as a result of this responsiveness to the needs of all ages. But it must be pointed out that an extensive, biased, and lasting predominance of the will over knowledge is profoundly at variance with the Catholic spirit.

Protestantism presents, in its various forms, ranging from the strong tendency to the extreme of free speculation, the more or less Christian version of this spirit, and Kant has rightly been called its philosopher. It is a spirit that has step by step abandoned objective religious truth and has increasingly tended to make conviction a matter of personal judgment, feeling, and experience. In this way, truth has fallen from the objective plane to the level of a relative and fluctuating value. As a result, the will has been obliged to assume the leadership. When the believer no longer possesses any fundamental principles, but only an experience of faith as it affects him personally, the one solid and recognizable fact is no longer a body of dogma that can be handed on in tradition, but the right action as a proof of the right spirit. In this connection, there can be no talk of spiritual metaphysics in the real sense of the word. And when knowledge has nothing ultimately to seek in the Above, the roots of the will and of feeling are in their turn loosened from their adherence to knowledge. The relation with the supertemporal and eternal order is thereby broken. The believer stands no longer in eternity but in time, and eternity is merely connected with time through the medium of conviction, but not in a direct manner. Religion becomes increasingly turned toward the world and cheerfully secular. It develops more and more into a consecration of temporal human existence in its various aspects, into a sanctification of earthly activity, of vocational labor, of communal and family life, and so on.

Everyone, however, who has debated these matters at any considerable length clearly perceives the unwholesomeness of such a conception of spiritual life and the flagrance of its contradiction of all fundamental spiritual principles. It is untrue and therefore contrary to nature in the deepest sense of the word. Here is the real source of the terrible misery of our day. It has perverted the sacred order of nature. It was Goethe who really shook the latter when he made the doubting Faust write, not "In the beginning was the Word", but "In the beginning was the Deed."

While life's center of gravity was shifting from the Logos to the Ethos, life itself was growing increasingly unrestrained. Man's will was required to be responsible for him. Only one will can do this, and that is creative in the absolute sense of the word, that is, it is the divine will.[5] Man, then, was endowed with a quality that pre-

[5] Yet even here reason affirms that God is not merely an Absolute Will,

sumes that he is God. And since he is not, he develops
a spiritual cramp, a kind of weak fit of violence, which
takes effect often in a tragic and sometimes (in the case of
lesser minds) even a ludicrous manner. This presumption
is guilty of having put modern man into the position of a
blind person groping his way in the dark, because the fundamental force upon which it has based life—the will—
is blind. The will can function and produce but cannot
see. From this is derived the restlessness that nowhere
finds tranquillity. Nothing is left, nothing stands firm,
everything alters, life is in continual flux; it is a constant
struggle, search, and wandering.

Catholicism opposes this attitude with all its strength.
The Church forgives everything more readily than an attack on truth. She knows that if a man falls, but leaves
truth unimpaired, he will find his way back again. But
if he attacks the vital principle, then the sacred order of
life is demolished. Moreover, the Church has constantly
viewed with the deepest distrust every ethical conception
of truth and of dogma. Any attempt to base the truth of
a dogma merely on its practical value is essentially un-
Catholic.[6] The Church represents truth—dogma—as an
absolute fact, based upon itself, independent of all confirmation from the moral or even from the practical sphere.
Truth is truth because it is truth. The attitude of the
will to it, and its action toward it, is of itself a matter of

---

but, at the same time, truth and goodness. Revelation seals this, as it does
every form of spiritual perception, by showing us that in the Blessed Trinity
the "first thing" is the begetting of the Son through the recognition of the
Father, and the "second" (according to thought, of course, not according
to time) is the breathing forth of the Holy Spirit through the love of both.

[6] Here nothing is said, of course, against the endeavor to exhibit the
value of dogma in the abstract and that of the single dogmatic truth for
life. On the contrary, this can never be done forcibly enough.

indifference to truth. The will is not required to prove truth, nor is the latter obliged to give an account of itself to the will, but the will has to acknowledge itself as perfectly incompetent before truth. It does not create the latter, but it finds it. The will has to admit that it is blind and needs the light, the leadership, and the organizing, formative power of truth. It must admit as a fundamental principle the primacy of knowledge over the will, of the Logos over the Ethos.[7]

This "primacy" has been misunderstood. It is not a question of a priority of value or of merit. Nor is there any suggestion that knowledge is more important than action in human life. Still less does a desire exist to direct people as to the advisability of setting about their affairs with prayer or with action. The one is just as valuable and meritorious as the other. It is partly a question of disposition; the tone of a man's life will accentuate either knowledge or action; and the one type of disposition is worth as much as the other. The "primacy" is far rather a matter of culture—philosophy, and indeed it consists of the question as to which value in the whole of culture and of human life the leadership will be assigned and which, therefore, will determine the decisive tendency; it is a precedence of order, therefore, of leadership, not of merit, significance, or even of frequency.

But if we concern ourselves further with the question, the idea occurs that the conception of the primacy of the

[7] This is said of knowledge, not of comprehension; of the primacy of knowledge over the practical, of the contemplative over the active life, in the way understood by the Middle Ages, even if it lacks the latter's cultural-historical characteristics. On the other hand, it is impossible for us to free ourselves sufficiently from the domination of pure comprehension, as it has endured for half a century.

Logos over the Ethos could not be the final one. Perhaps it should be put thus: in life as a whole, precedence belongs, not to action, but to existence. What ultimately matters is not activity, but development. The roots of and the perfection of everything lie, not in time, but in eternity. Finally, not the moral, but the metaphysical conception of the world is binding, not the worth-judgment, but the import-judgment, not struggle, but worship.

These trains of thought, however, trespass beyond the limits of this little book. The further question—if a final precedence must not be allotted to love—seems to be linked with a different chain of thought. Its solution perhaps lies within the possibilities we have already discussed. When one knows, for instance, that for a time truth is the decisive standard, it is still not quite established whether truth insists upon love or upon frigid majesty; the Ethos can be an obligation of the law, as with Kant, or the obligation of creative love. And even face to face with existence, it is still an open question whether this obligation is a final rigid inevitability or if it is love transcending all measure, in which the impossible itself becomes possible, to which hope can appeal against all hope. That is what is meant by the question whether love is not the greatest of these. Indeed, it is. Nothing less than this was announced by the "good news".

In this sense, too, as far as the primacy of truth—but "truth in love"—is concerned, the present question is to be resolved.

As soon as this is done, the foundation of spiritual health is established. For the soul needs absolutely firm ground on which to stand. It needs a support by which it can raise itself, a sure external point beyond itself, and that can only be supplied by truth. The knowledge of pure truth is the fundamental factor of spiritual emancipation. "The truth will make you free" (Jn 8:32). The soul needs that spiritual relaxation in which the convulsions of the will are stilled, the restlessness of struggle quietened, and the shrieking of desire silenced; and that is fundamentally and primarily the act of intention by which thought perceives truth, and the spirit is silent before its splendid majesty.

In dogma, the fact of absolute truth, inflexible and eternal, entirely independent of a basis of practicality, we possess something that is inexpressibly great. When the soul becomes aware of it, it is overcome by a sensation as of having touched the mystic guarantee of universal sanity; it perceives dogma as the guardian of all existence, actually and really the rock upon which the universe rests. "In the beginning was the Word"—the Logos. . . .

For this reason, the basis of all genuine and healthy life is a contemplative one. No matter how great the energy of the volition and action and striving may be, it must rest on the tranquil contemplation of eternal, unchangeable truth. This attitude is rooted in eternity. It is peaceful, it has that interior restraint which is a victory over life. It is not in a hurry, but has time. It can afford to wait and to develop.

This spiritual attitude is really Catholic. And if it is also a fact, as some maintain, that Catholicism is in many aspects, as compared with the other denominations, "backward", by all means let it be. Catholicism could not join in the furious pursuit of the unchained will, torn from its fixed and eternal order. But it has in exchange preserved something that is irreplaceably precious, for which, if it were to recognize it, the non-Catholic spiritual world would willingly exchange all that it has; and this is the primacy of the Logos over the Ethos and, by this, harmony with the established and immutable laws of all existence.

Although as yet the liturgy has not been specifically mentioned, everything that has been said applies to it. In the liturgy, the Logos has been assigned its fitting precedence over the will.[8] Hence the wonderful power of relaxation proper to the liturgy and its deep reposefulness. Hence its apparent consummation entirely in the contemplation, adoration, and glorification of divine truth. This is also the explanation of the fact that the liturgy is apparently so little disturbed by the petty troubles and needs of everyday life. It also accounts for the comparative rareness of its attempts at direct teaching and direct inculcation of virtue. The liturgy has something in itself reminiscent of the stars, of their eternally fixed and even course, of their inflexible order, of their profound silence, and of the infinite space in which they are poised. It is only in appearance, however, that the liturgy is so detached and untroubled by the actions and strivings and moral position of men. For in reality, it knows that those who live by it will be true and spiritually sound and at peace to the depths of their being; and that when they leave its sacred confines to enter life, they will be men of courage.

[8] Because it reposes upon existence, upon the essential, and even upon existence in love, as I hope to be able to demonstrate upon a future occasion.

General Index

Abraham, 295n11
absolution, 322
action, 291, 293, 316, 322, 324, 339, 341, 354–57, 360–61; existence and, 361; liturgical, 277, 287–88, 297, 310, 319, 330–31, 350
adoration, 287, 363
aesthetics/aestheticism, 329, 338, 344–45, 348, 351
Albigenses, 294
allegory, 318, 320n6
altar vessels, 308
angels, 332–33
Anselm of Canterbury, St., 308
antiphons, 280, 334n7
Apocalypse (Revelation). See Revelation, book of
Ark of the Covenant, 337
arrogance, 21, 224
art, 282n2, 293–94, 305–7, 315, 321, 329–30, 334–49
assimilation, 279, 299, 301–2, 315, 349, 355
atonement, 353
Aufklärung (age of enlightenment), 329
authority, 295n11, 297. *See also* power

Baptism, 288. *See also* sacraments
barbarism, 287n7, 295

beauty and the beautiful, 293, 313, 333, 337, 339, 341–51; soul of, 345; truth and, 342–51
being. *See* existence
Benedictine Order, 330n3
Bible. *See* Scripture
bishops, 297
Blessed Sacrament. *See* Eucharist
blessing, 277n1, 322
body (flesh), 275, 311–12, 316–24, 334
Body of Christ (*Corpus Christi mysticum*), 275–78, 280–83, 285–86, 288, 297–98, 301
breast, striking, 322
Breviary, 280, 286n6

calendars, 331
candles, 323
Canon, prayers of, 285
Canon Law, 329
Catharists, 294
cathedrals, 306, 343
Catholicism/Catholic Christianity, 277–78, 297–98, 309–10, 314, 340, 356–57, 359, 362. *See also* Church
Celestius, 295
charity, 277n1, 301. *See also* love
cherubim, 332
children, 295n11, 333–37

365